BREAKING

THE

MILITARY

COVENANT

(WHO SPEAKS FOR THE DEAD?)

David Hill

Nemesis Books

ISBN 978-1-9810-3842-8 (paperback)

Revised and updated - December 2021

This book was published in 2018 by Nemesis Books as a limited edition paperback. In 2019 it was published in an abridged form in paperback and e-book as **'Breaking the Military Covenant - Why British Servicemen are Dying Unnecessarily'** by Amberley Publishing. This authorised, revised and updated version of the original book is published by Nemesis Books. All proceeds will be donated to Help for Heroes.

The author spent much of his career as an avionics/aircraft programme manager in the Ministry of Defence. After retiring in 2004 he assisted families and Coroners in the Nimrod XV230 and Hercules XV179 cases, his evidence proving the aircraft unairworthy. This led to the Nimrod Review (2008-9) and the re-setting of airworthiness management. He submitted the same evidence to the Mull of Kintyre Review (2010-11), Lord Alexander Philip confirming it applied to Chinook ZD576. The pilots were cleared of gross negligence. In 2016 he published *Their Greatest Disgrace*, a personal account of that campaign. This inevitably touched on many accidents sharing the same root causes, and this new book develops the theme.

Also by the same author, and published by Nemesis Books:

Their Greatest Disgrace - The campaign to clear the Chinook ZD576 pilots
ISBN 979-8-8429-8674-3 (2016)

Red 5 - An investigation into the death of Flight Lieutenant Sean Cunningham
ISBN 978-1-7061-4923-1 (2019, updated 2021)

The Inconvenient Truth - Chinook ZD576: Cause & Culpability
ISBN 979-8-5184-5820-8 (2021)

A Noble Anger - The Manslaughter of Corporal Jonathan Bayliss
ISBN: 979-8-8342-7923-5 (2022)

As the issues discussed in these books are ongoing, they will be regularly updated. If you have purchased a previous edition, please contact the author for a free Kindle or pdf version. No proof of purchase required.

bigdee60@yahoo.com

https://sites.google.com/site/militaryairworthiness/home

This book is dedicated to:

Mrs Ann Lawrence and Mr George Lawrence, who lost their son Marc
in the Sea King ASaC Mk7 collision.

The late Rear Admiral Ron Holley RN, CB.

My daughter Jo, her late brother Andrew, and their late mum Annie.

Acknowledgements

Mr Keith Belcher.

Mr Tony Cable, retired Senior Engineering Inspector, Air Accidents Investigation Branch.

Captain Robin Cane, pilot.

Ms Jocelyn Cockburn, solicitor (Hodge, Jones and Allen), who represented families of servicemen killed in Snatch Land Rovers.

Mr Rob Cook, engineer.

Mr Geoff Cooper, retired RAF navigator.

Sir Roger Gale MP and Lady Suzy Gale, for the support they continue to provide to Mr and Mrs George Lawrence.

Commander (retired) Steve George RN, engineer.

Mr John Gray, engineer, formerly of GEC-Marconi Secure Systems.

Mrs Dorothy Holley, for her gracious permission to quote her late husband, Rear Admiral Ron Holley RN, CB.

Flight Lieutenant (retired) James Jones, engineer.

Mr Sean Maffett, retired RAF navigator, now an aviation journalist.

Mr Graham Miller, engineer.

Dr Susan Phoenix, retired military nurse (Queen Alexandra's Royal Army Nursing Corps), and now author.

Squadron Leader (retired) Chris Seal, pilot.

Squadron Leader (retired) Peter Skea, engineer.

Brigadier (retired) David N F Stewart, Late HIGHLANDERS.

Mr Brian Wadham, engineer.

Contents

List of Figures

Foreword

I consider it a great honour to be asked to write a foreword to this new book by David.

In the title he asks 'Who speaks for the dead?' In our own way, we both do. As a senior engineering inspector with the UK Air Accidents Investigation Branch, in 32 years I investigated, among others, the Pan Am Boeing 747 at Lockerbie, the Air France Concorde at Paris and the RAF Chinook ZD576 at the Mull of Kintyre. In the Chinook case, David wrote a splendid book *Their Greatest Disgrace* outlining the successful campaign to clear the deceased pilots of charges of gross negligence. He revealed perhaps the greatest breach of the Military Covenant - the aircraft was not airworthy, and this was concealed from the aircrew and passengers. In many ways, this new book is a follow-up. It cites, through a number of test cases (not all aviation related), over one hundred avoidable deaths of our servicemen.

Experience has made two matters clear to me. First, the root causes of most accidents are usually deficiencies in systems, whether these are systems for management, design, certification, maintenance, and/or operation. Second, those responsible can often find the most convenient approach is to blame the individuals at the coalface, commonly the pilot(s), either obliquely or directly. Often there is little or no evidence to support this (as was the case with Chinook ZD576). Doing so not only offends against natural justice but also defeats the basic purpose of investigating accidents, namely taking action to correct the deficiencies that led to the accident, thereby aiming to prevent recurrence. Fulfilling this duty is an essential component of the Military Covenant.

In this new book, David is both robust and compassionate. It is impeccably researched, revealing further cases of injustice that will fascinate and anger you in equal measure. One salient point he makes struck me - almost all the factors relating to the deaths were predicted and the warnings ignored.

I have known David for 10 years and am keenly aware of the direct assistance he has provided to bereaved families, helping them through the trauma of Coroner's Inquests and inquiries. He provided vital evidence to the Nimrod XV230 and Hercules XV179 Inquests, and the Nimrod and Mull of Kintyre Reviews, bringing substantial experience as an aircraft engineer and programme manager. His motivation is to

1

help prevent recurrence and ensure natural justice. I consider both to be most noble aims.

Tony Cable
30 November 2017

Prologue - Power & corruptible seed

The elements of the offence of misconduct in a public office are: (1) a public officer acting as such; (2) wilfully neglects to perform his duty and/or wilfully misconducts himself; (3) to such a degree as to amount to an abuse of the public's trust in the office holder; (4) without reasonable excuse or justification.

(Attorney General's Reference, No.3 of 2003)

Tuesday, 8 December 1992

St Giles Court, Central London - hub of the Ministry of Defence's Air Systems. Specialist avionic project managers, recently transferred to the RAF's support organisation, were on tenterhooks. Since 1987, the RAF had been implementing a policy giving rise to astronomical waste. Instead of rescinding the policy, it was now making savings at the expense of safety to generate compensatory funds. Only these few engineers had voiced dissent over this rush to the bottom.

Deputy Director (Avionics), Mike Weston, had been instructed to have seven named staff stay by their desks all day. Director General Support Management (DGSM), Air Vice Marshal Christopher Baker, was visiting and on the warpath, seething over these miscreants insisting on meeting legal obligations instead of implementing RAF policy. Throughout the day, one by one they were marched into an office. DGSM sat at a desk; almost laughably, with a lamp facing the single chair in the middle of the room. Behind him, to his right, two Air Commodores who had been involved in the escalation of complaints from *their* subordinates about these infuriating civilians. Against the wall to his left, six chairs.

The last, responsible for Fire Control and Surveillance radars, and Electronic Intelligence systems, was summoned at about 1600. Upon entering he saw his colleagues sat against the wall - explaining why no word had filtered out. It could not be a disciplinary matter, as no representation was offered. He was told to sit down, opposite DGSM.

He was immediately reprimanded for challenging this waste. Standing firm, he cited examples of being denied airworthiness funding, as it had been squandered. He reminded DGSM that his supply staff had recently procured 15 years' worth of spares for a front-line Royal Navy radar, which would be out of service within a year. And...

He was shut down. *'What you describe is fraud. As my staff act on my behalf, you are accusing <u>me</u> of fraud. If you cannot prove it, I have already made*

3

arrangements for you to be thrown out of MoD'. A craven act of bullying, the coward's management tool. Nevertheless, an undertaking was given to send DGSM the evidence; while pointing out his staff included those present. That, they had acted on his behalf to reduce waste and keep aircrew safe. That, he had now chosen sides.

Mike Weston was waiting outside and gathered his staff together. How to place on record what had occurred? And how to prevent DGSM carrying out his threat? It was suggested a senior auditing branch be called in - one reporting direct to the Permanent Under-Secretary of State (PUS, MoD's most senior civil servant). In January 1993, Director Internal Audit commenced a wide-ranging audit. His report, 'Requirement Scrutiny', was submitted to PUS, Sir Richard Mottram, on 29 June 1996.[1] It was comprehensive, supported the staff who met their obligations, and made 19 recommendations. Implementing one of them (#15) would have removed a major contributory factor to many of the deaths mentioned later. It was already mandated policy.

Meanwhile, contractors continued complaining about being asked to manufacture equipment they knew MoD did not need. Many refused, the only saving grace.

Asked what PUS's response had been, and how many of the recommendations had been implemented, on 15 October 2007 Director Internal Audit confirmed the report had been destroyed after seven years, as there was no reason why it should be retained (because it had not been actioned).[2] This correspondence was sent to the new PUS, Sir William Jeffrey. He did not reply, seemingly unconcerned that the money he was accountable for was being poured down the drain.

This 1996 report can be viewed as a direct descendant of the Nimrod Review of 2009. Same issues, same culprits. Same originator...

Thursday, 2 September 1999

MoD Abbey Wood, Bristol. Yet again, the same officer had refused to commit fraud. This time the directive was issued by his civilian line manager, who immediately reported this disobedience to *his* superior, a senior RN Captain.

A smaller room. Glass walls, so everyone in the open-plan floor plate could see. Again, sat facing his accusers, with no representation

---

1 Report D/DIA/5/295/10, 29 June 1996 'Requirement Scrutiny'.
2 Letter D/DIA(Bath)/6/5/2, 15 October 2007.

permitted. In fact, he had merely been asked to come in for a chat about a co-worker's personnel report all three of them had to sign. *'You committed insubordination and I am issuing you with a formal warning'*. No discussion. No questioning of witnesses. No consultation of regulations. Guilty as charged.

This misconduct was mentioned in the officer's next annual report. Marked down, he sought redress. An appeal was submitted, asking the Defence Procurement Agency's Executive Director 1, Mr Ian Fauset, which was the greater offence - the order to make false record, or the refusal to obey. On 10 January 2001 he ruled the refusal was an offence, but issuing the order and subsequent disciplinary action was not.[3] The Chief of Defence Procurement, Sir Robert Walmsley, upheld this; and again upon appeal.[4] This was then challenged at a formal hearing on 9 September 2002, chaired by the Director of Personnel, Resources and Development, Mr David Baker. A recording was made to preserve proof of misconduct. This was later justified when MoD denied all knowledge of the hearing.[5] Baker sided with the others. His decision was conveyed to staff by their Trades Union (Prospect) on 18 September 2002.[6]

On 28 October 2014, Sir Jeremy Heywood, Cabinet Secretary and Head of the Civil Service, ruled it would be *'inappropriate'* to rescind disciplinary action taken against MoD staff punished for this offence.[7]

*

If there is formal notification to the correct authorities of systemic failures in a Safety Management System, and the official response is to deny, lie, bully and harass, then the system has broken down and these actors are corrupt. As is anyone in possession of the facts who supports them.

There is a direct link between these events, MoD's fiscal troubles, deaths of servicemen, and breaches of the Military Covenant.

---

3 Loose Minute XD1(304), 10 January 2001.
4 Letters CDP 117/6/7, 19 November 2001 and 13 December 2001.
5 Letter DE&S 28-02-2013-121341, 18 March 2013.
6 Letter DPA/C175/JF/62/02, 18 September 2002.
7 Unreferenced letter from Sir Jeremy Heywood, 28 October 2014.

Introduction - The cover-up is worse than the crime

There are few things more stressful to bereaved families than dealing with a lying, obstinate bureaucracy. To appreciate why MoD resorts to this one must understand historical events, and that Covenant and duty are inextricably linked.

This book sets out inter-related cases, each characterised by wilful breaches of duty and law that resulted in harm. Proof is presented that senior officers, officials and Ministers were told by experts in the field that their prohibited actions would cause harm; yet continued with those actions and military personnel and civilians died as a result. The content has been submitted to numerous Coroners and Inquiries, and accepted by all.

It is structured so one can dip into case studies, although Part 1 explains some necessary background detail. Each case is approached from a new direction, revealing key facts that, had they not been concealed, would have resulted in investigations and legal proceedings taking a different path. Despite regular notifications of serious violations, MoD denied any problem existed. Parliament was misled and no corrective action taken. Fatalities multiplied.

But when Nimrod XV230 crashed in 2006, the truth was placed before the Oxford Coroner, Mr Andrew Walker. He confirmed the aircraft was not airworthy. Mr Charles Haddon-Cave QC was asked to conduct the Nimrod Review. He upheld evidence from the public, that MoD had failed to implement mandated airworthiness regulations.

The government accepted his findings. In 2009 MoD was told to implement the Review's recommendations, most of which were mandated anyway. Instead, it implied the regulations were faulty. This diverted attention from the real issue - the conscious decision to ignore them. It continues to resist, venting its spleen at those who identified and notified the failings in the first place.

Successive governments then changed tack, supporting MoD. The reason is simple. Knowledge of *when* these notifications were made, and *who* disregarded them, is too embarrassing. Knighthoods are at stake. Those who seek them. And those who should lose them.

*

The focus here is on MoD's refusal to implement airworthiness regulations, mainly because that is my area of interest. However, two

Land systems examples are included to emphasise that the underpinning regulations are universal. Arcane as the processes and procedures are, it is hoped they are explained in an accessible manner. The first example offered is one most members of the public will recognise - Snatch Land Rovers. This sets the scene.

Next, a section on MoD regulations and how they have been subverted. It explains why MoD has been called the *'citadel of waste'*, and who condones it. [8] Mr Haddon-Cave accepted the evidence of this maladministration, confirming MoD's policy of *savings at the expense of safety*. But readers were left to infer they were government ordered cuts. In fact, they were made to compensate for the waste mentioned earlier. Omitting this protected those responsible.

The main narrative discusses one accident in detail - the 2003 Sea King ASaC Mk7 mid-air collision, in which seven aircrew died. It is based on a report I prepared at the behest of Sir Roger Gale MP, representing Ann and George Lawrence, who lost their son Marc in the accident. Questions from recipients meant it was expanded to include the background to the Sea King AEW Mk2 upgrade programme (which produced the Mk7), and details of major programme elements. Three principal contributory factors emerged from the Royal Navy Board of Inquiry, all relating to the concepts of 'see and be seen' and 'see and avoid'. These interwoven factors are picked apart to reveal what went wrong to permit them to occur, concentrating on what latent failures and preconditions were known to exist, and what action was taken. Or not, as the case may be.

Next, a number of briefer chapters about other accidents, incidents and events. This approach avoids repetition, my point being all share common factors. To demonstrate this, the dots are joined and breaches of the Covenant highlighted.

Finally, and to avoid merely listing a raft of failings, a section outlining a proposed way ahead. Nothing too radical is suggested - mainly a return to implementing legal obligations. How to go about preventing, as far as possible, avoidable deaths is explained. The Covenant should be as much about this as the after-care of the injured and bereaved.

My primary source is formal evidence to legal authorities and Inquiries, and practical examples are used to illustrate points. These anecdotes are no more damaging to MoD than the criticism it has received on the

---

8 Commonly attributed to Gordon Brown MP when Chancellor of the Exchequer (1997-2007), reflecting the views of numerous government committees.

same subjects (mainly waste and failure of duty of care) by its own auditors, government committees, and accident Inquiries. In particular, the condemnation by the Nimrod and Mull of Kintyre Reviews makes the position of those responsible so poor, nothing I can say is any worse.

Certain principles are recognised:

- A practice is misleading by commission if it deceives, or is likely to deceive, the average person, even though the information may be correct.

- A practice is misleading by omission if it omits important information, or gives unclear or ambiguous information.

- Regarding duty of care, if a person asks a reasonable question and is lied to, the fault lies with the liar. However, if the duty holder could be reasonably expected to know he was being misled or had been lied to, and did not, he is incompetent. If he is provided with evidence of this, and takes no action, he is negligent and liable.

These principles underpin Queen's Regulations and the Civil Service Code, and are directly linked to the Covenant. However, there is no mechanism whereby a member of the public can complain if they are breached.

So, who is meant to speak for the dead? In England, Wales and Northern Ireland, Her Majesty's Coroners. In Scotland, the Crown Office and Procurator Fiscal Service. But having been routinely misled by MoD, their work is contaminated. The police and judiciary? Contemptuous of evidence, they are content for MoD to judge its own case. Government? Defence of our nation is not a vote winner. MoD? It views the dead as convenient scapegoats. All, to varying degrees, have concealed serious wrongdoing. It is said judicial truth and actual truth are trains on parallel tracks, but often reach the same destination. Here, these authorities combined to derail one and divert the other, succeeding in their aim of defeating the ends of justice.

Who is left? Bereaved families, with the help of a few retirees. Yet, in the face of such overwhelming odds, the victories have been astounding. Nimrod XV230. Chinook ZD576. Hercules XV179. And more to come. MoD never learns.

Snatch Land Rovers

It is important to first acknowledge a major difficulty MoD faces when specifying and selecting protected vehicles. It is not as simple as providing a vehicle with better protection. There must be a trade-off between weight, mobility, speed, protection, utility and transportability. This 'requirement setting' is a little understood part of MoD. Few are trained for it. Oversight is crucial, to avoid conflicts and duplication.

The alternative is often unattractive. For example, most infantry abhor the thought of being cooped up in a main battle tank. But, equally, they hate Snatch, as it has so many obvious shortcomings; among them no weapon mounts. A version exists with less protection, but improvements in other features - termed WMIK (Weapons Mounted Installation Kit).

Sir Michael Fallon, Secretary of State for Defence, on 18 August 2017:

> *'The government entirely accepts the findings of Sir John Chilcot in relation to Snatch Land Rovers. I would like to express directly to you my deepest sympathies and apologise for the delay, resulting in decisions taken at the time in bringing into service alternative protected vehicles which could have saved lives. The government must and will ensure our armed forces are always properly equipped and resourced'.*

Such apologies have one purpose. Damage limitation, as there is more to hide. The real issue is why MoD misled Ministers, families and courts over the timing of vehicle availability. This is what links Snatch to the other cases I discuss.

*

Snatch was introduced into the Northern Ireland theatre in 1992, intended for rural operations.[9] (The Tavern Armoured Patrol Vehicle was for urban use). Its vulnerability was soon recognised and within a few years a replacement programme was approved, Future Northern Ireland Patrol Vehicle (FNIPV), and an In-Service Date announced. This last is important, because dependent programmes must consider it in their planning and costings. Under the '5-year rule', Snatch support funding would be progressively cut in each of its five remaining years. If the new programme is delayed, both need more money; but seldom receive it.

FNIPV was justified by a vulnerability analysis showing Snatch to be inadequate against assessed threats, based on a concept of use. In these circumstances MoD staff are taught the clock runs on litigation and have a 'reasonable time' to mitigate the risk. Plainly, this process worked. As

---

[9] https://publications.parliament.uk/pa/cm200506/cmhansrd/vo060720/text/60720w18 45.htm

of June 2003, FNIPV remained viable. But at some point shortly thereafter it was cancelled, probably a result of planned 'normalisation' in Northern Ireland. But the geographic reference in the programme name gave MoD an opportunity to cancel without considering what use Snatch would then be put to.

*

The threat from Improvised Explosive Devices (IEDs) is well-known in military history. During the Aden Emergency (1963-67) Army Land Rovers were modified to fit frontal protection, a roll cage, and V-shaped protective armour to deflect blasts. They were de-modified afterwards, but the modification points to awareness and positive action. In Afghanistan, the Soviet Union faced IEDs between 1979 and 1989, a clue to the immediate threat.

MoD usually groups IEDs under the heading 'Mine Attack'. For example, in March 2001 the proposed Future Rapid Effects System programme (essentially a family of vehicles) set out the threat in three sections: First, Second and Third Generation devices. It was expressed in terms of explosive content of the device, and how far it would penetrate Rolled Homogeneous Armour. But Snatch is not armoured. It is 'lightly protected'. IEDs don't just penetrate Snatch. They pulverise it.

MoD claims Snatch was assessed as adequate against threats in Iraq and Afghanistan. This implies the threat assessment concluded these were more benign theatres than Northern Ireland - an unimaginable level of incompetence or complacency. Three possibilities exist. One, an accurate assessment was conducted but buried. Two, the assessment was flawed and/or directed. Three, no assessment took place. Following inevitable deaths, Ministers were misled. Senior staff indicated to the media this was a procurement failure, deflecting attention from the fact Snatch had already been declared unsuitable, and its replacement cancelled.

A further vulnerability analysis was conducted. On 16 March 2005, two years after the invasion of Iraq, an independent report commissioned by MoD described Snatch as 'overmatched', adding that merely issuing occupants with body armour was insufficient. Instead of prompting immediate action, on 28 June 2005 junior Minister Dan Touhig MP veered the other way, saying medium weight vehicle capability was to be 'bulged' at the expense of light (including Snatch) and heavy forces. In other words, funding was diverted. A year later, steps were taken to procure enhanced body armour. Much needed, but not addressing the basic problem.

On 12 June 2006, Minister for Defence Procurement Lord Drayson told the House of Lords:

'I do not accept that Snatch Land Rovers are not appropriate for the role. They provide us with the mobility and level of protection we need'.

He went on to confirm Snatch was now used in urban areas, perhaps unaware of the significance of this change in use.

The death toll increased. In 2008 a further review was announced, overlooking the previous work resulting in FNIPV being approved. A classic delaying tactic. On 16 December 2008 the Secretary of State for Defence, John Hutton MP, announced he would not be proceeding with a Public Inquiry into the 37 deaths (at that time) involving Snatch. Faced with possible legal action, it might be concluded he did not want the facts revealed. MoD's position was it did not owe a duty of care to servicemen killed or injured in battle as a result of inadequate equipment, by virtue of the 'combat immunity' principle. Nevertheless, on 10 July 2009 the families of three soldiers killed in Iraq won the right to a judicial review.

May 2011 saw the precursor to the Supreme Court hearing. In the High Court, Ms Jocelyn Cockburn, a solicitor representing several families of deceased soldiers said:

'MoD's defence is there was no particular threat to Snatch associated with Improvised Explosive Devices in July 2005'. (When the son of one of her clients died).

MoD also claimed in-theatre commanders made the decision to use Snatch. In fact, they had been given no alternative. The judge ruled:

'There can be no doubt MoD is under a general duty to provide adequate training, suitable equipment and a safe system of work for members of the Armed Forces'.

On 19 June 2013, after a series of hearings and appeals, the Supreme Court ruled claims could be brought against the government under legislation covering negligence and human rights. Importantly, it confirmed that duty of care has no geographical or time limit, rejecting MoD's claim that when in-theatre servicemen were outwith UK jurisdiction. The outcome was not entirely satisfactory, as cases would have to be decided on an individual basis. Perhaps inevitable, but MoD was content as it helped with its strategy of obfuscation and compartmentalising each case.

The Iraq Inquiry Report (2016) confirmed the pre-existing programme; but not by name, and wrongly attributed it to 2005. Patrick Mercer MP, a former Army Colonel:

> *'Myself and others pointed out (Snatch's) inadequacy as far back as 2005; that was only partially addressed by the wearing of extra body armour. It is not acceptable that this vehicle is still being used in the most dangerous of areas'.*

Others, including Lieutenant Colonel Stuart Tootal, commanding 3 Para, gave evidence of concern dating to 2003. Evidently, neither was aware of FNIPV. Correctly, Sir John Chilcot said:

> *'Delays should not have been tolerated. The MoD was slow in responding to the threat from improvised explosive devices'.*

But the delays were even worse than he revealed. The Military Covenant Commission knew this - it was advised repeatedly during its existence. Once again, MoD purred over adverse comments about alleged procurement failures. They diverted attention from the real issues, which occurred long before procurers ever got involved. Sir Michael Fallon's apology must be viewed in this light.

PART 1: FROM HERE TO THERE

'All officers well understand they are not permitted to participate in party politics, but that is a very different matter from publicly acknowledging the needs of the men engaged in combat, provided the publicity does not, of itself, endanger our forces'.

Rear Admiral Ron Holley RN, CB

1: The Military Covenant

In 2000 the term was coined in 'Soldiering - The Military Covenant'.[10] Now called the Armed Forces Covenant (allowing MoD and Government to avoid the period before the name change), the original is more commonly used. It is viewed as a way of measuring whether the government and society at large have met their obligations to members of the Armed Forces. The original intent was that the Covenant would include obligations owed to soldiers by their commanders and politicians (and hence the civil servants and servicemen charged with implementing government policies). Army doctrine stated:

'The country expects soldiers to be available at any time, to go anywhere and to carry out a wide variety of potential missions in support of government policy, often as the last resort. Such capability requires good equipment, organisation, training and leadership, and above all, soldiers with high degrees of personal and collective commitment, self-sacrifice, forbearance and mutual trust'.

Today, this has become:

'An agreement between the Armed Forces community, the nation and the government. It encapsulates the moral obligation to those who serve, have served, their families and the bereaved. The Covenant's twin underlying principles are that members of the Armed Forces community should face no disadvantage compared to other citizens in the provision of public and commercial services; and that special consideration is appropriate in some cases, especially for those who have given the most such as the injured or the bereaved'.[11]

Modern-day evolution

The events of 11 September 2001 brought wider conflict, and increasing losses in Iraq and Afghanistan through not having the *'good equipment'* in sufficient numbers. Prime Minister Tony Blair MP acknowledged the government's obligations - on 12 January 2007 saying the Covenant needed to be renewed, repeating:

'It will mean increased expenditure on equipment, personnel and the

---

10 DGD&D/18/34/71 Army Doctrine Publication Volume 5 'Soldiering - The Military Covenant', February 2000.
11 The Armed Forces Covenant (policy paper), 3 June 2016.

conditions of our Armed Forces, not in the short run but for the long term'.

This reaffirmed the original intent but omitted that many equipment programmes had been slashed, including the flagship programme intended to reduce casualties, Future Integrated Soldier Technology.

Following adverse publicity arising from a spate of avoidable deaths, the phrase became more widely known through its use by General Sir Richard Dannatt, the Chief of the General Staff; notably in a speech to the International Institute for Strategic Studies in September 2007. That same month, the Royal British Legion commenced its Honour the Covenant campaign, concentrating on welfare issues. This gave MoD an opportunity to quietly forget the prevention aspect, and shift many responsibilities to the Departments of Welfare and Pensions, Health and Education. At his party conference in October 2007, the Leader of the Opposition, David Cameron MP, accused the government of breaching the Covenant; implying he agreed with the original concept.

Responding to the British Legion's campaign, the Secretary of State for Health, Alan Johnson MP, announced in November 2007 that veterans would get priority treatment on the National Health Service, and those injured would be treated immediately in hospital rather than endure waiting lists. Prescription charges would also be waived. Well done Mr Johnson, but MoD had retreated into the shadows.

In late 2007 Gordon Brown MP, by now Prime Minister, ordered an Inquiry. This was largely a result of Harriet Harman MP, Leader of the House of Commons, asking difficult questions of MoD regarding its abrogation. Quentin Davies MP was asked to prepare a report intended to identify how the perceived gulf between the Armed Forces and society could be bridged, <u>without significant cost</u>. It was not revealed if a cost cap had been imposed.

Mr Davies published 'National Recognition of our Armed Forces' in May 2008. Two months later the government published 'The Nation's Commitment: Cross-Government Support to our Armed Forces, their Families and veterans'. In October 2008 it published a formal response to Mr Davies's report, 'The Government's Response to the Report of Inquiry into National Recognition of our Armed Forces'.

At this point, one could discern the move away from 'hard' issues such as good equipment in adequate numbers, to 'soft' issues such as *'transfer of ceremonies and parades to public venues'* and *'business breakfasts for Chiefs of Staff'*. (Recommendations 4 and 13). The *without significant cost* directive had kicked in. Although perhaps not to the breakfasts.

Upon coming to power, on 25 June 2010 Mr Cameron pledged to enshrine the Covenant in law. Such a development would allow service personnel to sue the State for breaches. [12] He set up the Military Covenant Commission, which reported in December 2010. However, it merely took forward the position inherited from Labour - the 'hard' issues were omitted. On the same day its report was published, so too was the Armed Forces Bill 2010. It further diluted the original intent and did not state what welfare provisions must be provided for under the Covenant, such as minimum standards of care. The British Legion characterised the Bill as *the beginnings of a u-turn'* on Mr Cameron's pledge. Unfortunately, the u-turn had begun much earlier.

After considering these representations, in February 2011 the Conservative-Liberal Democrat coalition decided there was no need to make the Covenant law, proposing instead to cover it in an annual report to Parliament. A Labour attempt to reverse this was defeated. The cross-party support of May 2008 had evaporated.

On 15 May 2011 Mr Cameron announced the principles of the Covenant would now be written into the Bill, meaning they need not be enforced. The following day, the government published the first Tri-Service Armed Forces Covenant, and defined it:

An Enduring Covenant Between
The People of the United Kingdom
Her Majesty's Government
-and-
All those who serve or have served in the
Armed Forces of the Crown and their Families.

The conflict between duty and Covenant

There are two distinct types of duty at play here, explaining why the 'hard' issues were omitted:

- The legal obligation placed upon MoD staff to adhere to and implement regulations. This sits outwith the Covenant.
- The moral obligation - duty one owes, and which one ought to perform, but which is not legally binding. This applies to the

---

12 MoD press release 'Military Covenant to be enshrined in law', 25 June 2010.

Covenant.

One can reasonably separate these duties in this way, so long as both are carried out. However, if either is breached the Covenant becomes meaningless. The government did not offer how, or even if, it would enforce MoD's obligations. While both claim a commitment to the Covenant, they are free to ignore it - and do so with impunity. Therefore, and while strictly speaking they are not covered by the Covenant, it is important to offer examples of legal obligations being ignored.

Returning to Sir Michael Fallon's statement of 18 August 2017:

'The government must and will ensure our armed forces are always properly equipped and resourced'.

Did he appreciate he had just re-written the Covenant? Can we expect another U-turn? Sir Michael resigned on 1 November 2017. It is yet to be seen if his successor(s) will honour this commitment.

Implementation

Many of these 'soft' issues, particularly in relation to veterans, rest with other government departments, devolved administrations and local authorities. Indeed, the Scottish Executive issued its own paper, 'Scotland's veterans and forces: meeting our commitment'. This proved the point, as defence is not a devolved matter. Faced with an increased burden, these other entities had their funding cut. Hence, the Covenant, ostensibly government policy, has been relegated to an aspiration because it is not properly funded. MoD and government stand back and plead innocence in the full knowledge it is being breached.

As if to make life even more difficult, servicemen are not employees but Crown Appointees, lacking many legal rights afforded the general public. If denied healthcare, a veteran might make representations to his MP. A diligent MP might pursue this with the local Health Authority. However, this diverts attention from prior negligence and maladministration; transferring the problem to an unprepared local authority, which sits at a great distance from MoD and cannot involve itself in its business. The soldier's immediate concern is his treatment, but who acts on his behalf against those who have abrogated their legal and moral duties?

2: If you think safety's expensive, try having an accident

The deaths I discuss arose from refusal to implement MoD's Safety Management System. The failure is of leadership, and management who urge staff to make savings while avoiding obligations. MoD and government conceded this after the 2009 Nimrod Review. That many years notice had been given was overlooked. The policy persists.

Safety management

This is concerned with having a consistent approach to potential causes of harm, and targeting effort where it will have most benefit. A balance must be sought, whereby safety does not dominate to the detriment of operational effectiveness. A proactive approach is necessary, minimising (eradication is impossible) the need to react to harm. Professional judgment is paramount. As a decision may have to be defended on the basis of that judgment, the process must be fully documented and assumptions validated. On aircraft and equipment this means primarily by engineers, but their derogation by MoD has diminished its corporate knowledge. Consequently, trainees have less access to advice and assistance.

The primary output is a Safety Case, which considers five basic questions: (1) What are we looking at, (2) What could go wrong, (3) How bad could it be, (4) What has been or can be done, and (5) What if it happens? It should answer these questions for the uses defined in the Statement of Operating Intent and Usage, and for each Build Standard.

At key points in a system or equipment's life, Safety Case Reports summarise the Safety Case and set out residual risks and hazards. Maintaining the validity of the Safety Case is a continual process - it is the requirement for a report that is periodic.

Both physical and functional safety must be addressed. The latter recognises an equipment or system may be safe in one application, but not in another. This is linked to the dangers of unverified read across, whereby equipments and their installation designs are simply copied from other, different, applications. Because its assessment requires exploratory analysis, functional safety cannot be assured by only complying with prescriptive legislation and regulations. The significance of this will become apparent in Part 2.

Risk and certainty management

A hazard is a potential source of harm, whereas a risk is a possible variation from a predicted outcome. A risk assessment establishes the likelihood of harm occurring and its impact, if exposed to a hazard. When known a risk will occur, or pre-exists, it is a certainty and must be dealt with before proceeding. MoD policy requires this, yet also militates against it. In the accidents I discuss, the hazards, risks and certainties associated with the contributory factors were identified early. Appropriate mitigation was initiated, but the work was cancelled - often by unauthorised persons - and no alternative put in hand.

Worryingly, since the early 1990s MoD trainees have increasingly been taught it is sufficient to populate a Risk Register. That, actually mitigating the risk is optional - although most intuitively see the need. A significant drawback is that project teams are manned according to cost, not content. And one cannot predict exactly what resources will be needed, which those holding the purse strings see as a weakness.

The Executive Board must manage certainties. Moreover, because risk management begins at the concept stage, the Service sponsor must initiate the Risk Register. In practice, the subject is often an afterthought, commenced some way through the acquisition cycle when the programme has been firmed up. Thus, the creation or upkeep of the Safety Case is often the aim of a risk mitigation plan, not a core activity. Essentially, this is what happened on Nimrod MR2, leading to the loss of XV230 in September 2006.

For current purposes, the most obvious certainty (or standing risk) since the early-1990s is that, as a matter of policy, airworthiness has not been maintained. The solution is to rescind this policy and get rid of those who still insist on it in the face of multiple deaths. The Executive Board and Ministers have consistently rejected this, protecting their own jobs. Therein lie the two greatest organisational failings - poor leadership and lack of independent oversight. Overnight, matters would improve considerably if these posts were just done away with. You might think this harsh, but everyone in the graveyard votes the same.

*

Risk Managers are seen as a nuisance. A typical reaction is to accuse them of thinking up problems which may not be there. This ignores that assessing *possible* risks is the core element of the job. (This should not be confused with 'paralysis by analysis'). The Risk Manager is better described as a collator. (And no matter his grade or rank he is the key member of the team, not least because he has an overview of the entire programme). Potential risks are reported to him. He allocates tasks and timescales, and people report back to him on progress. He must have commensurate authority to direct staff to undertake these tasks. MoD does not tolerate this.

Thus, a good Risk Manager in MoD will almost inevitably come into conflict with superiors. A common danger sign is when accused of not finishing what he starts - an alarming thought process brought about by the default position that he must carry out the entire process himself. Yet, whole projects can emerge from a single risk - the Full Mission Trainer in the Sea King ASaC Mk7 case is a good example - and the main programme may have hundreds of risks. This expectation is therefore unreasonable and is itself a significant risk - in fact, a certainty. The owner is again the Executive Board. To point this out is to be vilified and identified as a troublemaker. Consequently, many experienced staff avoid risk management posts, the task falling to whoever has the gumption, but not necessarily the resources or authority to do it. The same can be said of safety management.

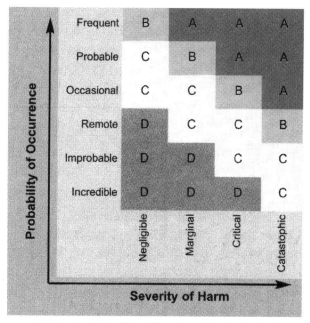

Figure 1 - Risk Classification Matrix *(MoD)*

Risks must be confirmed case by case as being tolerable and As Low As Reasonably Practicable (ALARP). Figure 1 is important to risk and safety assessment, classification and decision-making.

Each letter defines a Risk Class. Class A is unacceptable and *must* be mitigated before entering Service. B, C and D require a particular level of approval before being tolerated. (Generally speaking, Class A at 4-Star level, Class B/C at 2-Star, Class D at half-Star). If a Class A risk emerges during Service use, it can only be tolerated under truly exceptional circumstances. Toleration shall not be implied - it must be stated in writing in a Safety Statement. Each probability and severity band, and the criteria used, must be defined in the Safety Management Plan. As a certainty must be mitigated before proceeding, the probability of occurrence column stops short of 'always'.

Importantly, and where much confusion arises, a judgment is allowed as to how much risk reduction is reasonably practicable in B, C or D regions (i.e. where risk exists but may be tolerable if ALARP). And an intolerable risk can be ALARP, since there may be nothing more that can be done - but servicemen still expected to take that risk.

An intention to reduce a risk to ALARP, even if the required action is in hand, does not mean the risk has been reduced to ALARP. This is achieved only when the necessary control measures are in place. But in recent years MoD has adopted the concept of ALARP (Temporal), which it uses to justify carrying Class A risks while mitigation is being considered, but is not in hand. This may be acceptable given an operational imperative, but is routinely used to deal with risks that were understood from the outset but ignored. The political imperative is mitigating the risk of negligence being exposed, not the risk to life. This led to, for example, Tornado aircrew being deceived into believing mid-air collision risks were ALARP. Mitigation was available in 1991. Twenty-eight years later, and after a number of deaths, it has not been implemented, even on Tornado's successor. 'Extended Temporal'?

MoD is in a more difficult position than most when asking *What is reasonable and to whom?* Health and Safety legislation helps, linking this to context. That is, one considers the situation, the benefit to be gained from taking the risk, and whether further mitigation is impracticable or disproportionate. An oft-overlooked subtlety is that cost is a legitimate consideration, affordability is not.

ALARP is about the practicality of risk reduction, tolerability about the willingness to bear the risk - the link being the sacrifice required. In the military, especially, this involves placing a financial value on human lives, injuries or environmental damage, so can be an emotive subject. MoD issues guidelines (and the financial value has reduced significantly over the years); but they are just that, implying a higher authority decides case by case - which is unworkable. The persistent problem faced is the blurring of what is and isn't practicable and acceptable, caused by arbitrary and draconian cuts to safety related funding. The enduring question is - *Where does one stop?*

One could also ask - *Where does one begin?* Our servicemen face many scenarios where risk assessment is utterly futile. The hazards may be overwhelming. Often, an impossible dilemma is presented, and it is here the Covenant must be enforced. Today, lurking in the back of every commander's mind is the possibility of legal action sometime in the future. Decades after the event, servicemen are being pursued for actions taken in the heat of battle in Northern Ireland and Iraq. In the Mull of Kintyre case, for example, bereaved families continue to be door-stepped by investigators seeking to acquire old diaries in the hope they contain evidence against the deceased and their colleagues. Our political leaders could stop this at a stroke, but do nothing.

*

Risk management is not a one-way street. The process relies on constant feedback, continuous assessment, and robust corrective action systems - and the resources to manage this. A 'just' culture is necessary - where the organisation gives due regard to honesty rather than issuing censure, but where individuals are not free of blame if they are culpably negligent. In recent years, parts of MoD have tried this, their efforts undermined by high-profile cases in which it knowingly placed blame on the wrong persons; invariably subordinates in order to protect superiors. This book discusses the most infamous cases (Chinook ZD576 and Nimrod XV230) and reveals another (Sea King ASaC Mk7). Only in the Chinook case have those wrongly accused been cleared, and only then after a 17-year public campaign opposed, and actively impeded, by MoD and governments.

Post Design Services (PDS)

Having attained a tolerable and ALARP system, how does one keep it so? That is, primarily, maintain the Build Standard and Safety Cases. The contractual vehicle is PDS. It has 17 core components, and important threads such as Configuration Control and the Safety Case run through each core component. That is, they are fundamental to each component, not components in themselves, serving to emphasise that they must always be considered, no matter how minor the task.

PDS does not enhance the Build, Standard, it maintains it. It may develop a modification, but does not buy the mod sets, assemble mod kits, or embody them. It may develop a repair scheme, but not carry out repairs. By minimising volume-related activity, most of PDS, for a given equipment or aircraft, costs the same regardless of how many are in service. Hence, it must be separately funded. This is not generally understood or taught; indeed, the new Military Aviation Authority regulations get the definition wrong and disappear off at a tangent.

When PDS was subsumed into the wider support structure in 1991 (spares, repairs, etc. which *are*, broadly, volume related), it was subject to financial cuts each time there was a fleet reduction or savings measure. Thereafter, PDS (and hence maintaining airworthiness) was regarded as a waste of money. Inevitably, this compromised safety. The nadir was in January 1993, when RAF suppliers issued instructions that even safety related issues were not to be investigated or mitigated (missing the point that *all* PDS activity is safety related). This ethos remains.

*

A Technical Agency is appointed to manage this work and, uniquely, named in the contract. He is usually a civil servant, must be an engineer, and controls the Design Authority Build Standard. The only dedicated procedural Defence Standard is 05-125/2, plus an associated volume of 20 PDS Specifications. From 1991-on, MoD's Directorate of Standardisation was denied resources and last tried to update them in September 2004, but was instructed to desist. One difficulty was that 05-125/2 reflected the Secretary of State's regulations, but staff were under orders to ignore them. To accept the update task was a poisoned chalice. The Standard has now been cancelled. But all Technical Agencies had personal copies and, lacking a replacement, the wise continue to implement it. In part, this explains why some equipments are managed better than others.

An important role of the Technical Agency is to appoint and manage System Co-ordinating Design Authorities (SCDAs), responsible for complete systems. This is the basis of systems integration and, hence, functional safety. The components of a system (e.g. comms) are often supplied by different contractors, each the Design Authority for their own kit. Each aircraft fleet usually has a different mix and match so, while the individual components may be familiar, the system may (by design) perform differently in each application. An SCDA is appointed - typically the Design Authority responsible for the most significant part of the system. (Which in comms is generally the Intercom). Their role is to manage the other Design Authorities as sub-contractors, and maintain the Build Standards (including safety) of each configuration, in all applications. They deal with the Aircraft Design Authorities, and manage Interface Definition and Control.

Moving up a level, it can be seen that, for example, if air-to-air refuelling is required, the aircraft themselves must be integrated. In isolation each may be safe, but when joined the whole may become unsafe. Again, the Nimrod XV230 accident is a prime example, whereby the Nimrod fuel line couplings could not cope with the flow rate from the modified tanker. In short, there was no valid Interface Definition Document describing the interface. So basic is this, the decision to avoid this obligation can only have been deliberate, to save money.

The Technical Agency is (or was) one of the most carefully considered and controlled appointments in MoD. On avionics, for example, MoD had a centralised section within its Procurement Executive. A one-stop shop for practical airworthiness management. Today, the work is fragmented, a minor task to often unqualified and inexperienced staff. The entire subject has been marginalised, and a culture persists whereby the person who understands detail (and the Devil is in the detail) is belittled. Gaps occur in audit trails. The effect is cumulative, and most are never closed.

There is a truism in defence procurement. One can always tell the general background of a project manager by what he omits from the contract. Those who have been a Technical Agency seldom omit anything of importance, increasing the likelihood of time, cost and performance criteria being met. The crucial contractual milestone is successful Transfer to PDS. The hurdles the contractor and MoD must jump, together, ensure a seamless transition from Development and Production, to safe In-Service use. In the main case discussed (Sea King ASaC Mk7), a non-technical official cancelled this milestone. Yes, one can always tell.

Airworthiness

Airworthiness and serviceability are often used interchangeably, but the former facilitates the latter. Airworthiness is:

'The ability of an aircraft or other airborne equipment or system to operate without significant hazard to aircrew, ground crew, passengers or to the general public over which the airborne systems are flown'.

Military Airworthiness is therefore a matter of public interest. It is governed by Military Airworthiness Regulations (Joint Service Publication 553; prior to July 2003, JSP318B), which articulate the requirement to attain and maintain airworthiness. Also, by Defence Standard 00-970, Design and Airworthiness Requirements for Military Aircraft. How to implement these is set out in the 05-series procedural Defence Standards. All are mandated (as is any 'requirement') in aviation related contracts.

Airworthiness, and safety in general, rests upon four pillars: a Safety Management System, Standards, Independence and Compliance. Ensuring their integrity is money in the bank, providing warning of impending problems whereas the aircraft seldom does. Each pillar must have solid foundations. Weaken them, remove or shorten a pillar, and the edifice rocks. Eventually, it falls down.

MoD has always had an excellent *Safety Management System*, but implementation is inconsistent. As mentioned earlier, one of the main *Standards*, 05-125/2, so important that any project manager is at an immediate disadvantage if he doesn't know it backwards, has been outlawed since 1993. In June 1991, the main providers of *Independent* oversight, HQ Modification Committees, were disbanded, effectively rendering *Compliance* optional. The accidents I outline arose from concentrated attacks on all four pillars.

Already, we have established a timeframe and contributory factor, revealing prior negligence.

*

Airworthiness is not a one-off process. It is a through-life obligation requiring:

- An approved Statement of Operating Intent and Usage, which documents the military roles and missions; in turn largely dictating the aircraft specification.
- An aircraft and its equipment, at known and understood Build Standards.
- A Whole Aircraft Safety Case, subsuming subsidiary Safety Cases.
- Maintenance procedures and processes.
- A system that keeps this data up to date as the aircraft configuration

25

changes.

- A Release to Service built on these - the Master Airworthiness Reference. When issued, it must be accompanied by a letter of promulgation, which is the authority to commence Service regulated flying.

Lacking these outputs an aircraft is not airworthy, can never be acceptably safe, and cannot (lawfully) be released to service. MoD has routinely refused to meet this obligation, <u>but falsely stated it has</u>. This violation is central to the accidents discussed here.

Fitness for Purpose

To an engineer, this is the definition of quality. In a military context, it is an operational term. Yet there is a dearth of information on how it is attained and maintained, and who is responsible. Indeed, MoD has been unable to answer this question in court. (The Hercules XV179 Coroner's Inquest, discussed later). Nevertheless, it is generally held to refer to these scenarios, and variations thereof:

- When the aircraft does not comply with its specification; for example, it is carrying faults or not up to modification state.

- When the operational imperative requires it to be flown beyond the boundaries of the Release to Service.

- When, given new threats, its configuration must be enhanced to maintain its safety.

This last is important because fitness for purpose is usually seen as a temporary lowering of standards to carry out the immediate task. But it also refers to the need to raise those standards, requiring extra resources (noting the original intent of the Covenant, to provide the correct equipment). At this operational level, through a system of delegation, and within defined limits, temporary lowering of standards is acceptable; although more normally applied to serviceability.

Airworthiness is a non-negotiable legal obligation; fitness for purpose (and serviceability) is where acceptable variables may arise. An operational commander relies entirely on a stable baseline against which he can make a judgment to deviate. Put another way, when attaining and maintaining airworthiness, one must avoid the avoidable; leaving the commander to manage the unavoidable. One must recognise he is constrained. For example, he is in no position to procure and fit equipment he needs. He must be given the basic tools for the job

- an airworthy aircraft fit for the task he has been set. The deviation under consideration should be relatively minor and/or unforeseen. If predictable, the system has failed him. Aircrew place total reliance on each echelon doing its job properly. If others fail in this duty, it defies natural justice to place sole blame on the aircrew or the commander. This principle was at the heart of the 17-year campaign to clear the Chinook ZD576 pilots.

The four levels of failure

Most accidents can be traced to one or more of four levels of failure. Organisational faults or influences, unsafe supervision, preconditions for unsafe acts, and the unsafe acts themselves. The normal method of describing this is the Reason Model of accident causation, after Professor James Reason; more commonly called the 'Swiss Cheese' model or cumulative act effect.

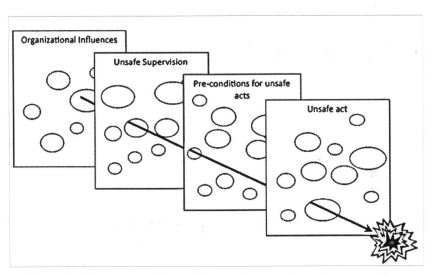

Figure 2 - The Reason 'Swiss Cheese' Model of accident causation
(Public domain)

Defences against failure are modelled as layered barriers, represented as slices of Swiss cheese. The strength of these barriers must always be known and maintained. The holes in the slices represent individual weaknesses in individual parts of the system, and are continually

27

varying in size. The system as a whole produces failures when a hole in each slice momentarily align, permitting the 'accident trajectory'; so a hazard passes through the holes in the defences, leading to a failure. The hazards/failures may exist all the time, but not every aircraft will crash because the holes are seen to be constantly moving and only rarely, if ever, align. The model includes both active and latent failures. The latter is useful in accident investigation, since it encourages the study of contributory factors that may have lain dormant for days, weeks, months or even years; until they finally contribute to the accident.

Each level is divided into categories:

1. Unsafe Acts. (Errors and violations). Errors are unintentional behaviours and may be skill-based, decision-making or perceptual. Violations are wilful disregard of rules and regulations; they may be routine (habitual and tolerated by the governing authority), or exceptional (isolated and neither typical of the operator nor condoned by management).

2. Preconditions for Unsafe Acts. Environmental factors (e.g. physical, technological), condition of operators (mental, physiological, and physical) and personnel (crew resource management, readiness).

3. Unsafe Supervision. Inadequate supervision (training, leadership, oversight), failure to correct known problems (e.g. ignoring safety hazards) and supervisory violations (e.g. bullying, illegal orders).

4. Organisational Influences. Resource management (e.g. equipment, information, facilities), organisational climate (culture, structure, policies) and processes (instructions, procedures, regulations).

In practice, defences should be strengthened in recognition errors will occur. Inadequate defences may make errors more dangerous, but some errors will overcome even the most robust defences. However, MoD staff face a huge difficulty when seeking funding, often confronted with obtuse demands to prove a given defence will prevent occurrence.

*

The model assumes several random events occur in such a way the holes align. But what if they are aligned by conscious acts, such as directives to make false declarations? When this occurs it is no longer an example of the Reason Model, since it is not random - it is gambling. MoD might advocate use of the model, but is a chronic gambler. For 17 years it blamed the two pilots for the Mull of Kintyre accident (29 killed), having gambled on the worst failure possible in aviation - the aircraft was not airworthy. This is where servicemen (ultimately) look to their leaders to

28

show backbone.

In the Sea King accident discussed in Part 2, the appointment of a non-engineer to a technical supervisory post automatically enlarged a hole in the *Organisational Influences* slice. When he self-delegated airworthiness authority, the *Unsafe Supervision* slice disappeared. When he overruled engineering design decisions, new and bigger *Precondition* holes were created. This breach of legal obligations was a significant *Unsafe Act.* Despite formal warnings as to consequences, management encouraged him and the *Organisational Influences* slice crumbled altogether. The layered defences against mid-air collision, put in place by engineers before his appointment, were systematically attacked on multiple fronts. If obligations had been met, these defences would have stood. Therefore, his behaviour was a root cause. While examples at all four levels are identified throughout, no unsafe act is attributed to any of the deceased. Rather, the sheer scale of prior negligence is emphasised, and the fact it was concealed from all Inquiries.

Technology and system maturity

Maturity (or rather immaturity) is key to the cases discussed here. How does one know when a design is sufficiently mature to progress to the next stage? Terminology has changed, but the approach remains the same. One applies tests to determine and demonstrate Technology Readiness Levels (TRLs) and System Integration Readiness Levels (SIRLs).

Both have nine levels, Level 9 being the most mature. TRL1 is the technology concept stage; TRL9 is the actual system qualified through successful mission operations. SIRLs are more complex because there are many domains. For airworthiness, SIRL1 is concerned with agreeing methods for safety management; SIRL9 is its verified In-Service implementation. For software, SIRL1 is the analysis of the potential role of the software; SIRL9 is software validation achieved. Two basic rules apply:

- The SIRL cannot be higher than the lowest contributing TRL.
- The SIRL of a system should be assessed as equivalent to the lowest SIRL of the contributing individual sub-systems.

Project managers must demonstrate Level 6 or 7 before proceeding to manufacturing, when the technical risk focus should shift to systems integration. While they can approve a temporary deviation during development, this cannot be extended into production and in-service use. Part 2 discusses the impact of unauthorised staff agreeing major deviations during development and permitting the associated risks to be carried into the in-service phase; which were then contributory factors in the accident.

As a further example, Chinook HC Mk2 was not permitted to fly on 2 June 1994 (the Mull of Kintyre accident), mainly because Safety Critical Software was at TRL4 so prohibited in the aircraft. Procurement and trials staff had applied the rules properly, and Lord Alexander Philip confirmed their statement, that the aircraft was unairworthy, was *'mandated'* upon the RAF.[13] Knowing this, a false declaration was made it *was* airworthy. Twenty-nine aircrew and passengers relied on that statement, and died.

---

13 Mull of Kintyre Review report, paragraph 2.2.8.

3: Is it MoD policy to waste money?

It is an aspiration within MoD not to waste money. That is not in doubt. However, an aspiration only becomes policy when properly resourced. The resources required to avoid waste include clear directives and procedures, top-down support, and retention of corporate knowledge. It has not been MoD practice to provide these for well over two decades.

The correct implementation of policy must be regularly verified. Every audit since 1988, conducted by both MoD (e.g. Equipment Accounting Centre, Director Internal Audit) and external bodies (e.g. National Audit Office, Committee of Public Accounts), has found MoD wanting. Their recommendations were ignored.

Now, one could leave it there and say *'discuss'*. MoD would brief Ministers, denying problems have ever existed. Ministers, despite knowing this to be untrue, would regurgitate the lie. But let us consider the evidence. What is the primary method for avoiding waste? The process is called Requirement Scrutiny, and it addresses three fundamental questions:

- Is it a proper charge to public funds and the defence budget?
- Is it affordable within budgetary constraints?
- Is it consistent with government/defence policy?

Conducting or contributing to scrutiny is an obligation placed upon all staff by the Permanent Under-Secretary of State for Defence (PUS), who is MoD's Chief Accounting Officer. That doesn't mean he is an accountant, or knows anything about Defence. He is accountable to Parliament, so it is he who answers before parliamentary committees. When conducting scrutiny, one is not working for one's line manager, but directly to PUS. (The basic principle behind the two events related in the Prologue). Those who sign requirements at the various stages have formal letters of delegation. They make a written declaration that scrutiny has been conducted in accordance with a set of rules. This applies to those who buy pencils or aircraft carriers. It is only the depth of scrutiny and level of approval that differ. This process is (in theory) overseen by the Defence Audit Committee, a sub-committee of the Defence Board (the highest committee of MoD); which in turn reports to the Defence Council.

If one makes a false declaration, one is avoiding an obligation to PUS; which is maladministration and fraud by misrepresentation. But, as we have seen, this is not considered wrongdoing. I disagree with this ruling, but concede many do not, and that members of the Defence Council have consistently upheld it. Given this, the inescapable conclusion is yes, it is MoD policy to waste money.

*

Government employees and Crown Servants who cannot bring themselves to implement its policies are required to resign. Why do we not see mass resignations? One reason is the waste described is mostly a consequence of local MoD policy, which conflicts with higher government policy. Also, types of policy may conflict. Avoiding waste is a financial policy, but disciplinary action for insisting on implementing it is a personnel policy: and never the two shall speak. With different parts of MoD responsible, it is difficult to reach resolution without falling foul of someone very senior. Often, staff just choose to avoid upsetting those who control their careers; and there can be no doubt there is a direct correlation between the willingness to commit this fraud to further personal advancement, and most of the deaths discussed here.

On the other hand, those who obey the law justify their actions by pointing to the legal obligations set out in their terms of employment. It is what prevents dismissal, because senior staff know it will be reversed at tribunal. However, this does not preclude reprisals, usually in the form of bullying and harassment; for example, by denying promotion, unwarranted criticism, and so on. The solution lies at government level. A cull is required, starting with those who advise Ministers this is acceptable behaviour. Followed by those Ministers who shamefully accept such advice.

4: Savings at the expense of safety - a pebble in a pond, long ago

In 1987 the RAF (who had control of tri-Service Air stores, and funding) introduced a policy termed 'DM87', inserted as a leaflet (DM87) in Air Publication 830 (the Supply Handbook). Contractors were to be denied access to MoD holdings of, for example, electronic spares. Those in MoD whom it affected most, the Service HQs and equipment project managers, were not told the policy was even being considered. Industry was 'advised' via a small ad next to an obituary in the 13 January 1988 issue of THESBAC, the circular of the Society of British Aerospace Companies. The RAF placed the onus on the Society to inform its members. Of what was unclear, because it had not circulated the actual policy or how it was to be implemented.

In most cases, these stores had been bought for the sole use of said contractors. Instructions were issued to destroy existing holdings. The immediate effects were:

- MoD was placed in contractual default (for not supplying spares).
- Extended repair times, which now included the time taken to source and buy replacement spares for those scrapped.
- Repair contracts had to be amended and funded to allow contractors to buy these replacements. Prohibited from buying economic quantities, unit prices increased.
- Air stations attempted repairs they were not capable of, often damaging the equipment even more and making it unsafe.

This ludicrous situation, whereby front line was desperate for kit, and contractors had the necessary spares to effect repairs but were under orders to scrap them, was compounded by Air Member Supply and Organisation (AMSO, in Harrogate) raising requisitions to replace the scrapped spares. Which, when delivered, would promptly be scrapped. Which would generate another requisition... This continued for at least eight years (evidenced by the 1996 audit report mentioned earlier).

Between 1988 and 1993, project managers escalated their concerns through MoD(PE) and AMSO management chains. It was recommended contractors at least be permitted to use up existing spares, or buy them. AMSO refused, so faced having to generate funding from within its existing budget to compensate for the waste. (It couldn't ask for more, as the idiocy would be immediately exposed). Something

33

had to give. What other source of funding was there to make these multiplicate buys, and fund the act of scrapping? The answer, initially (1988-1991), was that intended for attrition replacements and repairs. Because the Long Term Costings Instructions required the holding of a Contingency (16% of Depot Stock) and War Reserves, the effect was at first gradual, as these were consumed. All was exposed during Transition to War in late 1990. AMSO found itself unable to supply kit which should have been sat in store at immediate readiness. Front line and the media unfairly criticised politicians for unpreparedness and lack of funding. Those responsible stayed silent.

A key factor here is the typical two-year postings of military officers. Those who had developed and implemented the policy in 1987/88 were mostly gone by 1990. Their successors were left to carry the can, and they simply passed it to the civilians who knew the background, but whose suggestions had been rejected. When repeated, they were rejected again. This had nothing to do with right or wrong. The officers seeking advice were junior - typically Wing Commander and below. Upon finding out an Air Ranking officer had put his name to the policy, they walked away, unwilling to challenge orders. Legal and moral obligations were swiftly forgotten.

*

At this time, Post Design Services (PDS) funding was controlled by MoD(PE) in London; a huge organisation but with only a handful employed to understand these issues. The money was protected ('ring-fenced'). However, upon transfer to AMSO in 1991 the financial pots were combined, allowing PDS monies to be used to compensate for the effects of DM87. AMSO swiftly imposed cuts of ~28% for at least the next three years (to end of Financial Year 1993/94). Their view was PDS did not generate a 'due-in' on the stock computer (as maintaining the Build Standard is an intangible in that sense), so was a waste of money - fatally flawed reasoning which persists today.

These savings at the expense of safety were used to subsidise the, by now, runaway costs of repair contracts. This hid the problem for a while but, inevitably, the successive cuts bit, and the critical effect - compromised airworthiness - came to the fore. Developing modifications and investigation of faults ceased. Amendments to technical publications were stopped. Safety Cases became progressively invalid.

In the RN, nowhere was this RAF policy more apparent than the case of

Lynx helicopters making heavy landings due to smoke in cockpits, caused by crumbling Bakelite terminal blocks associated with the aircraft power supplies to the radar. With aircrew in sickbays, RAF suppliers refused to fund the investigation or mitigate this serious, and immediate, risk to life. (A disregard for fire hazards that has resonance with the Nimrod XV230 and Hercules XV179 cases). The Fire Control and Surveillance Radar team leader ignored them, suspended a low priority RAF contract (Hoffman Lightweight TACAN), and used the funding to make the Lynx fleet safe.

As far as the RN was concerned, the problem was reported on the Thursday and fixed by Ferranti Radar Systems Division over the weekend. However, in the background suppliers were livid, and the company targeted. Not blacklisted as such, but inundated with vexatious complaints about imaginary failings. On one occasion, an AMSO administrator attended a design meeting and demanded to know how the company would check a modified Sea Harrier radar power supply operated correctly at 45,000 feet; given the aircraft was single-seat and an engineer was required to conduct the test. The Chief Test Engineer's *'Using a bloody long cable'* seemed to suffice. While this might bring a smile, the company were furious at the implied impropriety.

In case you think this subject (spares, repairs, PDS) small beer, the annual waste on avionics ran to well over £100M (around £215M today[14]) - and Director Internal Audit confirmed the failings were pan-MoD. (The only part of MoD to receive a clean bill of health was Tornado engines, but that was more a case of desperation to find something right). A later chapter discusses another radar project, Cloud and Collision Warning Radar, which accounted for £3M of this in 1988/9. By contrast, PDS for all avionics cost around £12M per year (mostly man-hours). It can be seen that robbing this pot of 28% each year made little inroads into the cost of repairing the damage caused by DM87, but decimated airworthiness.

This was a contributory or aggravating factor in each of the accidents I discuss. DM87 was a pebble thrown in a pond long ago, and we are still seeing the ripples.

---

14 https://www.ons.gov.uk/.

5: Nimrod MR2 XV230 - Afghanistan 2 September 2006, and the subsequent Nimrod Review

Flight Sergeant Gary Andrews

Flight Sergeant Stephen Beattie

Flight Sergeant Gerard Bell

Flight Sergeant Adrian Davies

Lance Corporal Oliver Dicketts (Parachute Regiment)

Flight Lieutenant Steven Johnson

Sergeant Benjamin Knight

Sergeant John Langton

Flight Lieutenant Leigh Mitchelmore

Flight Lieutenant Gareth Nicholas

Sergeant Gary Quilliam

Flight Lieutenant Allan Squires

Flight Lieutenant Steven Swarbrick

Royal Marine Joseph Windall

On 2 September 2006 RAF Nimrod MR2 XV230 suffered an in-flight fire and crashed in Kandahar, Afghanistan, killing all 14 on board. This accident is fundamental to understanding MoD's ills. It led to the Nimrod Review, which recommended correct implementation of MoD's Safety Management System. It remains unclear when this will commence.

On 11 June 2007 I advised Graham and Trish Knight, who lost their son Ben in the crash, that the root cause was failure to maintain airworthiness, and to seek confirmation (or otherwise) that a valid Whole Aircraft Safety Case existed. It didn't. MoD and the Coroner now knew it was public knowledge that the aircraft was not airworthy.

On 4 December 2007 the Board of Inquiry's report was released:

'The loss of XV230 was caused by the escape of fuel during air-to-air refuelling'.

In his remarks, the Commander-in-Chief Air Command, Air Chief Marshal Sir Clive Loader concluded:

'The loss of XV230 and, far more importantly, of the 14 Service personnel who were aboard, resulted from shortcomings in the application of the processes for

assuring airworthiness and safe operation of the Nimrod. I am clear that further activity must be undertaken for our other aircraft types to check whether there is any read-across of lessons we have learned from this accident at such enormous [and immensely sad] cost'.

I explained to the Knights and their legal team that the systemic admission was key. (The reference to other aircraft types being affected). The failures were not confined to Nimrod. This is what a myself and a few colleagues had been fighting to highlight since 1988.

The same day, Des Browne MP, Secretary of State for Defence and Scotland, asked Mr Charles Haddon-Cave QC to conduct a Review. His remit was to study, in particular, Safety Cases, Hazard Analyses, and Maintenance practices. Mr Browne (now Lord Browne of Ladyton) was not told his junior Ministers had been given advance notice of the failings, but on MoD advice issued denials.

Importantly, Mr Browne effectively waived the Official Secrets Act so that past and present MoD employees could give evidence without fear of censure. This opened the door on other cases, such as Mull of Kintyre, because the systemic nature of the failings meant the same evidence was relevant in each case, and would now be in the public domain.

*

A little background is required to the air-to-air refuelling (AAR) system. Two weeks into the Falklands War, the first of the upgraded MR2s began replacing the MR1s. An AAR Service Designed Modification was embodied in early May 1982. This gave the Nimrod force the required reach, allowing it to operate off the Argentine coast. The operational sortie limit of 24 hours was now determined by engine oil consumption.

In August 1982, MoD asked British Aerospace (BAeS) to conduct a feasibility study into an AAR capability on the Nimrod AEW (Airborne Early Warning) Mk3 aircraft, which was then in development. In late 1982 BAeS presented a proposal, and later another for the installation of a permanent AAR capability in the MR2 and R1.

Nimrod AEW was cancelled in 1986. That year BAeS submitted its proposals for the permanent conversion, by formal modification, of both the MR2 and R1. The modification was in due course introduced across the fleets.

In 1984, MoD had purchased former commercial TriStar aircraft, gradually converting them to tankers to supplement the VC10 and Victor fleets.

The maximum permissible flow rate for the Nimrod fuel couplings was 1,052.7 kg/minute. But the TriStars delivered 2,100 kg/minute. During trials in the 1990s, it rapidly became apparent that the higher delivery pressure was too much for the Nimrod to bear, causing blow-offs and fuel line coupling failures. (Moreover, the TriStar's third engine caused the Nimrod's tail fin to flex, leading to handlings problems).

As a result, Nimrod was not cleared for tanking from TriStars. MoD has been reluctant to set out why, by 2005, this was taking place despite the incompatibility and critical safety hazard remaining.

But even in normal use, leaks were common; an inevitability given the complexity of the Nimrod's fuel system - in part due to the box construction of the mainplanes, necessitating joins in fuel lines between each box. Also, the difficulty of fitting and aligning the couplings. It merged at the Inquest that the requirement was one degree, but no instructions, tools or training were provided to achieve this, and four degrees and worse was the norm. And repairing leaks is a specialised task, but the experience and numbers of Nimrod maintainers was allowed to diminish. Poor practice and human errors increased, as did the leaks.

In summary, the fuel systems of both Nimrod and TriStar were understood in isolation; but when mated during refuelling the whole was a new, third, system that behaved differently. In other words, functional safety had not been assured, and this behaviour was not reflected in the Safety Cases. (Note: not only the Nimrod Safety Case, the TriStar's as well). It was later revealed that the figures had been removed from the Aircrew Manual, denying aircrew the opportunity to spot the risk.

At the Inquest in May 2008, and after listening to evidence, Oxford Coroner Andrew Walker ruled that the leak came from a coupling within the fuel feed system, and this fuel was ignited by a hot duct within, or closely associated with, Dry Bay 7 on the starboard side.

*

As mentioned previously, the way to avoid this is to prepare Interface Definition Documents. The flow rate from the tanker, and the maximum acceptable by the receiving aircraft, are presented side by side. It would be immediately obvious there was a mismatch. Failure, and in many cases flat refusal, to carry out this mandated work is widespread in MoD. Later, I explain the fatal consequences in the Sea King ASaC and other cases. In other words, XV230 was a recurrence.

Based on my evidence, Mr Walker asked about compliance with Military Airworthiness Regulations. MoD dismissed them as *'irrelevant'*. He disagreed, and instructed MoD to make them available to the court. He summed up:

> 'This aircraft, like every other aircraft within the Nimrod fleet, was not airworthy. What is more, the aircraft was, in my judgment, never airworthy from the first release for service in 1969, following its conversion from the Comet C4 civil aircraft to the Nimrod MR1, through the modification to the Nimrod MR2, completed in 1979, to the point where Nimrod MR2 XV230 was lost. I would be failing in my duty if I didn't report action to the relevant authority that would prevent future fatalities. I have given the matter considerable thought and I see no alternative but to report to the secretary of state that the Nimrod fleet should not fly until the ALARP standards are met'.

This is a fair assessment. The most relevant technical investigations, <u>by members of the public</u>, revealed a design defect had lain dormant for many years, manifesting itself when a series of factors combined on the day of the accident - a classic illustration of the Reason Model. Many, including Mr Haddon-Cave, criticised Mr Walker, but all missed the fundamental point he was making. It was for MoD to positively prove the aircraft airworthy. It could not.

The Chief of the Air Staff, Air Chief Marshal Glenn Torpy, briefed the media that the aircraft was *'safe to fly'*. He did not set out the expected use, or specify what risks he wanted his men to continue to run. On 23 May 2008, Minister for the Armed Forces, Bob Ainsworth MP, stated:

> 'I would like to reassure all those concerned that the Chief of the Air Staff has reaffirmed to me that the Nimrod is airworthy'.

Somewhat premature in the middle of a Review ordered by his superior, prompted by overwhelming evidence to the contrary. He later admitted he had not read the Coroner's report, and Air Chief Marshal Torpy did not reveal his reasons. Both were complicit in the concealment of prior negligence.

In December 2008, Secretary of State for Defence John Hutton was served with a writ by two families. Responding, in March 2009 MoD admitted liability, submitting papers to the High Court admitting the aircraft was not airworthy. The court ruled:

> 'The defendant owed to the deceased a duty of care and the accident was caused by this breach of that duty of care'.

*

But to regress. On 1 July 2008, a debate took place in the House of Commons on 'The Nimrod Fleet'. Angus Robertson MP (SNP), in whose constituency RAF Kinloss lay, took the lead. He has always been supportive of those striving to uncover the truth of these accidents, and XV230 in particular. Here, the main issue was a claim by Des Browne MP on 4 December 2007 that:

'QinetiQ has conducted an independent investigation into the fuel system and confirmed that, in light of the measures taken since the crash, the fuel system is safe to operate'.

Yet in the same breath he confirmed:

'Air-to-air refuelling has been suspended subject to further investigation".

The apparent contradictions are obvious, the main implication being that ceasing AAR suddenly made the Nimrod safe. This avoided the much deeper problem of organisational failures, and the decision being made by people who had failed to conduct systems integration or prove functional safety. What confidence could there be in them being right this time?

Mr Robertson cited a more recent event involving a serious fuel leak that a technical investigation had been unable to *fully understand'*. In reply, Mr Browne reiterated:

'I am assured...this aircraft is safe to fly and airworthy. I would not allow it to fly if I did not believe that to be the case'.

The report in question, 'Nimrod Fuel Leak Study', had been issued on 17 March 2006, almost six months before the accident.[15] It took many months to acquire a copy. It included 30 recommendations, and I mapped 29 of these directly to JSP553 'Military Airworthiness Regulations', which is mandated in all aviation contracts. Also, many were invoked by Defence Standards 00-970 'Design and Airworthiness Requirements for Military Aircraft', and 00-56 'Safety Management Requirement for Defence Systems'. ('Requirements' are also mandatory). The single recommendation that was not mentioned in the airworthiness regulations was mandated separately by the Chief of Defence Procurement.

The report concluded:

'The recommendations should be considered and acted upon before it can be considered the equipment risks are As Low As Reasonably Practicable.

---

15 QinetiQ/D&TS/Air/RF051726/14, 17 March 2006.

I offered my assessment to Mr Robertson, and in the debate of 1 July he repeated my conclusion:

'The Secretary of State assured the House that Nimrod was safe, citing a report by QinetiQ. To establish whether that was factually correct has been difficult, and it took a Freedom of Information request to establish that the report said that the aircraft would not be fully safe until its 30 recommendations were carried out. All but one of those related to a failure to implement mandatory airworthiness regulations'.

In reply, Bob Ainsworth MP stated:

'I am told that that is not correct. I do not know where (Mr Robertson) got that information from'.

Six of the recommendations related to AAR - they were discounted, implying the AAR suspension was to be permanent. MoD did not accept a further three; rejecting at least two of the Secretary of State's mandates and the regulations in which they were laid down. (Noting again that MoD had told the Coroner these regulations were irrelevant).

Mr Ainsworth said MoD was implementing the remaining 21 'as soon as is reasonably practicable'; completely ignoring that the Assistant Chief of the Air Staff, in signing the Release to Service, had confirmed they were already implemented - something that would have been re-scrutinised the previous year when assessing whether to cease AAR. Once again, MoD had lied to a Minister.

The Nimrod Review (2008-09)

Even after such a time, I remain in two minds about the Review. MoD serially misled Mr Haddon-Cave. While perhaps told the truth up to a point, a lie of omission is still a lie. He was provided with MoD offices, and advisors intent on minimising the damage to MoD. Immediately, he was difficult to contact, and it was only after Graham Knight hand-delivered a second copy that he wrote thanking me for my submission.

MoD provided his secretary, an official who had acted in the same capacity during the Deepcut Review. Perhaps more pertinent, he had been a contracts officer in his early career, with particular responsibility in 1990-91 for Nimrod support contacts. Therefore, he was an ideal first-hand witness to the evidence that these contracts had been curtailed due to the aforementioned savings; and that project managers had been complaining this directly affected airworthiness. It is unknown if he declared this.

Mr Haddon-Cave undoubtedly succumbed to this MoD influence, overlooking evidence (actual documents) revealing notification of systemic failings in the late 1980s. Instead, he claimed they commenced in 1998. Why? Who benefited? The answer is clear from his paragraph 13.124, discussing and praising two Chief Engineers, Air Chief Marshals Michael Alcock (1991-96) and Colin Terry (1997-99). The former had been heavily implicated in the rundown of airworthiness in the early 90s; the latter had, as Director General Support Management, overseen the third ~28% cut in direct airworthiness funding in 1993-94. (Particularly relevant, given the Review's criticism of General Sir Sam Cowan for a 20% cut, spread over five years). This chapter (13) is headed 'Cuts, Change, Dilution and Distraction (1998-2006)'. Had it correctly said '1988-99', the entire tenor of the report would have had to change. Also, the names of those accused of wrongdoing and incompetence.

Nevertheless, he did support most of my key points, reiterating:

'The shortcomings in the current airworthiness system in the MoD are manifold and include:

- *A failure to adhere to basic principles*
- *A Military Airworthiness System that is not fit for purpose*
- *A Safety Case regime which is ineffective and wasteful*
- *A series of weaknesses in the area of personnel*
- *A Safety Culture that has allowed business to eclipse airworthiness'.*

Most of the airworthiness system *was* fit for purpose - it just wasn't implemented correctly. Yes, the system is broken if it permits this failure, but it was essentially a single point failure and easy to fix - but less so with the passage of time. (The Compliance pillar). Those responsible were known, because they had placed their rulings and policy decisions in writing. He lauded these same officers, instead naming and shaming innocent MoD individuals. (I cannot speak for the QinetiQ and BAeS employees he named, although it is clear from his comprehensive assessment of their evidence that they, too, suffered from a culture of bullying and harassment if they dared raise safety concerns).

It went unsaid that these failings had been notified time and again by MoD staff, only to be rejected. Allowed to judge their own case, senior staff were insulated from personal accountability, forming the perfect recipe for repeated failures. To emphasise these prior notifications, in my submission I stated:

'The causes of this accident are rooted in MoD's systematic failure to implement the regulations designed to ensure airworthiness, despite many warnings of the consequences, over a long period.

On 15 September 2005 I wrote to my MP, who passed the letter to Adam Ingram, Minister for the Armed Forces: "In my experience, this ambivalent attitude towards safety is compelling evidence of a lack of robustness in the application of procedures within the MoD, which I have known to result in critical safety problems".

On 17 May 2007 Mr Ingram replied: "Mr Hill has stated that although the MoD has a robust airworthiness regulatory framework it is not applied robustly. I contend that the framework is applied robustly". [His emphasis]. Please note the delay between my letter and Ingram's reply. Nimrod XV230 crashed on 2 September 2006.

I tried again, to his successor Bob Ainsworth MP. "I contend that cultural traits and organisational practices which are contrary to sound engineering practice and detrimental to safety have been allowed to develop. Effective communication of critical safety information, and intelligent debate, is stifled. There is a lack of integrated management and oversight across programs and often an informal and uninformed chain of command and decision-making process exists outside the formal airworthiness and safety delegations". On 2 August 2008, Minister repeated his position'.

Again, had he mentioned this his report would have had to be completely different. He would have had to name those who continually took this line in ministerial briefings.

Messrs Ingram and Ainsworth were, tragically, proved wrong. Neither has apologised, and no action has been taken against those who misled them. An opportunity to prevent the accident was lost.

*

Mr Haddon-Cave cited the Nimrod Airworthiness Review Team (NART) report of 1996, and to his credit rejected an assessment by Reviewing Officers that the comments therein were crewroom *'gossip and whinges'.* However, while confirming these whinges were prescient, he did not mention the available ARTs dated back to August 1992, and had noted a series of fatal crashes caused by the same systemic failings. Citing this would have damned those he praised. He seemed oblivious to the fact NART was (by definition) reporting pre-1996 systemic failings (and the Chinook/Wessex/Puma ART of 1992 referred back to 1987), yet he had dated them at 1998. In this respect his report is like most Board of Inquiry reports. Obvious disconnects and contradictions exist.

Someone may have *proof read* it, but it was not *copy edited.*

Legal action was considered against those named. Investigations abruptly ceased when the RAF Provost Marshal, Thames Valley Police, and Crown Prosecution Service were informed of the truth.[16]

*

Turning again to fuel leaks, at paragraph 3.11.1:

> *The Nimrod Safety Case quoted the potential for a fuel system leakage as Improbable, which is defined as: "Remote likelihood of occurrence to just 1 or 2 aircraft during the operational life of a particular fleet". The Board of Inquiry's analysis of fault data, however, indicated an average of 40 fuel leaks per annum between 2000 and 2005'.*

Air Chief Marshal Torpy defended this on BBC Panorama, saying:

> *'The level of fuel leaks has remained constant'.*

Yes, <u>constantly high and constantly dangerous</u>.

Moreover, Nimrod was designed for a life of 10,000 flying hours. The fleet leader had flown over 19,000 hours, but no components had been cleared beyond the original 10,000. Flying an aircraft beyond its design specification, never mind nearly doubling the flying hours, without evidence of an Ageing Aircraft Audit, Life Extension Programme, and re-certification, is a major failing and <u>must</u> have involved numerous false declarations that compulsory regulations had been followed.

I have just outlined two serious offences - misleading/lying by omission (be it by Torpy, Ingram and Ainsworth, or those who briefed them), and making false record (*inter alia*, in the Release to Service, by Assistant Chiefs of the Air Staff). Worse, these were <u>repeat</u> offences. Senior officers and Ministers knew this, explaining their failure to act. That introduces an element of malice aforethought to the equation.

*

Unsurprisingly, the now Sir Charles is often invited to give talks on his Review. These are always excellent, although of course omit certain inconvenient truths. His manner is self-deprecating, compensating for the inevitably dry nature of the subject. He manages to inject gentle humour, and has settled down to a presentation of:

- 7 steps to the accident.
- 7 themes.

---

16 For example, letter to Thames Valley Police Chief Constable, 6 October 2010, copied to Mr Charles Haddon-Cave.

- 7 lessons; one of them, organisational, broken down into 12 failures, with parallels drawn to the Space Shuttle Challenger disaster.

He properly places more emphasis on certain issues, such as the irreversible damage caused by outsourcing and *'too little appreciation of specialist skills and hoary-handed aged engineers, and too great a reverence to young soft-handed MBAs'*.[17] But, he continues to date the beginning of these failings to 1998, despite the privatisation of MoD's workshops in the mid-90s (from whence the hoary-handed, and often not too aged engineers came from), and the introduction of a 2-tier engineering stream (the 'MBAs' and the 'specialists') in 1991. Overnight, the hoary specialists, MoD's experience and corporate knowledge, were deemed incompetent and unnecessary, cast aside in favour of the 'MBAs'. (In fairness, many had good engineering degrees, but that is no preparation for practical airworthiness management).

Particularly relevant to any MoD accident, he reiterates that one must not simply blame the final act, but look higher at organisational failures. Also, to be aware of normalisation of deviance. The most obvious example of this is senior staff instructing subordinates to violate airworthiness and requirement scrutiny regulations, they do, and it becomes the norm; although at no point in his Review is there mention of this, despite it being a root cause of many deaths. Similarly, he correctly talks of the *'dilution of risk management processes'*, while overlooking that projects are routinely denied risk manager posts, and staff instructed to ignore the subject.

Suffice to say, his 7 themes, 7 lessons, and 12 organisational failures, were contributory factors in the main accident discussed here, the 2003 Sea King mid-air. All were predicted, notified, and ignored. Mr Haddon-Cave knew this, but a feature of his report is that he did not articulate the linkages to other fatal accidents, despite confirming the failings were systemic. Oddly, for a QC, he did not set out his argument sufficiently. He accepted my headline points, but had he repeated my detailed justification for each he would have, for example, revealed the truth behind the Chinook Mull of Kintyre accident of 1994 (29 killed); casting doubt on the innocence of those he praised.

The report added nothing to what was known, but was of huge value. It is still largely ignored by MoD; which would soon stop if, in his day job, .

---

17 The Hon. Mr Justice Haddon-Cave to the Piper 25 Conference, June 2013 'Leadership and Culture, Principles and Professionalism, Simplicity and Safety - Lessons from the Nimrod Review'.

Sir Charles ever got the opportunity to sentence the offenders to a few years in prison.

Why was Nimrod MRA4 cancelled?

The requirement to replace Nimrod MR2 can be dated to the 1980s. The MR2 was a modification to the MR1, itself based on the commercial Comet design. There is a saying - *don't modify a modification*. It is not set in stone, but intended to warn of the high probability of certain risks materialising; chief among them obsolescence, a poor audit trail, and weak Safety Cases. It indicates what risk reduction work must be undertaken, in preparation for the main contract.

The problems with the MRA4 are legend, and revolve around the failure to mitigate not only risks, but certainties. In fact, in 1996 BAeS recommended establishing a new production line and building from new, to modern standards, not those of the 1940s and 50s. Both they and MoD's own engineers knew what was coming. That prescience again. MoD declined. Not by coincidence, that same year the Chief of Defence Procurement launched an extraordinary attack on his engineering staff, saying he did not want engineers managing technical programmes. Technical advice of any kind was dismissed out of hand. It is very disconcerting suddenly working in such an environment. At the time, myself and colleagues were employed for our programme management and engineering background in all parts of the procurement cycle. Overnight, non-engineers (in our case, a physiologist) were permitted to overrule our engineering and airworthiness decisions, very often cancelling contracts without considering the consequences. I explore this further later.

*

On 1 July 2008, Bob Ainsworth MP stated:

> 'It is the view of all those involved in the Equipment Safety and Environmental Working Group, which includes QinetiQ, BAE Systems, the RAF and the (MoD) Integrated Project Team, that the Nimrod is tolerably safe and ALARP, and is therefore safe to fly. No member of the group demurs from that view'.

Except... On 19 October 2010 the MRA4 programme was cancelled, wasting over £4Bn, and the entire fleet publicly scrapped. The government 'spun' this as a part of the Strategic Defence and Security Review, claiming the UK did not need a core fixed wing maritime patrol capability. On 27 January 2011, MoD claimed:

'The severe financial pressures and the urgent need to bring the defence programme into balance meant we could not retain all existing programmes'.

Several retired senior officers protested in the media against this loss of strategic capability. They criticised the government for not making provision to avoid the capability gap, missing the point that their former colleagues (and possibly themselves) had known for some years this outcome was inevitable, but had misled Ministers.

The truth emerged on 3 February 2014, during an exchange between Kevan Jones MP (Labour) and Philip Hammond MP, Secretary of State for Defence. The latter stated:

'It is a bit rich for him to say that the gap in maritime patrol cover was created by this government. What this government did was to recognise the reality that <u>his</u> government had been investing in aircraft <u>that would never fly, would never be certified and would never be able to deliver a capability'.</u>

(That a previous Conservative government initiated the programme apparently escaped Mr Hammond. Mr Jones, who had been a junior Defence Minister from 2008-10, plainly did not appreciate he had been handed a gift, and did not reply).

In other words, the MRA4 could never be certified as airworthy. Yet, two years before, Hammond had echoed the MoD claim that the decision was for financial reasons:

'Scrapping the ill-fated Nimrod MRA4 was one of many tough but necessary decisions we had to take to deal with an equipment programme that was out of control'.[18]

Did he not appreciate he had given Parliament two different stories?

This admission warrants a full Inquiry. It should begin with the *'several hundred design standard non-compliances'* cited by MoD shortly before the cancellation announcement.[19] On 13 October 2010, close to cancellation, an internal MoD report listed examples. Only the unclassified part has been made available, so presumably there are worse problems than those affecting bomb bay doors, Aileron Feel and Trim Unit, Ram Air Turbine, icing clearance, inability to correlate finite element modelling and wing fatigue tests, hot air pipe in forward intake zone, inadequate drainage in forward intake zone, HP8 hot air pipe clamp, nose landing gear, and engine bay firewall. Also, under-tension fuel pipes, which is uncomfortably close to the cause of XV230. The report lists only two

---

18 https://www.bbc.co.uk/news/uk-16965450, 10 February 2012.
19 Letter report DES/11/06, 13 October 2010.

47

issues that have been resolved - aerodynamic design and flap hinge failure.

Whoever in MoD was faced with the decision would not have got a warm feeling, and it is easy to see why he cancelled.

Bad enough, but even worse is that the Design Review process, to be conducted at configuration milestones throughout the development programme, broke down completely. These reviews culminate in an Installation Design Conference. The Trials Installation aircraft is presented to MoD, offering the final opportunity to identify such failings before drawings are sealed. *'Several hundred non-compliances'* is a damning indictment.

*

What was the problem? Contractually, Nimrod MR2 was Government Furnished Equipment to the MRA4 programme, and the contract had to set out the defined design baseline; which would be modified to create the MRA4. That is, MoD had to agree what it would deliver to BAe, and the contract would say something like:

'Quantity (x) Nimrod MR2 to be fed in at the following Build Standard...'.

Complementing this, other contractual obligations would be delivery of an up-to-date drawing set and valid Safety Case to BAe (because the design was Under Ministry Control, not Under Contractor Control). This would be Government Furnished Information, and without which Service regulated flying of the MR2 would be prohibited. The obvious risk, in fact certainty, encountered by almost every other aircraft and avionics programme at the time, was that it was no longer funded policy to maintain Safety Cases.

The agreed baseline was Issue 26 of the Nimrod MR2 General Assembly Drawing, dated January 1996. (There are a number of ways of expressing this, and this is acceptable so long as the GA drawing references the required detail). But no-one, not MoD, nor even BAe Chadderton, Design Authority for Nimrod, could define 'Issue 26', as configuration control had not been maintained. By definition, therefore, there could be no valid Safety Case or Release to Service.

This should be the first question asked by any investigation into the failure of the MRA4 programme. The second would be why MoD offered a contract with an unverifiable and impossible to achieve condition (placing itself at enormous risk), and why BAe accepted it (rendering it impossible to meet its contractual obligations). And if one cannot define the Induction Build Standard, how on earth can the work package be determined or costed? I can't, so the contract is open-ended, and the cheque book blank. Which is exactly what happened.

This was confirmed when, in March 2008, a query from production engineering (BAe Woodford) led to the discovery that they were using the latest issue of MR2 drawings (2007) to build PA4 (the first aircraft to be delivered). That is, in design terms there was an unexplained and undefinable gap between what was contracted and what was used. That's (at least) 11 years of unknowns, with each one potentially increasing the price and adding to the probability of slippage, and ultimately not being able to produce a Safety Case.

This explains why the Nimrod MR2 Integrated Project Team (IPT) was frantically trying to generate a Safety Case in the early 2000s. Had Mr Haddon-Cave noted this background in his report, he would have not been able to justify criticising the IPT leader, Group Captain George Baber. He would have had to ask who abrogated their legal obligation to produce and maintain one in the first place, and what policy led to the decision. And why that person signed to say one existed.

*

How to avoid the problem? A risk reduction programme was required to stabilise the Build Standard, but was not conducted. Yet, as you will learn, this was the basis of the success of a concurrent and a related (through radar design commonality) programme within the same Directorate General, the Sea King ASaC Mk7.

Why was this mandated procedure implemented on one programme, but not the other? Who knew of this? At a management oversight level, Director General Air Systems 2 (a 2-Star). But the buck cannot stop there because, due to the procurement strategy (dual single tender), the Chief of Defence Procurement (a 4-Star) had to personally approve the main technical and contractual pre-requisite Mk7 programme.[20]

Where is the proof senior management knew of this in time to influence Nimrod? First and foremost, the pre-requisite programme was subject to weekly review due to the procurement strategy, and was also reviewed by the Public Accounts Committee, to whom the Chief of Defence Procurement, Sir Robert Walmsley, gave evidence on the subject on 3 March 1999.

Moreover, the final report for the said pre-requisite was issued

---

20 Submission D/DHP 24/4/93, 25 July 1995, resulting in contract H11a/809 and subsequently H11a/838.

internally (within the Sea King IPT) by the programme manager on 22 October 2000. His formal Post Project Evaluation report, which is the main 'lessons to be learned' document, was sent to the Deputy Chief Executive of the Defence Procurement Agency (a 3-Star) in May 2001.[21] (DPA had replaced MoD(PE) in April 1999). It stated:

'Advance funding was committed to a 4-phase risk reduction programme to assess and stabilise the Build Standard. The primary risk areas were (a) poor Configuration Control, (b) component unavailability and (c) equipment not up to modification state. All risk predictions proved valid, were mitigated, and read-across to other Sea King projects'.

Who was responsible for this policy, and the lack of management oversight? The first is easy, because it is a matter of record - Air Member Supply and Organisation (RAF), whose *savings at the expense of safety* policy was developed in 1987. But when the Public Accounts Committee asked in 2010 who had management oversight of MRA4, MoD claimed not to know; although it conceded its own guidelines required each project to have a nominated Senior Responsible Officer. In practice, this is at 1-Star level (Air Commodore or equivalent). Above him, the 2-Star is required to assess the top 10 risks under his remit every month. The Committee reported:

'There were inadequate records kept of who had been responsible throughout a project's life'.[22]

But those who could read the MoD telephone directory or the project files knew. The 1-Star was Director Maritime, also responsible for Merlin. And, as stated, his 2-Star was Director General Air Systems 2 (later Executive Director 1), whose rulings are a recurring feature of this book. Rather conveniently, all Nimrod records originated by him have now been destroyed.[23]

*

What of the 2008 assertion by the Equipment Safety and Environmental Working Group? Each member was now seen to be completely wrong - staggering given MoD's most junior engineers were required to understand the subject implicitly. In the real world, one might expect questions to be asked and Group members relieved of their duties. But that would reveal Ministers were given advance notice of the failings, and that senior MoD staff had blatantly lied in briefings.

---

21 ES(Air) 24/4/93 (D/DHP/24/4/93), May 2001. 'ECS Post Project Evaluation report'
22 Committee of Public Accounts, Major Projects report 2010.
23 Letter FOI2018/01835, 10 April 2019.

That, the failings repeated those of other fatal accidents - again, and most notably, the 1994 Mull of Kintyre crash, which at the time was gaining a higher profile due to precisely the same lies being exposed.

Cancellation was a neat way of sweeping a lot of legacy issues under the carpet, especially if there was to be no Inquiry into the general MRA4 fiasco, and no prosecutions on XV230. And this has since been repeated on other aircraft fleets, and other fatal accidents.

In 2008 the House of Commons Defence Select Committee described Chinook Mk3 as the *'gold standard cock up'*. One assumes Nimrod MRA4 inherited this mantle. After all, failure was a certainty and it cost over £4Bn to prove it. Either way, same 2-Star.

6: The Military Aviation Authority (MAA)

The MAA was formed in April 2010, as a result of the Nimrod Review. It has full oversight of Defence aviation activity, and undertakes the role of the single authority responsible for regulating all aspects of Air Safety across Defence. Mr Haddon-Cave had recommended an independent Military <u>Airworthiness</u> Authority, but that would provide a clue to the real problem and those responsible. In 2016 a further restructuring saw it subsumed into the Defence Safety Authority, and its head downgraded from 3-Star to 2-Star.

The Secretary of State instructed the MAA to implement the recommendations of the Nimrod Review, most of which were mandated anyway. One was to update the regulations, which the MAA set about with gusto. Some were certainly dated, mostly due to MoD's constant reorganisations (one of Mr Haddon-Cave's seven themes, and a lesson it steadfastly refuses to learn), but they were still fit for purpose to a competent and experienced user. Would it not be better to provide engineering staff who satisfy MoD grade minima? And suitable leadership? In effect, regulations are being re-written to compensate for no longer providing either. Infinitely worse - staff may refuse to implement them, but make a false declaration they have. Also repulsive is the immorality of forcing this maladministration upon servicemen, to their detriment. The MAA refuses to discuss this, despite so many deaths. It's supposed independence is a distinction without a difference.

*

In October 2019, Dr David Snowball of the Health and Safety Executive (HSE), who had recently chaired a panel auditing the MAA, was invited to speak at a conference hosted by the Royal Aeronautical Society. A few weeks before I had asked him: *'Would the new regime under the MAA have prevented these accidents?'*. He replied saying his remit was *'confined to the implementation of the Haddon-Cave recommendations'*. But what if the MAA will not admit the recommendations are mandated policy anyway? Lacking that acceptance, any audit is worthless.

My letter was copied to the Chief Executive of the Royal Aeronautical Society, Mr Simon Luxmoore. He replied saying the content (discussing airworthiness) was *'none of my or the Society's business'*; which might come as a surprise to its Airworthiness Group. I replied:

'I am aware the RAeS is hosting the forthcoming MAA Military Air Safety Conference, and you are giving the opening address. In that context, I thought

both you and the Society would regard aviation safety as relevant to your business. The evidence I have offered is based on MoD's own papers. I hope none of it is contradicted'.

Delegates were duly misled. It was a backslapfest.

Another speaker was Director General-elect of the MAA, Air Vice Marshal Barry North. In the event, he did not take up post as planned, instead becoming Deputy Commander (Personnel). The brief prepared for him claimed <u>Mr Haddon-Cave</u> had identified systemic failings. In fact, <u>civilian MoD staff</u> identified them, from the late 1980s-on, and advised them to senior civilian and Service staff, Ministers, the Coroner; and then Mr Haddon-Cave.

It was also claimed there was an inability in MoD to *'recognise that risks were building'* prior to the loss of Nimrod XV230. This was untrue, evidenced by numerous internal reports of the late 1980s/early 1990s - not least by the RAF's Director of Flight Safety. These had been submitted to those directly responsible for airworthiness oversight, but buried by the senior officers whom the Nimrod Review later applauded.

*

The following year, MAA Technical Director Air Vice Marshal Martin Clarke, claimed:

'We've asked some difficult questions. That's why we were created'.[24]

Wrong again. You didn't ask difficult questions, the public did. You were created after MoD lied when replying, and Nimrod XV230 crashed. Catch yourself on. It's embarrassing.

Why say this? It is difficult for a senior RAF officer in the MAA to acknowledge the only reason his post exists is because his superiors have erred to the point of committing serious offences, causing avoidable deaths. There is a solution, and it is linked to a more basic question - why are there so few civilian specialists in the MAA? Such work is a vocation, not something for a two-year military posting. MoD, and especially the RAF, do not like admitting it was civilian staff who met their legal obligations, and whose evidence Mr Haddon-Cave and Coroner Andrew Walker accepted over official denials.

So, how many in the MAA have in the past reported these systemic failings? MoD's official position is that only one employee met this

---

24 Aviation International News, 13 July 2014.

obligation, and I was wrong to do so.[25] At the very least, the Director of Flight Safety's notifications from 1992-98 give lie to this. Yet, MoD continues with this allegation; implying MAA staff have either failed in their statutory duty, or have no relevant experience. Surely a truly independent MAA would challenge this? It is demonstrably aware, in fact now contributes to these briefings, yet says nothing. That silence speaks volumes.

Knowing the root failure, why does MoD/MAA refuse to address it? The answer is the same. Identifying failures by Air Ranking officers does not sit well within a Service-led organisation. This cultural barrier becomes insurmountable because it is necessary to publicly rescind the policies, and outlaw the practices, of those who caused the failings. To do so, one needs to be free from fear or censure; which often means waiting until the perpetrators are retired. We already know the attitude of a recent Chief of the Air Staff - he publicly supported the very officers who caused the problem.[26] His message was loud and clear to those aspiring to Air Rank.

*

It can be seen why the MoD/MAA is openly hostile to the edicts of the Secretary of State, and why it denigrates those who reported the failings, while protecting those who ignored the warnings.

Overall, however, and subject to the right leadership and political support, the MAA must be seen as a force for good, although wholly unnecessary had MoD allowed its staff to meet their legal obligations. Safety in general has regained a higher profile, with the worldwide resetting of aviation safety directly traceable to the evidence given to Andrew Walker and Graham Knight's legal team in 2007.

However, the lack of understanding, experience and training means MoD staff are now reluctant to make decisions - fatal in aviation. A key aim, which MoD/MAA cannot even discuss, must be that the safety of equipment and personnel should no longer have to rely on the willingness of civilian project managers to disobey orders. The main benefit so far is improved consistency. But the bar has been set extremely low, and later I cite very serious failings that have occurred on the MAA's watch. There is a long way to go.

---

25 Directorate of Personnel, Resources and Development briefing to the Under Secretary of State for Defence, 23 April 2003.
26 Air Chief Marshal Stephen Dalton letter to the Guardian, 6 January 2010.

The elephant in the room is this. To understand the way ahead, one must accept what caused the problems. The MAA simply will not admit that written warnings were given to Ministers <u>before</u> Nimrod XV230 crashed. Today, few in MoD know why the MAA was formed. Including the MAA.

PART 2: SEA KINGS ASAC MK7 XV650 AND XV704 - IRAQ, 22 MARCH 2003

Lieutenant Thomas Adams, United States Navy

Lieutenant Philip Green RN

Lieutenant Antony King RN

Lieutenant Marc Lawrence RN

Lieutenant Philip West RN

Lieutenant James Williams RN

Lieutenant Andrew Wilson RN

On 22 March 2003, two Royal Navy Sea King ASaC Mk7 helicopters collided off the Al-Faw Peninsula in the Northern Arabian Gulf, killing all seven crew. The Board of Inquiry concluded that, due to lack of evidence, the events of the last few minutes could never be fully understood, and the precise cause could not be determined. On 8 January 2007 the Oxford Deputy Assistant Coroner, Sir Richard Curtis, concluded the collision was an accident.

*

This section contains the main narrative of the book. It discusses elements of the case in some detail, emphasising the common factors between it and others; and links these to breaches of the Military Covenant. It reveals the evidence concealed from the Board of Inquiry, Coroner and families, and seeks to rationalise why the integrity of the Mk7 programme was compromised from mid-2001, allowing known risks to manifest themselves on 22 March 2003.

I will take you through the history of the Sea King AEW Mk2 and various upgrades leading to the Mk7 standard, describing MoD's structure at the time, its policies, and their effect on aviation safety. Key decisions, events, and the linkages to wider organisational faults are explored. This background is necessary before we can assess the Board of Inquiry report and the proceedings of the Coroner's Inquest, and reinforces the principle that the final act is rarely to blame for accidents.

Extracts from the 2007 Inquest are discussed where relevant. Please bear one thing in mind... MoD conducted an investigation into what it considered the main contributory factor - the High Intensity Strobe Lights being unairworthy. It then denied all knowledge of this investigation to families, and its outcome remains suppressed.

The Board of Inquiry itself raised the subject of airworthiness failings. (Hence, I do not allege or seek to argue the point). What sets this case apart is their nature. In 1994, Chinook HC Mk2 was so immature it was three years away from satisfying the regulations when ZD576 crashed on the Mull of Kintyre. Nimrod never did. Sea King ASaC Mk7, having been upgraded from the AEW Mk2, was close - frustratingly so. The failures that plagued the others were well-known, and at first had been avoided by simply implementing regulations. Unfortunately, in fact criminally, this risk reduction work was later cancelled without alternative mitigation, weakening defences designed to prevent collision. At night, at low level, with sensors unavailable, and anti-collision strobes switched off, the eyesight of the four cockpit crew became critical. In darkness, that was the weakest link.

My central point is this. Known performance degradation between the AEW Mk2 and ASaC Mk7 wholly coincided with the Board's three main contributory factors.

7: The eyes of the fleet

Sea King AEW Mk2

The 1982 Falklands War in the South Atlantic confirmed a known gap in capability, absence of an effective Airborne Early Warning capability to get inside the enemy's decision cycle. As the new Invincible Class Carriers lacked catapults or arrestor gear, only a helicopter could be considered. In May 1982, while hostilities were ongoing, Westland Helicopters converted two Sea King HAS Mk2s to undertake the AEW role; ironically, XV650 and XV704. The radar, Searchwater LAST (Low Altitude Surveillance Task), was an adaptation of Searchwater in Nimrod. This had been suggested in 1979 by Thorn-EMI, who made the radar, after the Fairey Gannet AEW Mk3 was withdrawn from service. Belatedly, MoD agreed. The concept was proven, and a further eight aircraft were converted. Of these ten, eight were fully fitted AEW Mk2s and two were attrition airframes, without the radar and other mission system avionics. (Fitted for, but not with).

Figure 3 - XV650 as a Sea King AEW Mk2 (2001). To the casual viewer the main difference between AEW Mk2 and ASaC Mk7 is the latter does not retain the dorsal radome. Other external differences are mainly communications antennae. *(Public domain)*

In August 1985 an Inertial Navigation System and G8 Autotrack Computer enhancement was approved. Further minor changes followed, mainly to the communications system by Naval Service Modification. In the late 1980s, development of a colour display upgrade commenced. Low radar transmitter power (and hence range) was recognised, and a high-power design was undertaken in 1990 as a private venture by Thorn-EMI Varian, with MoD oversight at the company's invitation.

In 1992 a Radar System Upgrade (RSU) was endorsed. Essentially, this was the consolidation of these relatively minor tasks, coupled with better processing to handle the resultant increase in targets. In addition, a number of technical pre-requisite projects were endorsed separately, without which RSU would have no real benefit - secure communications, Joint Tactical Information Distribution System (JTIDS), (another) Inertial Navigation System, GPS, and Mode 4 Combined Interrogator Transponder Identification Friend or Foe (IFF) being the most significant. Management of RSU, and some of the other projects, was tasked to the Directorate of Helicopter Projects (DHP) in MoD's Procurement Executive. The important point, at this stage, is the endorsements were piecemeal - they did not form a coherent programme. This fragmented, uncoordinated approach arose from the 1988 disbandment of the RN's HQ section responsible for oversight - Materiel Provisioning and Support Policy (MPSP), whose job it was to identify such linkages and reconcile them within the Naval Air Programme, and thus task them to the correct procurement offices.

Most of the pre-requisites were (correctly) contracted without competition, due to intellectual property ownership. Pre-development commenced in 1994 with a series of risk reduction contracts; mainly to resurrect and stabilise Build Standards (and hence Safety Cases). However, RSU was competed, which meant it naturally lagged. Again, correctly, as much of the existing design was owned by MoD.

The In-Service Date was declared in 2002, Full Operating Capability in 2006. The new ASaC Mk7 was widely regarded as the most advanced capability of its kind. The RN's claim it was two generations ahead of the RAF's Airborne Warning and Control System (AWACS) aircraft was not entirely inter-Service banter. In September 2018, after nearly 50 years' illustrious service, the Sea King left service. Last to go were the Mk7s; but the heart of the capability, the avionics suite, is to be retained in an updated form, in a new host, Merlin.

The requirement

The endorsement was for eight fully fitted aircraft (i.e. retain the *status quo*). The actual requirement was 16, needed to sustain 96 hours continuous air coverage from two carriers. The shortfall was recorded as a Critical Operational Constraint and uplifted to 10, plus three attrition airframes to be converted from surplus anti-submarine aircraft. However, the necessary top-up equipment buys were low and uneconomic, as none would be procured for the attrition airframes.

An Alternative Assumption was successfully staffed, increasing the endorsement to 13 fully fitted aircraft. (An Alternative Assumption is an amendment to the Long Term Costings Main Assumptions; sometimes correcting obvious errors, sometimes adding detail or urgent requirements, but often reflecting politically motivated cuts). This new full Fleet fit policy (13 of 13) was a significant change from the Mk2 partial fit policy (8 of 10). It made the top-up buy economic, and rendered the overall programme far more than a routine upgrade.

The project office was not advised why the *actual* requirement was rejected, so the programme manager included the other three as an option in subsequent contracts. This was not taken up, but at least registered the shortfall. In early 1996, under pressure from MoD Centre in London to revert to 10, he prepared a counter-argument and the 13 survived.

*

Here, it is beneficial to know how aircraft are categorised and used. Normally, a fleet has Front Line aircraft, plus Training and In Use Reserve (IUR) (both allocated fewer flying hours), and IR6 (held at six months readiness, although the original intent was six weeks). An assumption is permitted that 14% of the total are in the Repair Pool at any one time - which sets support baselines. (A figure unrecognisable to today's front line, who are more used to 50%+ unavailability).

However, the nature of the AEW Mk2 fleet, and its rapid creation in 1982, meant it had no IUR or IR6 aircraft to fall back on. It had two 3-aircraft front line flights (A & B), plus a 2-aircraft HQ/Training flight - hence the shortfall. A little bit of devilish detail. 14% of eight is 1.12. Prior to 1988, the Long Term Costings Instructions permitted this to be rounded-up - which attracted more funding for support. This was changed to rounded-down. In an 8-aircraft fleet the effect is huge.

Lacking endorsement for the correct quantity, and given the need to maintain AEW Mk2 operational capability throughout the programme,

Boscombe Down were tasked to modify the Sea King 'Hack' aircraft. It was used to test, primarily, the radar transmitter chain and navigation system. There is no expectation of the Hack ever being suitable for operational use, but it is maintained in an airworthy condition as a test vehicle. Its use is not regulated by the Service, but (at the time) by MoD(PE) Directorate of Flying. On equipment, the Hack (properly, the Sample) is complemented by the Reference, which is maintained at the latest Design Authority Build Standard and available at 48 hours' notice for front line use. Mk7 was a major programme, requiring the Hack (ZD570) and two Trials and Proof Installation aircraft (XV707 and, later, XV672). In configuration control terms, ZD570 was between a HAS Mk1 and Mk2, jokingly a 'Mk1.5'.

*

In early 1994 the RN's Aircraft Support Executive (ASE) disagreed with the programme manager's estimate that each conversion would take around three months; sequentially, to maintain AEW Mk2 fleet readiness. Their planning assumed all aircraft would be converted, and aircrew re-trained, over a single week-end. In effect, they never accepted the scope changed from the original transmitter power modification. At the same time, the original plan for an Intensive Flying Trials Unit was cancelled, indicating ASE were not alone in their misconceptions. This gets to the root of why, in 2003, ship procedures did not reflect the form, fit, function and use changes between AEW Mk2 and ASaC Mk7.

It is important to explain why Director General Aircraft (Navy) played little or no part only a few years later. The Hallifax Savings of 1988, aimed at reducing Fleet Air Arm support costs by 33%, had abolished many specialist posts, including the entirety of its key section, MPSP (above). The roles were not replaced in the newly formed Aircraft Support Executive. By the time the equivalent savings were imposed on the RAF, Air Member Supply and Organisation (AMSO) had taken over all aviation support funding and the RN took a second hit, forced to share the RAF cut.

When this raid was visited upon RN funding (1989-on), only a handful in the RN, or MoD as a whole, understood the risks. The penny never dropped until matters came to a head during Exercise ReGen in 1996, a largely paper exercise to determine if the RN could meet the Draft Naval Regeneration Plan. Flag Officer Naval Aviation asked the Sea King avionics programme manager to submit a paper explaining why vital avionic assets for Sea King, Lynx and Sea Harrier could not be located or were unserviceable. All paths led back to the Hallifax Savings and AMSO's DM87 policy of 1987.[27]

That FONA had to seek advice on Lynx and Sea Harrier from the Sea King office merely confirms my comments about retention of corporate knowledge. Rather than approach the offices charged with managing the subject, the Senior Service now had to resort to seeking out an individual who someone recalled having worked in its HQ many years before. It can be readily seen where cracks begin to develop.

---

27 Loose Minute D/DHP 69/1/1, 10 July 1996.

8: They put their trust in us

Servicemen place total reliance on those who deliver their equipment and ensure its safety. This chapter introduces these staff, and how they ensure that safety. If permitted.

Programme management

By 1990 entire functions within MoD had been abandoned, part of draconian savings measures brought about by Options for Change - a reaction to the military draw-down as a result of the end of the Cold War. The basic mistake, as ever, was to chop posts in areas that were not volume-related. More cuts followed in 1994, via the Front Line First initiative. Between 1990 and 1993 a series of moratoria on recruitment and promotion were introduced, forcing programmes to be frozen for up to five years - including most of the pre-requisites. In financial terms there were short-term savings, but a huge bow wave developed. In capability terms, equipment quickly became obsolescent. The endorsement of Radar System Upgrade forced the issue, as it could not proceed without the pre-requisites being delivered.

*

The Directorate of Helicopter Projects (DHP) delivered all MoD helicopter programmes except Merlin, essentially a decision to balance workload between DHP and Director Maritime (who managed Nimrod MRA4). Both reported to Director General Air Systems 2 (DGAS2), in turn responsible to Controller Aircraft and, thence, the Chief of Defence Procurement.

In November 1993 DHP (Dr David Hughes) completed the formation of his own Sea King avionics sections, under Assistant Director Helicopter Projects 2 (AD/HP2, Kevin Thomas), with responsibility for Sea King-peculiar equipment programmes. Head of Sea King (H/SK, Keith Newton) had two two-man sections; one managed Radar System Upgrade (H/SK1 and H/SK1a), the other all other RN Sea King programmes, including the pre-requisites (H/SK2 and H/SK2a). (The RAF Search and Rescue variant was managed separately, as the RAF always sought to have its programmes managed by RAF officers).

This innocuous-seeming reshuffle recognised the inherent risk of the programmes resting with Air Member Supply and Organisation (AMSO), who tended to be hostile towards what MoD(PE) was trying to achieve, and towards the RN in general. (In 1994, AMSO was rebranded as Air Member Logistics). The main risk (in fact, certainty) arose from AMSO's policy to run down the management of airworthiness, successfully completed in early 1993; a policy which its successor perpetuated. This process had to be resurrected, insofar as it applied to Sea King programmes; which is what Dr Hughes had anticipated. But therein lay a major stumbling block. The failures were systemic, requiring Executive Board management. A single aircraft office had no control over the wider MoD.

In early 1994, during Radar System Upgrade Cardinal Points Specification preparation, H/SK2 suggested those programme elements which could be contracted in a single package be drawn together. This became known as Mission System Upgrade (MSU), but this *project* was still only part of the overall Mk7 *programme*.

However, there remained a significant shortfall in resources, the endorsement providing only around 30% of the true cost. Hence, the Mk7 programme could be said to be grossly over its original budget, but did not exceed a fair and reasonable price - a distinction lost on those who criticise 'cost overruns'. This does not mean someone erred. As already mentioned, the RN section responsible for articulating and quantifying the requirement no longer existed. Lacking this input, how can anything be costed accurately? The initial budget, and what is contracted, becomes a wet finger guess.

What was 'Mission System Upgrade'?

This is important, because what the Sea King ASaC Mk7 Release to Service (the Master Airworthiness Reference) termed 'Searchwater 2000 Radar Mission System Upgrade', plus the Inertial Navigation System/GPS, had an INTERIM clearance on 22 March 2003. This is defined:

'The aircraft must not be operated in any way that places any reliance whatsoever on the proper functioning of this equipment'.[28]

As you read the following chapters, please bear this in mind. Were the crews having to rely on equipment they were not permitted to rely upon?

Put simply, MSU was the Radar System Upgrade, Joint Tactical Information Distribution System, and Man Machine Interface. Due to system dependencies, Electronic Support Measures, Communications,

---

28 JSP318B Regulation of Ministry of Defence Aircraft.

Navigation, Active Noise Reduction, Identification Friend or Foe, and Airborne Video Recording System were affected. The Release to Service did not define MSU in this (or any) way.

It is too simplistic to say it was the systems new to Mk7, because legacy systems now *behaved differently*, especially those that were upgraded versions of Mk2 Naval Service Modifications. For three years there was to be a dual Mk2/Mk7 fleet, so the risk of confusion had to be mitigated.

At this point, an indication of what was legacy and new to the Mk7 is useful. Only differences immediately evident to the crew are included.

Upgraded AEW Mk2 Systems

- Searchwater LAST radar.
- Airborne Video Recording System. Recorded different data to the Mk2 version - so much so it was essentially a new design.
- Identification Friend or Foe Mk12, Mode 4. Not airworthy in the Mk2, but made safe, with different functionality and use.
- AN/ARC164 UHF radio. Not airworthy in the Mk2, but made safe, specified performance restored, and relocated.
- Orange Crop Electronic Support Measures. Not airworthy in the Mk2, but made safe, performance improved, and relocated.
- Clear (non-secure) Intercom, and in the process the HF and UHF radio sub-systems, updated and performance restored.
- Mk4A aircrew helmet with Active Noise Reduction. Battery operated in the Mk2, but fully integrated with the aircraft communications system, using aircraft power, in Mk7.

Systems new to Mk7

- Joint Tactical Information Distribution System (JTIDS).
- Enhanced Comms System. Added a secure overlay to the clear Intercom, new UHF Homing, additional UHF radio, and JTIDS voice channels.
- Ring Laser Gyro Inertial Navigation System, with embedded GPS.
- Man Machine Interface. This might be viewed as the most significant achievement of the programme, designed by RN AEW Observers.

Plus, a series of modifications to the airframe, and changes to the support infrastructure, including ships, to accommodate the Upgrade.

As I said earlier, each Build Standard (Design Authority, As Trialled, In-Use) has its own issue of the Whole Aircraft Safety Case. But in conversion programmes such as this, there is another - the Induction Build Standard, which is not necessarily any of the above. An aircraft project office cannot dictate this Build Standard, merely advise what is acceptable and legal. Here, the Mk2 fleet had to be at a known, airworthy, and contractually agreed Induction Build Standard. This process allows the work package, and hence timescale and price, to be agreed with industry. In addition to stating the deliverable (the Mk7 and sustainability packages), MoD had to say what it would provide in the first place. Three main organisations were responsible:

1. <u>Director General Aircraft (Navy)</u> Availability, maintainability and reliability. Articulating quantitative and qualitative detail. Seen to be the 'owner', dictating disposition and support policy, so was customer of...

2. <u>Air Member Logistics</u> Supply Management Branches for existing systems. Director Support Management 3 (Avionics/PDS) (RAF); comprising the former MoD(PE) airworthiness specialists. DHP fulfilled the same role for the airframe.

3. <u>Defence Helicopter Support Authority (DHSA)</u> At the time, a new organisation, drawing together support staff from the three Services. Here, the important deliverable was to be a Whole Aircraft Safety Case Report, based on the In-Use Build Standard.

However, the boundaries of responsibility between the three were poorly drawn, with both overlap and significant gaps. As explained, the most important DGA(N) posts had been abolished in 1988. Similarly, most Avionics/PDS functions in 1991-3 as part of the airworthiness rundown. None of these staff transferred to DHSA, because they were already too senior. DHSA's 'solution' was to over-grade many posts, but that does not guarantee quality of applicants. In fact, quite the opposite. All tasks defaulted to DHP; specifically H/SK2.

I will return to this later, in chapter 13, when discussing the contributory factors. But, briefly, DHSA refused to advise the programme manager of the Induction Build Standard, meaning he had no current Safety Case Report. This is where matters became difficult for him. Officially, he was required to declare planning blight until a satisfactory report could be produced. But, this would have meant delaying the programme for around two years, playing into the hands of those who were trying to derail it at every turn. This is where broad and deep experience of every engineering domain is required, and a willingness to trust one's engineering judgment.

What baseline existed? The basic one was Westland's Whole Aircraft Safety Case at their Design Authority Build Standard. Their Chief Designer was content with it; and that, more than anything else, provides sound foundations. But using that meant the programme manager had to regress further than should have been necessary, risking time and cost penalties. He had to assess the differences between this and the other Build Standards - mainly Naval Service Modifications which had not been appraised by Westland, so were not in the drawing pack. Some of these, such as the Interim Lamberton secure speech fit, would be superseded anyway. But others, such as the AN/ARC164 UHF radio fit, and Orange Crop Electronic Support Measures, were functionally unsafe. He had to anticipate what reasons Westland would give for rejecting them - and there was no doubt they *would* reject them. Also, there were parallel projects to monitor; for example, a new Combined Interrogator/Transponder IFF. (See next chapter).

Put another way, the safety evidence would be lacking in some areas, and reliant to a greater degree on his judgment. Crucially, he would have to be willing to make this decision; and be able to justify it, even into retirement. He decided to proceed, and dealt with the unknowns by including detailed aircraft surveys in the work package. Again, knowledge of Service procedures was important, and with the help and cooperation of the 849NAS Air Engineering Officer and Commanding Officer, the induction programme was constructed around the Scheduled Unit and Scheduled Base Maintenance programme of the aircraft. Delays, and huge cost overruns, were avoided completely, but at the cost of significant disruption to the squadron.

The bidding process

On an Invincible Class carrier, onboard commonality was critical. The avionic workshop was small and there was only room for two Automatic Test Equipment Suites - and they already existed; MATS for Merlin and BVATE for the Sea Harrier's Blue Vixen radar. So, while the RN was not permitted to specify what it wanted (something the general public will find strange), in practice this mandate meant the requirement was Merlin, fitted with a radar and other avionics that could be tested with a modified MATS or BVATE. However, the focus of the Invitation to Tender was Radar System Upgrade, not the wider programme (or even

Mission System Upgrade) meaning bidders had to have an innate understanding of many issues not mentioned in the Cardinal Points Specification.

Four companies responded:

1. GEC-Marconi (formerly Ferranti), bidding a variant of the latter's successful Blue Vixen radar, including the option to use Merlin.

2. Thorn-EMI, bidding a modification to their existing Searchwater LAST radar.

3. Lockheed-Martin of Los Angeles, bidding a modified, and very capable, version of the mature Hughes APG-63 radar.

4. Thomson-CSF, effectively part of the French government. It became evident at the Bidders' Conference, held in St Giles Court, London in 1994, that they were not serious contenders, and withdrew. This becomes relevant later.

Only GEC-Marconi demonstrated wider understanding, submitting the only complaint bid; although it suffered by being run from Milton Keynes, not Edinburgh where the radar was designed and manufactured. However, assessors (the H/SK teams, plus RN specialists and scientific staff) were told to overlook the major non-compliances in the other bids, because the Merlin programme was running late and it was thought, correctly, that Sea King would have to be retained. An unintentional side-effect was to hand the advantage to Thorn-EMI.

Even so, the outcome (in terms of marks awarded) was close between GEC-Marconi and Thorn-EMI, with Lockheed a slightly distant third. However, there were too few differentiating questions - ones that would inform MoD as to suitability and robustness of the bid. At the RN's insistence, the vast majority (in excess of 600) related to Integrated Logistic Support, where the bidders simply answered 'Yes' and gained full marks, but without having to demonstrate any practical knowledge of the subject. There were too few questions where a reply of 'non-compliant' or 'partially compliant' was conceivable; and assessors were not permitted to take into account their experiences of the bidders' past performance. The two leaders could only be separated at the second decimal point yet, demonstrably, only GEC-Marconi understood the broader requirement (the onboard commonality mandate, and the fact that what they bid for was about a third of the programme). In truth, they won by a large margin.

Meanwhile, retention of Sea King was confirmed. Two consequential risks materialised immediately:

- If GEC-Marconi were not selected, the winner would have to enter into a sub-contract arrangement to modify and use MATS or BVATE, which was not costed in their bids. Had this been taken into account, GEC-Marconi 'won' by a significant margin.
- The 8+2 had been original Mk1s, which would see them remain in service until almost 50 years old, but newer airframes disposed of. Also, they represented five different production runs, with different configurations. This was the time to rationalise the Sea King fleet and use the most suitable airframes. Sufficient were available. The cost would be minimal. In the medium/long term it would save money. But the suggestion was not taken up. Managing the resultant configuration control issues was made pain-free by Westland's flexibility; especially that of the Chief Design Engineer, Gus Jay; but the through-life costings had to be adjusted upwards.

Abrogation

In late 1995 the programme was dealt a significant blow. Not only was Sea King to be retained, but the RN Aircraft Support Executive's Engineering Weapons Authority (ASE EWA) demanded MoD(PE) buy new airframes, not modify the old ones. This was impossible, even if endorsed and funded, because Westland had announced the current contracts (for the RAF and Norway) would be the last, releasing factory capacity for Merlin, Apache and forthcoming Lynx upgrades. This emphasised that the Naval Air Programme was not being managed in any meaningful way.

A meeting was convened, chaired by Kevin Thomas (AD/HP2). It was short. As DHP could not buy new aircraft, EWA, Mr Mel Doidge, formally withdrew all support to the programme. An extraordinary decision, which Mr Thomas assumed his superiors would challenge. They did not - in fact, the Chief of Defence Procurement actively supported it.

Director General Aircraft (Navy)'s Future Projects section stepped in, providing an Integrated Logistics Support Manager, a Lieutenant Commander; demonstrating the wider RN knew of EWA's actions. But this was but one EWA function. Their biggest task was to have been the management and provision of over 3,500 items of Government Furnished Equipment (assets in the MoD inventory that must be supplied to the contractor so he may fulfil his contract - which EWA also wanted bought new). It was also their job to, for example, manage equipment modification programmes.

ASE had a large section under a Commander RN to do this. It now fell to DHP, who had been allocated no resources. But in MoD *any* civilian project manager is expected to be able to undertake *any* job in the team. H/SK2 was told to do it at home, in the evenings and at week-ends. He had done the job before when in DGA(N) HQ, and knew what to do. But he needed commensurate control over RN resources, and the *at home* bit would be difficult when the necessary information was highly classified.

The RN's Director of Operational Requirements (Sea), Commodore (later Rear Admiral) Rees Ward RN, was supportive. Given H/SK2's background, and after presenting his proposals, on 4 December 1995 Commodore Ward agreed to him formally taking the place of his Aircraft Support Executive, with authority to speak for the RN. Highly unusual, perhaps even unique, but needs must if entire functions crucial to the success of a programme are suddenly ended.

It says much that in 1995 DOR(Sea) were still struggling with the 1987 decision to abandon these commitments. Every time they initiated a new project, their own key player was nowhere to be found. It must have been a blessed relief for the solution to be handed to them on Sea King, by far the biggest and most diverse fleet. *Can you do it? Yes. Thanks, please carry on. Next? Lynx? Do you have anyone? No?...*

H/SK2 was stood down from this task five years later, on 30 November 2000, and not replaced. But the need continued, revealing a lack of understanding of the issues. The Board of Inquiry report unwittingly revealed the effect - most of the work simply ceased.

Contractor 'selection'

Any argument over who won the bid swiftly became academic. In early 1996 an 'industrial impact' paper was prepared. Need to know basis, Director and above, so nobody conversant with the programme was permitted to contribute. The contract was to be awarded a company in Crawley, West Sussex. Coincidentally(?), Thorn-EMI were relocating from Hayes in Middlesex to Manor Royal, Crawley, becoming Thorn Radar, part of Thorn Sensors Group, after acquiring MEL, formerly Mullard Electronics Limited.

The reasoning was... If the contract went to Edinburgh (GEC-Marconi), everyone at Crawley would be made redundant. If the contract went to Crawley, no-one at Edinburgh would be affected, as there was no radar capability there anyway. This was arrant nonsense, which any MoD employee working in Air Systems would know - presumably why they were excluded. The operation in the Edinburgh area, spread over a dozen or so sites and employing up to 12,000 staff, supplied airborne radars for Sea Harrier, Merlin, Lynx, Eurofighter (Typhoon) and, in the recent past, Buccaneer, Phantom and Lightning. (H/SK2 had been project manager for five of these, and before that RN customer for three). Also, variants were supplied overseas - in the case of Lynx alone to over a dozen other countries. It was purely a political decision, although there is no suggestion the Minister of State for the Armed Forces, Nicholas Soames MP (Conservative, Crawley) lobbied in any way.

This event illustrates how often the criticism levelled at MoD's procurers is unjustified. Two years had been wasted on a tendering exercise, depriving the RN of capability. In an industrial relations sense, bidders had not realised they were in an unfair competition, spending millions on their bids. Dr Hughes had an awkward lunch with the GEC-Marconi board.

Another factor was deemed important. Overseas sales of over 100 systems were predicted by the (imposed) contractor, which would generate considerable commercial exploitation income as MoD owned Intellectual Property Rights. If accurate, this would have made the Full Mission Trainer a prime candidate for a Private Finance Initiative (PFI) agreement. Ignoring this claim, H/SK2 annotated the 'Overseas Sales' box on the PFI form 'No', and calamity was avoided. In contrast, the ongoing Apache Attack Helicopter programme embraced PFI for its Trainer, delaying the In-Service Date by some years, at significant cost. It is unclear how many ASaC or UK standard Apache Trainers were sold overseas, although commonly held to be less than one.

*

More changes were afoot. Racal Radar Defence Systems (RRDS) acquired Thorn Sensors Group. DHP were instructed to negotiate with Racal, who of course had not bid for the job. A 6-month 'freeze' was imposed to permit them to assess the programme, the secondary 'benefit' being to delay MoD expenditure. The MSU contract was let in February 1997 - bearing in mind this was but one of many required. To place this timeframe in context, that month five productions sets of the pre-requisite secure comms equipment had already been delivered.

Later, Thomson-CSF were rebranded as Thales, and acquired RRDS. A significant concern will be evident. Thomson-CSF had withdrawn from the competition, but were now the prime contractor, albeit under a different name. Clearly, the distance of Racal and then Thales from the bid and selection process introduced a major risk. In fact, it could, and was, argued this should have been a showstopper. But a supposedly unbreakable contracting principle was flouted for political expediency.

This is where the experience of bid assessors becomes essential. Company ethos and past performance is crucial but, as mentioned, this was not to be taken into account. One consideration would have been that, only a couple of years before, Thomson-CSF had badly let MoD down on an obsolescence issue that brought the Sea King Search and Rescue fleets to within a whisker of being grounded, and the Anti-Submarine Warfare fleet severely role-limited. Contracted to develop a replacement Silicon Control Rectifier for the radars, against a strict deadline, they pulled the plug literally at the last minute. It was only the initiative of an MEL Marketing Executive, Ian Loakes, that saved the day, tracking down a Westinghouse shipment of the old device through various owners to a backstreet electronics shop in Lagos. With the approval of the radar project manager (H/SK2 in a former role) he there and then bought the entire stock on behalf of MoD, giving the RN and RAF 15 years breathing space. Hitherto, such an episode would have allowed any project manager, especially if also the Technical Agency, to blacklist the company until it demonstrated better commitment; and ensure future contracts carried hefty penalty clauses. These are not trivial matters. Trust is a key component of any partnering arrangement between MoD and Industry.

Structure of the Sea King teams (Bristol 1996-2001)

It is important to first emphasise a subtlety. The main part of the aircraft programme - induction of the Trials and Proof Installation aircraft, stripping, survey, rectification, modification, re-build to initial Mk7 standard, and then trialling - was contracted direct to Westland under the Enhanced Comms System programme. This was completed successfully in January 2000, five months ahead of schedule and 30% under budget, establishing the performance baseline for the next phase. In mid-2000, the trials aircraft were transferred to the Racal contract (with Westland as a sub-sub-contractor) and fitted with the final Mission Systems. This is the last date the Aircraft Document Set was reconcilable. That is, the Mk7 was airworthy at this mid-2000 Build Standard but, according to the Board of Inquiry, became progressively less so.

In July 1996 MoD's Procurement Executive in London relocated to Abbey Wood, Bristol, most Sea King staff taking the opportunity to move on. Only H/SK2 remained. The two main tasks were the Mk4 and Mk7 upgrades. (Mk4 was the Commando variant, its primary role being to 'effect a simultaneous two-company lift of Royal Marines'). Essentially, both were avionics programmes; with expertise required on radar, communications, navigation, electronic warfare and software; plus airframe, electrical and hydraulics. Also, sonics, to complete existing tasks on Sea King HAS Mk6.

These demands considerably narrowed the field of suitable replacements. An experienced avionics technician and Tornado project manager was appointed H/SK1; joined by a young engineering graduate in what was essentially a training position. H/SK2 remained in post; later joined by an engineer regarded as the best radar diagnostician in MoD (and recipient of a commendation for maintaining RAF Search and Rescue fleet capability, having prevented imminent grounding in February 1989). Their line manager, from July 1996, was David Horsey; replacing Keith Newton. This post had been changed to non-technical, so H/SK1 and H/SK2 were not considered. Alas, Mr Horsey moved on the following year, replaced by Mr Robert Eason.

By end-1997 the Sea King management chain in the Directorate of Helicopter Projects was:

> Dr David Colbourne, Director Helicopter Projects (DHP). Sea King, Lynx, Chinook, Apache, VVIP Helicopter (Queen's Flight Replacement) and Helicopter Health and Usage Monitoring System (HUMS).

> Assistant Director Helicopter Projects 2 (AD/HP2). Sea King, VVIP, HUMS. Kevin Thomas passed away that autumn and was not replaced. In line management terms AD/HP1 Colonel Barry Hodgkiss (Chinook, Lynx) took over, but played no part in the programme management.

> Mr Eason, Head of Sea King (H/SK). His non-technical status restricted him to administrative tasks normally the role of junior staff.

> H/SK1 and H/SK1a - Radar System Upgrade, Joint Tactical Information Distribution System, Man Machine Interface. H/SK2 and H/SK2a - Delivery of pre-requisite projects, the Aircraft programme, management of the consolidated Mk7 programme. Also, Sea King HC Mk4 Avionics Upgrade Programme and Mk6

sonics programmes.

Notably, no Safety, Risk or Configuration Management posts were allocated, senior management deeming them an unnecessary extravagance. These major tasks defaulted to H/SK2. The Quality/Software Manager was shared with other programmes.

The Directorate Management Plan required that H/SK2 report direct to AD/HP2, although H/SK remained his line manager. The main consideration was his roles included resolving novel and contentious issues that could not be delegated to a non-technical post. The most pressing were that most of the programme was unendorsed and unfunded, and that the main technical risks related to airworthiness. Also, he and H/SK2a had to carry out most of the Aircraft Support Executive (Navy)'s functions, while also acting as Technical Agencies *in lieu* of Air Member Logistics.

In short: H/SK delivered his and H/SK1's equipment to H/SK2, who integrated it with his own into a coherent package (the Mk7). The larger Mk4 upgrade programme (in the sense there were 36 aircraft and multiple programme phases) was quite separate, H/SK playing no part.

By way of contradiction, the H/SK2 and H/SK2a posts were only funded to the end of 1998. Mr Thomas disagreed and managed to delay implementation, but his illness and untimely death bolstered the campaign to break up the teams. Its ultimate success meant that by June 2001 MoD had lost all its corporate knowledge, at a critical point in the programme. This is the most important organisational failure. Thereafter, no-one picked up crucial elements of the work, and defensive barriers broke down. One tangible outcome was that the risks relating to the contributory factors were not mitigated. This gave rise to the situational awareness failure noted by the Board of Inquiry as most likely cause. This is a good example of events, leading to factors, leading to cause. The warning signs were evident and the programme was increasingly relying on luck. It only needed a slice of bad luck...

A bum deal

During contract negotiations, in December 1996 the Sea King teams were directed to participate in the ASPECT programme - A Suite of PE Computer Tools. Each engineer was required to allocate 20 hours per week to the assessment of these new software tools, while maintaining timely progress on all programmes. The taking of leave was prohibited for six months. Quite how they were to achieve this, given the instruction to devote evenings and week-ends to the unendorsed programme elements, was unclear. Matters deteriorated on 28 August 1997, when they were directed that ASPECT took priority over all risks; an illegal order which they ignored.

A particularly unhinged requirement was for staff to stop work every ten minutes, log on, and type what they'd just been doing. This took about five minutes; and assumed they were always at their desks, not out and about managing contractors throughout the UK, and working on design matters at Air Stations and Boscombe Down. Forcing time management on productive employees is non-productive.

As H/SK2a memorably observed, ASPECT is what happens when you bend over in a chicken run. It brought no benefit to MoD, and most of it was ingloriously scrapped. One component that did survive was an 'initiative' to standardise the format of Invitations to Tender and contracts. This had already been achieved in 1991 by a contracts officer in the Directorate of Air Radio, Ray Skipp. His version remains superior.

Dependencies

Having made the decision to ignore illegal orders, matters were plain sailing in the Directorate of Helicopter Projects; although the directives continued. Infinitely more challenging were external dependencies. These fell into three categories - other MoD(PE) Directorates, other MoD agencies, and Industry.

Industry dependencies are facilitated by MoD, as it must let suitable enabling contracts. Even so, contractors must often be persuaded to commence work and trust MoD to come up with a contract. This requires a sensible contracts officer who knows when to turn a blind eye to restrictive directives. The teams got lucky with Mrs Gill Doherty. However, in 2000, contracts work, but no staff, was transferred to Yeovilton, where staff were told it was optional to support the Mk7.

As Build Standards were no longer maintained, MoD was constantly in default as it could not provide the necessary information to allow industry to build accurate quotations. Most companies were understanding, but gently pointed out they had not been under any contractual obligation for some years. Many provided their services free of charge, the overhead involved in negotiating a relatively low cost (man-hours only) contract being disproportionate and largely unrecoverable. They might bloat the next formal quote, but the wise project manager would let it go. Trust and mutual professional respect, built up over many years, played a significant part in oiling these wheels.

*

On the point of commencing equipment conversions (with the aircraft to follow), on 11 August 1997 Mr Geoff Noad of the RN Aircraft Yard Fleetlands advised the programme manager:

'We no longer regard MoD(PE) as a customer and do not want this work'.

The Fleetlands Avionic Business Unit Manager (ABUM), Mr Iain Gray, took notes and issued minutes. This was the first he had heard of the decision, taken while he had been actively planning the forward loading of his avionics shop, and recruiting.

This affected both Mk7 and Mk4. Fleetlands had signed up to over 25,000 man-hours work on the communications systems alone. At the time, they were 'free' to MoD(PE), funded from the central Rotary Wing Support budget. Suddenly, H/SK2 had to find millions to pay industry; GEC-Marconi Secure Systems to modify the avionics, Westland the aircraft. This decision stemmed from the RN's Aircraft Support Executive withdrawing support for RN Third Line workshops (Fleetlands and Almondbank) - an indirect attack on its own front line. (Two examples have now been cited of the Aircraft Support Executive making Executive decisions to withdraw Support for Aircraft. Begging the question...).

*

Air Member Logistics (AML) were unhelpful, which had been anticipated and largely mitigated by 1996 during the risk reduction programme. The only difficulty was having to justify expenditure on the grounds an RAF department *will* abrogate responsibility with impunity. The prime example occurred on communications equipment procured for RN Sea King Mk6 and Lynx Mk3/8, and RAF Nimrod MR2.

Nimrod MR2 embodiment was cancelled altogether. As its equipment was to a large extent incompatible with the helicopters, more than £40M was wasted. Both RN programmes were cut; 82 to 53 Sea Kings, and 84 to 48 Lynx. Sensibly, the Sea King AEW and Mk4 upgrades were predicated on using most of the resultant surplus. On 28 February 1992 it was directed that some £25M worth of this be placed in quarantine, for future use by AEW and Mk4.[29] (1985 prices, ~£77M at 2018 prices, not taking into account non-recurring development costs and Department

---

29 Letter D/ASE/901/141/1/c, 28 February 1992 to DGSS(RAF).

of Trade and Industry indices). This is why the Enhanced Comms upgrade only cost £20M (1994 prices, ~£39M today) - that was merely the balance required to redesign and upgrade the equipment for AEW and Mk4, and upgrade the aircraft installations.

However, much of the surplus was misappropriated and fitted to RAF and Army aircraft. To conceal this, AML destroyed records, including the 10ZZ Register recording temporary Section (10ZZ) and Reference numbers; allocated to, for example, equipment delivered early under Diversion Order. But not before H/SK2 visited RAF Wyton on 24 January 1996 and viewed it. (He was given the heads-up on AML's intentions by the RN's sole representative at Wyton, a Chief Petty Officer). The information gleaned from this fleeting glance at, in practice, a large computer print-out, was used to recover a significant amount of equipment. But kit worth tens of millions remained unaccounted for. This concealment had security implications, as much of the new secure comms kit could not be at the new Home Office-mandated Build Standard. This arose from the TEMPEST specification being changed midway through production.[30]

Kevin Thomas chaired a meeting on 30 May 1996. Deputy Director Support Management 11 (RAF) (a Group Captain G. Morton) denied the existence of the RAF aircraft (Nimrod R1) some of the RN's equipment had been fitted to. Pointless, given H/SK2 had been the project manager for its Electronic Intelligence equipment in 1990-91. He also claimed vital integration rigs were funded, serviceable, and under full Post Design Services (PDS); despite his staff, the RN and MoD Quality Assurance audits openly admitting they had not been since 1991. He demanded of Mr Thomas (who was senior to him) that MoD police be asked to instigate criminal proceedings against GEC-Marconi Secure Systems for theft of the RN Sea King and RN/Army Lynx rigs.

Not unreasonably, Mr Thomas thought him barking mad and politely declined. But to prevent further embarrassment a post-meeting note was appended to the minutes stating he had undertaken his own audit, confirmed the rigs had been dismantled by Air Member Logistics, and

---

30 TEMPEST is a codename, not an acronym, for the study of compromising emanations (unintentional intelligence-bearing signals). In practice, to achieve TEMPEST clearance certain equipment, such as secure communications and their installations, must meet a stringent specification relating to cross-talk. In Sea King ASaC Mk7, the TEMPEST boundary encompassed the Mission System, secure comms, AVRS, IFF and (uniquely) aircrew helmets.

PDS was inadequate.[31] That is, ultimately, Safety Cases were not up to date. Rebuilding the rigs cost around £1M; work that GEC-Marconi completed on trust before a contract could be arranged.

Notably, the RN Aircraft Support Executive (ASE) representative at the meeting was the same official, Mr Doidge, who had earlier withdrawn support for Mk7. Despite being the owner of the (former) rigs and the equipment, he sided with DDSM 11. Mr Thomas asked H/SK2 why ASE would side with the RAF department that was royally shafting the RN at every turn. He replied that they (the Directorate of Helicopter Projects) were the greater threat, aware of ASE's abrogation and maladministration - practices they shared with the Group Captain's department. MoD(PE) was their common enemy.

The wider RN was reluctant to challenge the RAF's actions. On 5 June 1996 H/SK2 was asked by the Directorate of Operational Requirements (Sea) (his customer) to cost the cancellation of the Sea King HC Mk4 comms upgrade in its entirety, despite this being the highest priority Support Helicopter requirement in the MoD. In reply, he successfully made a case for retention, forcing the RAF to initiate replacement of the equipment it had misappropriated.[32]

This is a good example of measured attempts to derail programmes for no other reason than to conceal prior negligence and maladministration. Casual acceptance of these violations lies at the root of many deaths.

*

In April 1999, the Sea King Integrated Project Team was formed in yet another restructuring of MoD. The inaugural leader, Captain Nick Marks RN, refused to support his staff. He declared he had authorised the destruction of around 100 surplus AD3400 V/UHF radios, costing over £130k each (a small part of the above surplus, and also required for Merlin and Lynx). He asserted this when dealing with H/SK2's refusal to obey Mr Eason's order to make a false declaration that the surplus did not exist (in effect freezing both programmes for around five years).

Three weeks later H.SK2 unearthed 13 radios languishing in a store under a 10ZZ number. A minor victory, but serving only to annoy those whose fraud it confirmed.

---

31 D/DHP/24/4/93/25, 3 June 1996.
32 Loose Minute D/DHP 24/4/93/25, 5 June 1996.

Oversight

Before restructuring, Dr Colbourne took a sporadic interest in all this. His (and Barry Hodgkiss') main concern was dealing with the Mull of Kintyre aftermath, and the looming fiasco that was Chinook HC Mk3 (another known certainty). Nevertheless, on 25 August 1997 he sought a written brief from H/SK2 on all Sea King programmes, to concentrate on risks. This one-off was prompted by Mr Thomas's poor health. The brief gave advance warning of what became the Board's contributory factors. Each of the notified risks materialised exactly as predicted. This indicates maturity of understanding, because one would normally expect a few prophecies to be optimistic, pessimistic, or mistaken. The important point, at this remove, is that the Executive Board took no action. Its strategy was to wait to see if a risk occurred, then think about dealing with it.

This usually meant burying the notification in a bottom drawer and telling staff to ignore it; or, more commonly, simply not replying. Seven crew died when three known risks manifested themselves at the same time. The difference between this and most other cases is that, here, H/SK2 planned and commenced risk mitigation, only for his RN customer to claim one risk would never arise, and for Mr Eason to cancel work on the other two. That is, conscious decisions were made to remove viable defences against collision. If even one had remained in place, it is likely the accident would have been avoided. I discuss my justification later.

As risks occurred, so too did gaps in the programme. This would only become apparent when other contractors - mainly Westland - asked why work had not been carried out. This was taken to a dangerous extreme when the Critical Design Review (CDR) for the Mk7 aircraft installation design was waived. The CDR was the final programme management defence in depth that would have *emphasised* the risks associated with the contributory factors. A written declaration was required confirming the CDR was successful. It was false. On 4 June 1998, H/SK2 wrote to Mr Eason pointing out concerns that he, Boscombe Down and the RN had over safety, arising from his decision. [33] He concluded:

'To not even insist on a CDR when the main subject is electrical and structural integrity of the aircraft is beyond me'.

---

33 Loose Minute D/DHP/71/1/5/2, 4 June 1998.

He received no reply.

Management and Leadership

People are motivated by leadership; not management, which is the sound of one hand clapping. 'Programme manager' is an incongruity. He/she must be the programme leader; the difference being the latter, in addition to organising and managing resources, shapes the overall programme, displays integrity, honesty and moral courage, and leads by example.

The good leader recognises that people must not be thought of as resources. They are *resourceful*. It is they who finish the job, and are then given another. MoD and government are fixated on cutting people, when the first question should be *Have we enough of the right people to do the tasks?* If not, there are too many tasks. The procurement/acquisition arms of MoD lack leadership, but have many good project managers. Everyone else, from top to bottom, forms their support arms. If they do not provide that support and leadership, then they do not contribute and are surplus to requirements. Two anecdotes...

*

On 27 February 1998, Director General Air Systems 2 (DGAS2, Ian Fauset) held a 'coffee with the DG' gathering in his conference room. Periodically, he would invite a selection of grades/ranks to discuss matters of concern, (theoretically) without fear of censure. On that day, the only two technical staff were H/SK2 and a Squadron Leader working on Nimrod MRA4. The others were administrative support staff.

Admin went first. A banana cost too much in the staff canteen - Sainsburys were 5p cheaper. Their sandwiches were better quality. Captivated, DGAS2 promised immediate action. This took up most of the allotted hour.

Next, the Nimrod officer. Before he could speak, DGAS2 announced:

'Ah, Squadron Leader, I've just spoken to your Director and he tells me Nimrod is on schedule'.

'So he didn't mention the 4-year slippage?'

End of discussion.

Finally, H/SK2:

'What action is being taken to implement the recommendations made by Director Internal Audit in his report into wasted money?'

Completely ignored, coffee removed, meeting closed. Nevertheless, he handed Mr Fauset the Director Internal Audit report 'Requirement Scrutiny' of 27 June 1996, which had confirmed the waste to the Permanent Under-Secretary of State (PUS).

A few days later he returned it: *'This is of no concern to PE'*. That is, the systematic waste of public funds was of no concern to the Chief of Defence Procurement, who was responsible to PUS for that expenditure. Reinforcing his views, on 15 December 2000 Mr Fauset confirmed that refusing to obey an order to waste this money was an offence.[34] You might think placing this in writing utterly deranged, but it indicates the top-level support from *managers* the policy enjoyed.

*

On 11 December 2000, General Sir Sam Cowan, Chief of Defence Logistics, visited the teams. He asked for a progress report. The new H/SK1 replied that the radar worked (it didn't), therefore the Mk7 programme was complete - further proof that, even so late in the day, most staff looked upon Mk7 as a simple radar upgrade. In fact, not even that, as the programme was apparently complete before the radar was tested, never mind manufactured, fitted to the aircraft, and trialled.

4-Star Generals tend not to descend on individual project offices unless made aware of serious issues. With a glint in his eye he asked:

'How long has it taken to come to this successful conclusion?'

H/SK2 interjected, stating the systems integration process, by far the riskiest technical work, had yet to commence. General Cowan replied, *'Ah, the big I'*, and asked if this was recorded in the Risk Register. H/SK2 replied *'Yes'*, but simultaneously a young graduate said *'No'*.

It transpired a second Risk Register had been created under Mr Eason's direction, removing embarrassing MoD-owned risks. The General had obviously been shown a sanitised list of risks omitting this, and instinctively didn't believe a word of it. A wise *leader*. He was perhaps satisfied someone had their finger on the pulse, but would not have been happy at the poor oversight and determination of (absent) *managers* to impede their subordinates.

Shortly before General Cowan's visit, the new H/SK1 had circulated an outline strategy for contract acceptance, disregarding all systems integration and functional safety.[35] That is, it ignored the entire concept

---

34 Loose Minute XD1 (304), 15 December 2000.
35 Loose Minute ES(Air)(ABW)/71/10/2/2, 30 November 2000.

of delivering a different Mark of aircraft, with a different form, fit, function and use. There is only one person who would have told him to do this - his line *manager*. H/SK2 responded by circulating a reminder of what was required to mitigate these risks, a pre-requisite to even considering acceptance.[36]

But in April 2001 a third Risk Register was contracted, further blurring (falsifying?) the audit trail. A consultant had been engaged, unaware two previous versions existed until advised by the teams' Quality Assurance Officer, who had asked who he was and what he was doing searching classified project files without supervision.

This practice of multiple, progressively sanitised registers was notified to Mr Fauset, the Chief of Defence Procurement (Sir Robert Walmsley), and the Director of Personnel, Resources and Development (Mr David Baker). All three of these *managers* endorsed it, displaying complete disdain for the gravity of the violations and potential for harm.

The direct warnings were ignored, and the flawed contract acceptance strategy prevailed. The certainties and risks remained, were carried forward into the trials, production and in-service phases (something that is strictly prohibited when relating to maturity of design), and manifested themselves on 22 March 2003.

*

At this time, preparations were being made to transfer the work, but not the posts - and especially not *leaders* - to Yeovilton. Experience and corporate knowledge left the building. The lights were switched off. Nobody noticed.

---

36 Loose Minute ES(Air)(ABW)/71/10/2/2, 18 December 2000.

9: Notes on programme elements

Programme Element Costing was a formal discipline, to be carried out by the Service HQ. The output was data to Resources and Programmes (Navy); assisting in formulating a coherent Naval Air Programme and, importantly, identifying duplication and gaps. The RN ceased this activity in January 1988, explaining why so much of the programme was a MoD(PE) initiative. This section discusses three key programme elements, whose significance will become apparent.

Full Mission Trainer (FMT)

In February 1994 the RN's Aircraft Support Executive (ASE) had been reminded it must make provision for a new AEW Observer Trainer, as the Mk7 and Mk2 would be very different, and both would be in service together for around three years. There was a more mundane reason - the old portacabin hosting the Mk2 Trainer was rotting and falling apart.

ASE disagreed. An FMT was never endorsed; leading, for example, to the unedifying spectacle of H/SK2 and H/SK2a phoning round MoD units trying to beg a new portacabin (or one with fewer holes in it). By January 1997 Racal understood the risk and (correctly) inserted *'use of Full Mission Trainer'* in the Government Furnished Facilities list. The onus was now on MoD to buy one, and its status was henceforth access to a single item of yet-to-be-procured MoD equipment, commencing month 42 of the programme. Yet, it was a significant project in its own right (£xxM).

On 25 August 1997, Dr Colbourne directed: *As the RN had not asked for it, there was no endorsed requirement, and hence no funding or allocated staff, H/SK2 should do nothing*. The immediate effect would be contractual default. Why FMT was picked on, when the same applied to most of the programme, wasn't revealed.

It is believed this edict originated from the Executive Board. To it, Mk7 was a nuisance. While there were major obstacles to overcome, successful progress was *'an embarrassment to the department'*, conveyed to staff by an uncomfortable Kevin Thomas. You see, lesser programmes such as Chinook HC Mk3, and in many ways Nimrod MRA4 (as it did not have to cope with a dual-fleet), were faltering. Dr Colbourne was assured his staff were not working on FMT. However, in the background H/SK2 had Boscombe employ a retired AEW Observer, Colin Richardson, and charge his time to 'materiel'. Eventually, in February

1999, DHP's ruling was rescinded, and a formal post established. This was due to the on-going work to stand-up the new Integrated Project Team in April, and the acknowledgement that H/SK2's team was four men short.

In 2006, Colin and colleagues at Boscombe were awarded the Johnston Memorial Trophy *'for an outstanding performance of air navigation or airmanship or for the development of new air navigation techniques and equipment'*. Seldom has an award been more deserved.

Identification Friend or Foe (IFF) Mk12, Mode 4

The term IFF is a misnomer. It cannot positively identify a foe. And if an IFF interrogation receives no reply, or an invalid reply, the target cannot be readily identified as friendly. Complications arise if a 'friend' has a default policy of engaging a target that has not responded properly. This occurred when a US PATRIOT (Phased Array Tracking Radar to Intercept on Target) missile battery shot down RAF Tornado ZG710 over Kuwait on 23 March 2003; discussed later.

APX-113(V) Combined Interrogator Transponder was being procured for Sea King <u>AEW Mk2</u> and a Tornado variant, by the Directorate of Military Communications Projects (MCP). (Most aircraft only have a Transponder). As MCP and the Defence Helicopter Support Authority had the necessary funding, Mk7 costings had to assume the new system would be physically and functionally safe, fully integrated, simulators modified, Safety Cases updated, support in place, and the Military Aircraft Releases valid. When asked to confirm this, both declined to comment - always a bad sign.

In May 1998, Flag Officer Naval Aviation staff expressed concern that support would be lacking. They, too, had been unable to elicit a helpful response, even from their own Aircraft Support Executive. H/SK2's reply to the Active Fleet Manager explained the boundaries of responsibility and the actions required.

Consequently, on 22 July 1998 a meeting took place between the Sea King project teams and MCP. Asked by H/SK2 if they were buying new test equipment or modifying (for example) the existing Interrogator Test Set Type CRM612, MCP (Mr Mark Elliott) stated the latter. But added that the RN did not know how many there should be, or where, and could only find four. H/SK2 had the information to hand - nine had been bought on contract A54C/1817, and issued to carriers and RNAS Culdrose under temporary Section/Reference Number 10ZZ/210574.

Mr Eason told MCP not to believe him, but didn't offer his own thoughts; so H/SK2 annotated the Risk Register *'The risk is now one of timescale'*. This bullying style of *management*, born of weakness, inadequacy and a desire to control, is directly linked to the contributory factors. Three years later it was revealed Sea King Integrated Project Team support staff at Yeovilton were procuring a new IFF test set, not MCP. The risk had materialised.

*

On 18 January 1999, Lt Neale Hargreaves RN was assessing the Sea King AEW <u>Mk2</u> IFF installation at Boscombe Down. (It was primarily Neale who specified, designed and built the Man Machine Interface rigs at Boscombe Down, an astounding feat. He features again later).

His airworthiness recommendations report to MCP and DHSA concluded that Mode 4 failure warning integration was unsatisfactory, describing it as sounding like *'crap with a dink'*. An extraordinary yet perfect description, which would result in an 'Essential' during the release process; meaning it must be rectified before entering service. Furthermore, this racket could be switched off by turning a spare, unmarked switched volume control on the Intercom. This exacerbated the problem, as it should not be possible to unwittingly disable a critical warning tone (or even crap). His concerns were multiple, but centred on:

- The aircraft he would be flying in operationally was <u>functionally unsafe</u>, <u>vulnerable to friendly fire</u>, and increasingly so to <u>collision</u>.
- MCP and DHSA had rejected his requests to make the aircraft safe. (Westland were not involved, as it was a Naval Service Modification).
- He was aware this presented a significant risk to the programme.

H/SK2 postulated that the warning output was being routed direct to the Intercom, without a tone generator. The *'dink'* was the switching signal, the *'crap'* electrical noise caused by breaking into the Intercom ring main to splice the cable from the IFF. (Another prohibited practice). This proved correct, and MCP were asked to insist on the installation being made safe. They replied: *'It worked on the bench, so it'll work in the aircraft'* - a view ignoring (a) they knew it did not, and (b) the entire concept of systems integration, installed performance, and functional safety. Knowing the Mk2 was functionally unsafe, it was declared airworthy - leaving H/SK2 to find the funding to fix the problem in Mk7.

*

At this point, a series of problems had been notified over a period of nine months. All were red flags, but H/SK2's concerns were rejected. The strategy, supine appeasement and sacrificing safety to meet financial and timescale targets, continued. *This is precisely the criticism levelled at MoD in the Nimrod Review, almost 11 years later.*

H/SK2 agreed a solution for Mk7 with Westland and GEC-Marconi Secure Systems. An external tone generator was to be incorporated. (The aircraft has a readily accessible bank of generators, as they must be easily changed). GEC-Marconi were contracted to modify the Intercom and comms integration rig, Westland the aircraft installation. The cost was minimal - time was the issue.

He was overruled. Mr Eason contracted Racal to implement an alternative design by incorporating the tone generator circuit in the Combined Interrogator Transponder; but omitted the Intercom changes, rig upgrade, systems integration, testing and trials. This meant most of the work still had to be carried out by Westland and GEC-Marconi, but now with a Racal dependency at extra cost. Having agreed a solution costing under £30k, £xM (again, figure commercial-in-confidence) was spent effecting the simple integration of a warning tone. When approving this, a written declaration had to be made that, *inter alia*, no viable, more cost-effective alternative was available or already in hand. Any such declaration was false.

*

Having declined to comment the previous year, MCP now conceded they had not provided technical publications, Interface Definition Documents, Post Design Services, or a Safety Case. The Mk2 simulator, Observer Trainer, and rigs were not modified. Crucially, they confirmed this applied to other aircraft as well, such as Tornado. The effect was immense. Tackling a poor, unsafe IFF installation design in Sea King was straightforward, but time consuming. Tackling a systemic breakdown of the airworthiness process would require lengthy and expensive regression, overseen by the Executive Board. The Mk7 installation was made safe, but H/SK2 had no control over anyone else.

Military personnel are in no position to argue with superiors, be they Service or civilian. They are taught 'don't fight the white', a reference to government White Papers setting out policy. This is why Lt Hargreaves had to be seen to accept what MCP and DHSA were doing on Mk2, while in the background privately plead with H/SK2 that Mk7 be made safe. But his actions should not have been necessary. Senior staff had a legal and moral obligation to accept responsibility and instruct their subordinates to do their jobs properly. Three members of the Executive Board rejected this notion, with malice. If *they* won't do their jobs, get rid of them. It would solve many problems and save a lot of lives.

Airborne Video Recording System (AVRS)

Lacking Flight Data and Cockpit Voice Recorders, inbound XV704's AVRS was the only internal aircraft data source. XV650's had not been switched on. Despite being described as a Cockpit Voice Recorder by the Coroner, it was designed to record video from both radar displays, plus *'all that the Observers hear and say'*. Rear crew could deselect cockpit audio by enabling an Intercom Privacy Zone. It was not designed to be crashworthy.

AVRS was endorsed for Sea King HAS Mk6 in 1990, and AEW Mk2 in 1991, in two separate programmes; and were promptly victims of the imposed freeze mentioned earlier. When asked to comment on the Defence Helicopter Support Authority's proposed Mk2 specification, on 24 February 1997 H/SK2 outlined several incompatibilities with the known Mk7 aircraft Build Standard. This meant starting afresh on Mk7 while the Mk2 AVRS was still in development. Marconi Electronic Systems, Edinburgh (formerly Ferranti Display Systems Division) were contracted to develop and produce the system, with excellent support from Westland, Racal and GEC-Marconi Secure Systems. Lacking a funded RN endorsement (as the money was being spent on AVRS for Mk2, which the RN had assumed would be compatible with Mk7), the programme was progressed at risk (i.e. anticipating offsets or underspends elsewhere in the Directorate).

*

The Board of Inquiry stated, variously, the last 50/48/41/38 seconds were missing from the AVRS audio. The RN Flight Safety and Accident Investigation Centre (RNFSAIC) said 50% of the last two minutes was missing. The Board was saying there was a hard cut-off point, after which there was no audio on the tape. The RNFSAIC was saying fragmented and gradually degraded audio remained; which is technically more accurate.

All one can say is this. If an XV704 (inbound) voice is heard on the tape, it can be a radio transmission or Intercom. If an XV650 or Ark Royal voice is heard, it must be on a frequency monitored by XV704. If XV650 and Ark Royal cannot be heard, that does not mean they were not communicating with each other. MoD failed to correct the Coroner, so he, the families, and most witnesses thought Ark Royal and both aircraft heard everything on the tape; and that this was the sum of all communications. In fact, it is likely transmissions took place which were neither recorded nor disclosed.

Moreover, each of the crew could be monitoring a different radio. However, at the RN's request only one of the three radios (excluding JTIDS and HF) could be encrypted at any one time. This was set out in the RN's SIMOPS statement (Simultaneous Operations), the basis of all comms system design. The RN's Maritime Warfare Centre disagreed with this (wanting all three, and that they should be multi-mode V/UHF), but were unable to persuade the Directorate of Operational Requirements (Sea).[37] Nevertheless, H/SK2 had such a system designed and expansion capability built-in, should it be endorsed.

*

Technology maturity assessments and trials took place between March and September 1997, with the full participation of RN aircrew at Boscombe's Rotary Wing Test Squadron. There were two major issues to consider - how to capture both of the new hi-definition radar displays, and the recording medium.

For the former, three options were considered. Two were quickly rejected - a video standards converter, and a camera mounted behind the Observers. Vibration with the camera, insufficient horizontal resolution with the converter. A specialist video software house (Prima Graphics Ltd) was engaged to demonstrate the latest frame grabbing technology. This was relatively immature at the time, with at least one line of pixels from each frame lost in the 'stitching together' of the frames. In Mk7 one pixel could represent a target, so no loss could be tolerated and the frames had to be stitched seamlessly. Prima were contracted to mature the technology.

For the medium, the starting point was that Hi-8 magnetic tape was the standard used in existing replay and analysis systems in both the RN and Defence Evaluation and Research Agency. A change to any other format, and the knock-on effect on processing, playback and support, could not possibly pass scrutiny. Reinforcing this, the necessary degaussing equipment (Bulk Tape Erasers), an important security consideration, had been procured by H/SK2 in 1994 against the RN's stated requirement to use Hi-8. (Not VHS, as stated at the Inquest).

---

37 Loose Minute D/DHP/24/4/93, 17 March 2000.

In anticipation of questions being asked about an alternative, the investment appraisal assessed, and rejected, solid state memory and hard disk drives; due to the sheer cost/weight/size, and (again) the effects of vibration, respectively. Nevertheless, a parallel task was let to track the maturity of the technology.[38]

The procurement strategy was drawn up by H/SK2 and approved on 27 October 1997 by AD/HP2, with the Director's oversight due to the financial strategy. DOR(Sea) RNA7 and H/SK concurred.[39] As ever, additional manpower was refused. Once again, a significant programme element was to be managed from home.

On 12 May 1998, H/SK2 made one final assessment of crash survivable Military Standard re-writable solid state memory. The time, cost and performance risks were still too great; not least because AVRS was required well before the Mk7 In Service Date, for use in the Sea King Hack radar and navigation trials. Development proceeded, with AVRS passing Critical Design Review in March 1999; by which time the Military Integrated Logistic Support Manager (MILSM) had taken over support aspects.

*

The longest available tape (120 minutes, giving four hours in Long Play mode) was less than the Mk7's required mission duration. 120-minute tapes were stipulated at a design meeting on 1 July 1998. However, XV704 was using a 90-minute tape, meaning it was even more important instructions be provided *when* to switch on the device. The RNFSAIC noted crews 'usually' switched it on at the beginning of the mission, implying no firm instructions existed.

It was important to use a cassette without clear leader tape, as this resulted in an erroneous broken tape warning. Despite the correct tapes being specified (TDK), it was noted on 24 April 2001 that the wrong tape was being used during trials.[40] The RNFSAIC report offers an image of XV704's Sealed Video Module, containing a Sony E6-90HMEX tape (HME = Hi8 Metal Evaporated), which were manufactured with clear leaders. (It does not mention XV650's).

There are two basic tape formulations - Metal Particle and Metal Evaporated. The specification assumed the former, as it is more reliable, durable, and tolerant of temperature and humidity fluctuations.

---

38 Loose Minute D/DHP/24/4/93/25, 3 June 1996.
39 Loose Minute D/DHP/71/5/1, 27 October 1997.
40 Development Event Note #12.

Whereas, the latter's performance relies to a greater degree on the lubricant in the tape coating; which is thinner and more susceptible to damage through winding and rewinding while in contact with heads when reviewing the video. The Board did not comment on the incorrect tape being used.

Finally, the Board criticised the lack of technical publications and operating instructions. The minutes of the 1 July 1998 meeting reveal Marconi were contracted by H/SK2 to provide updates for the Aircrew Manual and Aircraft Maintenance Manual, and a new Operating Manual. Also, while the Defence Helicopter Support Authority had not upgraded the Mk2 Mission Trainer to reflect AVRS, he directed that the Mk7 Full Mission Trainer must be.

It should be asked why, apparently, this support package was not delivered, and how its deletion passed scrutiny. It would appear the Board did not speak to the MILSM who, once it was contracted, was responsible for such matters; but, like his colleagues, subject to constant overrule. When the Board's report was finally made available within the RN in early 2004, it was he who instantly spotted that the main contributory factor, High Intensity Strobe Lights (discussed later), had been identified as a risk by H/SK2, but the mitigation plan overruled by H/SK. It is not known if he notified the Board President.

*

At each stage, the correct Service and civilian staff were kept informed. It therefore came as a shock when the Board criticised the use of magnetic tape. Boards must ensure *individuals whose professional reputation may be affected by findings are afforded the rights of reply*. However, this does not extend to civilian staff. Nor do the regulations address the concept of errors or false allegations being made, or how this is dealt with. The Board offered no opinion on what medium *it* thought should have been used. It failed to mention the RN's formal requirement to use the *same* medium in Sea Kings AEW Mk2 and HAS Mk6, and Merlin. Which is what, ultimately, renders the criticism facile.

It is unclear who advised the Board on this matter. Their ill-informed criticism was shameful, on a number of levels. It called into question the integrity and professionalism of a number of staff (including the late Kevin Thomas), all the while omitting that the RN had not endorsed a requirement. The Board would have been better asking *How on earth did we get AVRS in the first place?*; and recommending that the strategy adopted by H/SK2 be studied for future benefit.

10: The events of 22 March 2003

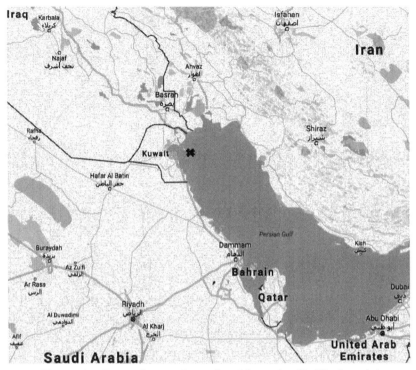

Figure 4 - General overview of accident site *(Public domain)*

'A' Flight, 849 Naval Air Squadron, based at the Royal Naval Air Station Culdrose, Cornwall, was embarked on HMS Ark Royal, an Invincible Class carrier. The carrier group was one week into operating in the Northern Arabian Gulf, its role to guard the right flank of the coalition push through Kuwait into Iraq. The Flight consisted of four newly converted Mk7s, and this was their first operational deployment. Their role was to support land forces operating on the Al Faw peninsula, using the aircraft's new capabilities to provide real-time tactical data.

The operation being supported became known as the Battle of Umm Qasr, lasting from 21-25 March 2003. The port of Umm Qasr was a primary objective, being the main entry point and supply route from the Arabian Gulf. It was taken by a joint amphibious landing force, spearheaded by Royal Marines of 3 Commando Brigade. This facilitated the advance on Basra, to the north. Controlling the Al Faw peninsula was of strategic importance, as it is bounded by Kuwait to the south and Iran to the north.

One aircraft had to be maintained on task at all times, perfectly illustrating the concept of use - 96 hours continuous coverage. A 30-minute overlap was required, to permit an electronic handover. It had to be carried out while airborne, as certain systems are disabled by safety interlocks while on deck, only released when the radome swings down. XV704 had been due to launch at 0200, but this was brought forward to 0130. Her mission was due to finish at 0430. XV650 was to launch at 0400, but was delayed on deck by a software loading failure and took off 22 minutes late. No handover took place because the necessary systems were not available to her at impact, as the problem(s) had not been resolved.

*

The XV704 crew comprised Lt West as senior Observer and aircraft captain, Lt Wilson as pilot (the Mk7 is operated as a single-pilot aircraft, discussed later in chapter 17), and Lt Lawrence as second Observer. For most of the mission Lt West would be in the rear, right-hand Observer seat, next to Lt Lawrence. However, during launch and recovery he had to move forward and occupy the left cockpit seat to act as lookout. The XV704 mission briefing was not retained.

The XV650 crew comprised Lt King as senior Observer and aircraft captain, Lt Green as pilot, Lt Williams as second Observer, and Lt Adams, an exchange Observer from the United States Navy. Lt King was in the left cockpit seat, Lts Williams and Adams in the Observer seats. The XV650 mission briefing was withheld. Why only one briefing was retained was not addressed by the Board of Inquiry.

*

The night was dark. Visibility was variable, and the previous days had seen a severe sand storm with particulate matter remaining in the air. The sorties were conducted under Visual Flight Rules. While returning to Ark Royal, XV704 descended to around 230 feet. Upon launch, XV650 proceeded at around 194 feet, her delay placing both aircraft in the same airspace at the same time.

Shipping had to be avoided, requiring a degree of weaving and knowledge of where the shipping was. The ships were running with reduced and deceptive lighting, making identification difficult. XV650's only available sensors were the cockpit crew's eyesight. It is likely Lt

King was partially distracted from his lookout role by the problem the rear crew were experiencing with systems initialisation, and may have been on his Intercom helping them. He had latterly been seconded to the MSU team, working at Racal's factory in Crawley, so was more familiar with the equipment than most. The Board did not mention this, but did comment on the advisability of the aircraft captain remaining in the rear. The possibility of having to abort the mission would be on their minds.

At approximately 0425 the aircraft collided around 4.35nm from Ark Royal, sinking in 15-19m of water. Several coalition units carried out search and rescue operations. Two RN minesweepers quickly located the wreckage with sonar equipment. US and UK salvage vessels attended, arriving on 22 and 23 March respectively. Dives were limited to a 3-hour window during each tidal cycle, made more difficult by poor underwater visibility and strong currents. Recovery was prioritised, concentrating on crews, classified equipment and items of wreckage that would offer most clues. Six crew were recovered and repatriated quickly, however the last was only recovered on 1 June. During this period his family were excluded from MoD briefings, on the grounds he may have been alive and captured. They were told he had been *thrown clear*. On the day he was repatriated, MoD arranged a meeting with the other families to discuss the Board of Inquiry report. The family chose to be at their son's side.

Event timeline

The following timeline collates *all* timings listed in MoD's reports, but is constrained by the Oxford Coroner's Office refusal to release the Coroner's notes (although it agrees they exist). MoD claims it has retained no files relating to the accident. Discrepancies are noted in the narrative.

01:38	XV704 launches eight minutes late, on scheduled 3-hour mission.
02:45	XV650 crew briefing.
04:00	XV650 due to launch. Held on deck due to JTIDS software loading failure.
	Watch change on Ark Royal.
	Witness (HMS Liverpool Lynx pilot): Lynx launch,

airborne for 5-10 minutes. If correct, this means she landed at **04:10** at latest. Radar shows her still airborne after the collision, over 15 minutes later and 0.5nm from HMS Liverpool.

04:01	Board of Inquiry and RNFSAIC: Lynx launch.
04:07:14	XV704 changes radar operating mode.
04:10	Witness (HMS Ark Royal Air Traffic Control): Lynx launch.
04:11	XV704 switches off lower forward strobe as aircraft descends to ~230 feet.
04:14:14	XV704 AVRS video ends due to salt water damage. Audio continues for another 10 minutes.
04:18:21	XV704 requests clearance to close with Ark Royal. Air Traffic Control replies: *'Playmate about to launch, standby for clearance to close'*; but XV650 is held on deck for a further four minutes. XV704 is not informed of this further delay, so has an expectation of encountering XV650 earlier; witnessed by XV704's crew actively searching for XV650 while the latter is still on deck.
(shortly after)	XV704 on Intercom: *'We are* (redacted) *with mother'* (meaning Ark Royal). Unlikely XV704 is looking at Ark Royal. Possibly HMS Ocean, dead ahead, ~20° to the right of Ark Royal.
04:20:40	XV704 rear Observer (Lt Lawrence) on Intercom: *'Nothing Mode C'*, referring to no IFF Mode C information (XV650's identification code and pressure altitude) on his radar display.

Shortly after this, XV704's front Observer (Lt West) on Intercom: *'I'm starting to see a flashing red light, or I just could be seeing things'*. The red light cannot be XV650, as she is still on deck. At this point, one might expect XV704 to carry out a comms check with XV650, but this is not mentioned.

RNFSAIC: Lynx enters Ark Royal Carrier Control Zone (CCZ). The radar plot provided by the Board of Inquiry shows **04:19:20**. (Figure 6).

04:21:21	XV704 front Observer (Lt West) on Intercom: *'Oh yeah, visual now. Visual the ship'*. Then, rear Observer (Lt

Lawrence): '*Still 10nm to mum. Seven minutes flying time*'. This is correct, indicating Lt Lawrence is clarifying Lt West's visual call.

Witnesses later stated Ark Royal would only be visible at 2.5nm, at most, due to deceptive lighting. Asked if there would seem to be confusion over which ship XV704 is visual with, Lt Cdr Dale (Air Traffic Control) replied: '*I would say so, yes*'. The Inquest inferred, wrongly, he heard this call.

04:21:24   XV704 front Observer (Lt West) on Intercom: '*Ok, got visual on playmate as well now*'.

At the Inquest, Mr Benson QC: '*But, playmate* (XV650) *did not leave Ark Royal until 04:22. So, how can they be visual with an aircraft that hadn't taken off?*' Witness Lt Cdr Dale: '*I can't help you. Might be visual with Liverpool's Lynx*'. This confirms XV704 was not notified XV650 had been further delayed.

04:22   XV704 appears on Ark Royal radar. Lt Cdr Dale informs XV704 that XV650 has just launched. Lt West would now be aware he had misidentified XV650, and situational awareness had suddenly degraded. At this point, one would expect the aircraft to contact each other, to deconflict and start arranging handover.

04:22:44   XV704 on Intercom: '*Visual playmate, just <u>right of nose</u>*'. Rear Observer (Lt Lawrence): '*I don't know if they're squawking yet*'. Pilot (Lt Wilson): '*Is mum just about to be in line with Coastguard cutter?*'

XV704 is over 8nm from Ark Royal and, given the stated visibility, unlikely to have visual with XV650.

XV650 is not '*right of nose*', she is ~20° left of nose; although the precise heading (where her nose is pointing) cannot be known due to the effect of wind.

The squawking comment refers to XV650's IFF. See **04:20:40**.

Lt Wilson is correct about alignment - Ark Royal is ~5nm beyond the US Coastguard Cutter Aquidneck - but this does not mean he has visual with XV650.

04:23:00   RNFSAIC: Lynx exits Ark Royal Carrier Control Zone -

confirming she was inside it at XV650 launch. The radar plot provided by the Board of Inquiry suggests nearer **04:24:15**.

Note: The Board of Inquiry and RNFSAIC timelines are not consistently ahead or behind one another. Here, the Board is 1m 15s later. At **04:20:20** it is the RNFSAIC which is later, by 1m 05s.

04:23:05	Board of Inquiry: XV704 turns left to bearing 045°, on an approach path to Ark Royal and a heading that would still have XV650 left of nose. The radar trace suggests this was before **04:22:40**.
~04:23:20	XV650 calls Ark Royal requesting a Flight Information Service. Informed XV704 is returning. At this point, at latest, one would expect both aircraft to be speaking to each other, to co-ordinate and deconflict. This <u>might</u> indicate UHF comms problems in XV650.
04:23:35	2.5nm from impact. In response to advice from Lt Lawrence, XV704 pilot makes a slight course alteration. Front Observer (Lt West): *'It's all guesswork with this lighting'*. At this point, the front crew have <u>not</u> positively identified XV650.
04:23:36	XV650 first appears on Ark Royal radar due to radar minimum range. But this is later contradicted, the Board of Inquiry stating it was at **04:24:30**. That is, Air Traffic Control had XV650 on screen for between 45s and 1m 39s.
04:23:45	XV650 executes an unexplained 20° right turn.
04:24:00	Board of Inquiry: XV704 cockpit crew see red flashing light. (Possibilities include HMS Liverpool's Lynx, XV650 or another aircraft).
	RNFSAIC: Approximate time Lynx turned off her anti-collision light. The Board of Inquiry placed this at *'probably'* **04:24:30**.
04:24:30	Just over 1nm to impact. Lt Lawrence advises front crew Ark Royal is *'050° at 6nm'* (which is accurate). Front Observer (Lt West): *'Oh, zero five five at six, not where I've been looking at all'*. This suggests Lt West was unsure about Lt Wilson's (correct) assessment at **04:22:44** that

Ark Royal was *'in line with the Coastguard cutter'* and continued looking elsewhere (which he would do anyway). The Board of Inquiry does not mention any discussion between the two.

XV650 calls Ark Royal (redacted). Air Traffic Control: *'Playmate 12 o'clock 2.5m'*. Due to radar update latency, the true figure is nearer 2nm. Also, the aircraft were not at 12 o'clock, but on parallel tracks ~0.35nm apart. By now, XV650 is on a frequency monitored by XV704 (see **04:23:20**).

04:24:37	XV704 AVRS audio ends. <u>At this point XV704 had not positively identified XV650</u>.
04:24:41	0.4nm from impact. XV704 executes 17° left turn.

The Board of Inquiry calculated that, just after the turn, aft strobes would become obscured: *'It is very likely that at no point has the front seat crew actually seen XV650'*. <u>Lacking radar/IFF they are, in effect, flying blind</u>.

04:25:15	RNFSAIC: Impact.

Board of Inquiry says, variously, **04:25:18** and **04:25:25**. The RNFSAIC report is more consistent.

04:25:30	Radar trace shows Lynx still airborne.

Discussion

The main sources were the Airborne Video Recording System (AVRS) tape from XV704 (inbound), and a recording of Ark Royal's Type 996 radar. Unverified AVRS extracts were discussed at the Inquest. Evidence indicated XV704's mission critical (No Go) avionic systems were working, although subject to limitations. XV650's were not available to the crew, meaning several defences against the collision were missing.

However, the Board contradicted itself, claiming that, because there were (apparently) no radio communications regarding equipment problems, this meant XV650 was fully serviceable and fit for purpose. But where would such transmissions be recorded? As a matter of policy, Sea Kings did not carry Cockpit Voice Recorders. XV650's AVRS was not recording. And Ark Royal's recorder was not set to the Air Traffic Control channel, compounded by the Air Traffic Control logs being destroyed.

*

There are significant timing discrepancies between evidence sources. The Board acknowledged this. The Coroner postulated the Airborne Video Recording System timings were out by *'a minute or two'*. Plainly he had been told this, but offered no further comment. One cannot avoid that many unexplained aspects revolve around GPS Time of Day. When asked about this by Mrs Lawrence, MoD refused to answer.

All investigations focused on the same core issue (visibility), but did not seek to understand the points each made, or establish the facts. This mirrors criticism of other accidents, notably Chinook ZD576, Nimrod XV230 and Hercules XV179, where the underlying reasons why the aircraft were not airworthy have not been investigated.

The most important point here is the Board's assessment that it was *'very unlikely'* XV704 had seen XV650. The evidence strongly supports this view. In press briefings, correspondence with families, and in court, MoD consistently ignored this, making unverified claims that each aircraft had visual - in effect placing sole blame on the pilots.

*

The regulations dealing with vision, and the requirement not to interfere with it, are well-defined. The risk under consideration is collision. The key is provision of defences in depth, because no single defence is 100% effective. All rely on human interpretation and are therefore subject to human error. The status of these defences on 22 March 2003 was:

- Inbound XV704's radar, and hence Identification Friend or Foe (IFF), were degraded due to necessary operating mode changes.
- Outbound XV650's radar, IFF and Joint Tactical Information Distribution System were not available.
- Radio and Intercom services in both aircraft were degraded due to the wrong Build Standard being fitted.
- Ark Royal's IFF was unserviceable, and her Air Traffic Control capability limited.
- The horizontal and vertical deconfliction regime was ineffective.
- The endorsed anti-collision lights had been replaced with a rogue and unairworthy High Intensity Strobe Light installation.
- The lower strobes were switched off.

This removal of defences fatally degraded situational awareness. There was little the pilots could do. Each category, in each of the four levels of failure in the Reason Model, had been violated - most of them consciously - long before 22 March 2003.

Air Traffic Control

The following services are available to aircrew:

- Flight Information Service - The most basic, non-radar service, and what XV650 (outbound) requested of Ark Royal.
- Radar Information Service - The pilot is informed of the bearing, distance and, if known, the flight level of conflicting traffic. No avoiding action advice is offered. He is responsible for maintaining separation from other aircraft whether or not the controller has passed traffic information; although the regulations assume he has been provided with the wherewithal. MoD made much of this responsibility, omitting to mention viable defences against collision had been pulled down.
- Radar Advisory Service - In addition to the above, the pilot is given advice on action necessary to resolve confliction.

The Board of Inquiry stated:

'The reason for the aircrews requesting a Flight Information Service appears to have much to do with the categorization of the ASaC (and ASW) helicopters as being radar equipped, as it does with the flight conditions'.

This refers to the Mk7's radar taking longer to come on-line after take-off than either the AEW Mk2 or HAS Mk1/2/5/6. Also, the need to operate in modes that limit the display of primary returns from other aircraft when recovering to the ship. (The Board was brief on this aspect and did not discuss the aircraft's radar enhancement transponder, specifically designed to allow ships to more easily see friendly aircraft on their radars).

The Board claimed a Radar Advisory Service (RAS) was available, ignoring that the Release to Service prohibited the Mk7 from seeking a RAS. It concluded:

'Safety margins for this aircraft have been inadvertently eroded in the Carrier Control Zone in Visual Meteorological Conditions at night'.

But not entirely inadvertently.

The Board was rightly critical of the scope for confusion. However, the decision to omit that seeking a RAS was expressly forbidden tainted its report and, hence, the Inquest proceedings.

*

This brings us to the concept of 'Super FIS'. The Board stated:

'The Senior Air Traffic Control Officer... provided a local CVS [aircraft carrier] variation of Flight Information Service, dubbed Super FIS; it is not formally laid down. This has developed within the CVS Air Traffic Control cadre precisely because of concern over aircraft proximity to each other at night under a Flight Information Service. The existence of such a local variation raises concerns in the Board's mind that the required clarity of Air Traffic Control (ATC) service, and the "contract" between aircraft and ATC as to precisely what protection ATC is affording the aircraft, is being blurred in practice, however worthy the intent. This has the potential to breed complacency. The critical point here is that a Flight Information Service provides no conflicting aircraft advice and a Super FIS does - the quality of that information being discretionary and at the judgment of the ATC Officer. The existence of such a grey area in such a safety critical environment deserves immediate attention'.

The Board noted <u>six</u> times that XV650 was under a Super FIS. But at the Inquest a procession of witnesses claimed there was no such thing. Except, and to his credit, 'A' Flight's Senior Observer (the aforementioned Lt, by now Lt Cdr, Neale Hargreaves):

'It refers to a moral obligation whereby even if a pilot calls Flight Information Service, the Air Traffic Controller is obliged to advise of problems'.

On the final morning, Richard Benson QC, representing the family of XV650's pilot, asked the Board President about it. He replied:

'It is a colloquial term for local flight service. The controller will give more information than strictly necessary'.

But apparently not *that* colloquial.

On MoD's own admission, controllers in the past had expressed concern over aircraft proximity. That is to say, a hazard had been identified. Did they report it? To whom? What was the reaction? If it *was* reported, nothing was done, as an unofficial Super FIS concept had to be developed. Its application could only be subjective, and depended on Air Traffic Control's interpretation of what they *thought* the aircraft wanted or needed. There is a reason why these terms are defined - so everyone knows what is expected of each other. Collision avoidance should not have to rely on an unofficial procedure. All Super FIS did was add a further weak defence. But when something went wrong, and fatalities occurred, it was a junior Air Traffic Controller who had to answer in court; not those who signed to say the risk had been reduced to 'tolerable and As Low As Reasonably Practicable'.

11: The Investigations

Accidents rarely have a single cause. They often have many contributory factors, a situation or circumstance that contributes to one or more causes. There may also be events that are related to factors or causes. Other indirect events may occur which may still be significant in preventing recurrence.

Of particular importance is the existence of latent human errors, which we are disposed to making. Any management system that establishes, tolerates, or fails to detect latent errors is an accident-enabling system, and is the most serious deficiency. Pilots are the last link in the chain of events, which may originate from design, maintenance or organisational weaknesses. Usually, they act to salvage the situation and all is well, but sometimes the outcome is an accident.

However, there is no category for something that has a bearing on the accident despite the hazard or risk being identified, but mitigation cancelled by an officer or official lacking the authority to do so. The 'system' assumes no-one would commit such an act.

*

Three investigations took place:

1. The Board of Inquiry (March - April 2003).
2. Royal Navy Flight Safety and Accident Investigation Centre (RNFSAIC) (March 2003 - October 2006).
3. High Intensity Strobe Lights (HISL) (January - February 2004).

These are discussed separately, followed by an overview concentrating on the main contributory factors, digressing only when it aids understanding.

The Board of Inquiry

The Board was convened on 24 March 2003 and conducted in accordance with The Queen's Regulations for the Royal Navy, and JSP318 (Military Flying Regulations). A US observer was present. The President was Captain (later Commodore) Richard Hawkins RN. The RNFSAIC provided assistance.

The Board did a reasonable job in trying circumstances. Not only because seven colleagues had died, but because information was concealed by parts of MoD. Also, it clearly suspected the US of withholding evidence - again, a common occurrence, made worse by one of their own being killed. Its report is heavily redacted, however many gaps can be filled by reference to other sources, such as replies to Parliamentary Questions. For example, the term *'HISL'* is completely redacted, as are the aircraft tail numbers. What MoD redacts is not necessarily classified, but often to misdirect certain readers, at a particular time.

Boards do not conduct Root Cause Analysis, so events leading to the contributory factors were ignored - which is why I dwell on them. (An event or factor is considered a root cause if its removal from the problem-fault sequence would have prevented the accident). MoD as a whole only looks at the final act. Any attempt to uncover the deeper truth is not tolerated. Here, most of the Board's assertions and conclusions were too simplistic, and some completely wrong. And hence, so too was the evidence to the Inquest.

It found the precise cause was *'indeterminable'* but in its opinion:

'The collision was caused by the loss of an accurate and timely appreciation in each aircraft of the other's relative situation between reporting visual with each other and the impact'.

That is, they lost situational awareness.

Royal Navy Flight Safety and Accident Investigation Centre

The RNFSAIC reported on 18 October 2006, 43 months after the accident - which is why the Coroner's Inquest was delayed until January 2007. It is unclear why it took so long. In a written reply to Andrew George MP on 11 February 2004, Adam Ingram MP predicted completion later that year. Like the Board, the RNFSAIC suffered from vital evidence being actively concealed. One cannot criticise it for this, but it too would have benefited from speaking to those who knew the answers to the questions it left hanging, particularly on contributory factors.

While there is overlap between the two reports, there are also significant gaps and major contradictions. It is important to note the RNFSAIC did not report to the Board of Inquiry, but to FLEET HQ, whose job it was to ensure all reports could be reconciled. Sixteen years on, and despite family representations, this task has not commenced; and is unlikely to.

More worrying are the differences between what the reports say and what MoD presented in evidence at the Inquest. For example, the

RNFSAIC claimed XV650 (outbound) was *'in the LINK picture'* with XV704, but at the Inquest it was firmly stated XV650 was <u>not</u> in the LINK picture. That is, its Joint Tactical Information Distribution System was not yet functioning, *degrading situational awareness*. Even if those present in court had read the RNFSAIC report, few would pick up on this anomaly or understand the terminology.

In a report prepared between 2003 and 2006, the RNFSAIC knows why and how High Intensity Strobe Lights (HISL) were fitted; but in 2003 the Board of Inquiry could only speculate, and in January 2004 the Sea King Integrated Project Team (IPT) denied all knowledge of HISL.

The investigators seem unaware that the aircrew helmets, previously classified as Aircrew Equipment Assemblies (AEA), are also part of the aircraft comms system in the Mk7, due to the fitment of Active Noise Reduction. Therefore, the statement *'The nature of the accident excluded the successful operation of aircrew safety equipment, AEA and egress and they were not factors for consideration by the investigation'* is flawed; meaning the investigation overlooked a worthwhile line of inquiry which would have revealed root causes. Admittedly, this is a rather obscure subtlety, and unique to the ASaC Mk7 (at the time), but serves to emphasise that Boards would be wise to consult with MoD's own experts. It's what they're there for.

The High Intensity Strobe Light (HISL) investigation

Notably, and perhaps a first, the Board cited the airworthiness regulations the HISL design did not satisfy. No praise can be high enough for this brave decision - elsewhere it would attract severe sanction, and end one's career at a stroke. An investigation was then undertaken in January/February 2004 as to *who fitted it to the Mk7, when and why*. MoD now denies all knowledge of this.

The investigator was Lt Cdr John Bramwell RN, a Directorate of Equipment Capability officer embedded within the support element of the Sea King IPT at Yeovilton. He did not know anyone in the project teams at Abbey Wood, and was informed that H/SK2, alone, specified, procured and fitted HISL to the Mk7 - a degree of multi-tasking that immediately aroused his suspicion.

The truth was quickly revealed. Photographs (including Figure 5) showed the first Mk7 on her maiden flight in January 2000, <u>without</u> HISL. Yet as recently as 16 November 2017, in reply to Sir Roger Gale

MP and Mrs Lawrence, MoD rejected this evidence.[41] Minutes of meetings in May/June 2000 revealed H/SK2's directive that it should <u>not</u> be fitted until proven safe in Mk2. That is, he and Westland needed a baseline (and a funded RN endorsement). Advised to look at the data pack, which would reveal the answers to his questions, Lt Cdr Bramwell could not find it. Part of the airworthiness audit trail had gone missing.

Asked on 28 January 2004 who had deceived him, he named a civilian Senior Professional and Technology Officer. He cannot be named here because this is hearsay. However, he had previously been the subject of a complaint over his refusal to correct unsafe Naval Service Modification designs.[42] In line with MoD policy that safety is optional, and staff may abrogate legal obligations, it was rejected.

H/SK2 was asked to submit a letter report outlining the events leading to his refusal to grant read across from the Mk2. It is dated 25 February 2004, was copied to two senior officers and two civil servants, and intended to be seen by FLEET as part of Lt Cdr Bramwell's own report.[43] In accordance with guidance issued to staff with airworthiness delegation, a personal copy was retained, as a false accusation had been made which would need to be defended. It was brief - partly because there was little to say beyond pointing to the written and photographic record, but also to draw comment. In a later letter to Mrs Lawrence, and despite the report being copied to the Sea King Integrated Project Team Leader, Commander-in-Chief FLEET Deputy Command Secretary Mr Simon Routh claimed the Sea King Project Team:

'Despite extensive enquiries, have been unable to identify any knowledge of such a report'.[44]

Before he could speak to Mr Eason, who had 'authorised' HISL be fitted, Lt Cdr Bramwell was stood down. IPT staff had panicked. They knew what the underlying issues were, and that they had been withheld from the Board. False record had been made that the regulations were obeyed. H/SK2's report/testimony was buried. Despite offering himself to the Inquest as a witness, he was not called. Instead, the primary focus was on an Air Traffic Controller. But afterwards, in correspondence with

---

41 Letter D/Min(DPV)/TE MC2017/10496e, 16 November 2017, from Tobias Ellwood MP to Sir Roger Gale MP.

42 Loose Minute D/DHP/24/1/28, 24 January 2000.

43 Letter report SPCISR2f-pf, 25 February 2004. Report to HISL investigator, copied to Brigadier David Stewart, Captain Roger Powell RN, Mr Lee Nicholls and Mr Robert Eason.

44 Letter FLEET-DCS 48, 8 February 2010, to Mrs Ann Lawrence.

Mrs Lawrence, MoD reverted to its unfounded accusation. She and other families (and H/SK2) are entitled to ask why; and MoD should be answering this in court.

*

Upon circulation of the Board's report to families, MoD claimed to Mrs Lawrence that Defence Standard 00-970 (Design and Airworthiness <u>Requirements</u> for Military Aircraft) *'does not contain requirements, merely recommendations'.* It is mandated in all aviation contracts.

On 4 August 2003, Mrs Lawrence asked MoD:

> *'If the anti-collision system was fitted as a Naval Service Modification, has it ever been formally assessed as fit for purpose?'*

> *'Yes, it has been tested'.*

This did not answer the question. Testing is entirely different to a functional safety assessment, which did not take place prior to the accident.

> *'Who authorised this modification?'*

> *'It would be authorised at Headquarters'.*

Authority to accept a change to the aircraft design was vested in H/SK2. He prohibited HISL on airworthiness grounds in 1997, and again in 2000.

The review process and actions of Commander-in-Chief FLEET

Before continuing, it must be emphasised that FLEET staff sit at a remote distance from most of those in the Service and project offices. Much of what they write, particularly to families, is provided in briefings by people they seldom have contact with, or even know. (This is nothing new, but it is only right to acknowledge their difficulty). This has pros and cons. It offers a degree of independence, but they have no direct access to knowledgeable advice. Misleading statements are often inadvertently perpetuated. However, failure to correct mistakes when they are pointed out is routine.

*

Upon completion, reports are submitted to the Convening Authority, FLEET's Assistant Chief of Staff (Aviation), who issues the definitive list of recommendations. Progress is reviewed every six months, under the direction of the officer-in-charge of RNFSAIC. This is a robust process, although assumes all relevant evidence has been provided to, and

105

considered by, the Board, RNFSAIC and FLEET.

As the main contributory factor, according to MoD, was the High Intensity Strobe Light installation, let us discuss one Board recommendation:

'Immediate action should be taken to replace the forward Sea King HISL with a lower intensity anti-collision light'.

This is quite different to its previous recommendation to relocate HISL. FLEET substituted:

*'The design aspects of **HISL** are to be reviewed to establish its suitability for purpose'.*

So, three opinions from two entities. The Board reveals a lingering school of thought that strobes are unsuitable. The Reviewing Officers ask for the entire design review process to start again, *oblivious to the fact it has not been carried out in the first place.* MoD presented this to Mrs Lawrence as evidence of action being taken, and up to a point it is laudable. But the fact remains investigators were misled.

On 2 August 2002 FLEET issued Service Deviation 002/7, dealing with *poor pilot vision and reflections* by instructing the pilot to switch off his lower forward HISL. That is, on that date FLEET knew the design caused problems. But instead of querying the basic design, and even the concept, the 'solution' was to remove a defence (switching off the light).

As signatory to the Service Deviation, and Convening Authority for the Board of Inquiry, FLEET <u>must</u> have been involved in the decision to launch the HISL investigation. After all, the outcome directly affected the validity of its Release to Service (including the Service Deviation), the safety of its aircraft, and what would be offered in evidence at the Inquest. It was seen to:

- Disagree with the Board of Inquiry, and the Design and Airworthiness regulations they were bound by, while offering no alternative proposals.
- Agree with the decision to ignore these regulations and make false record, to the detriment of aircrew.
- Fail to reconcile safety and design conflicts, leaving aircrew with a non-compliant aircraft and poor operating instructions.
- Reject its own Service Deviation.

Whether FLEET realised this is debatable. But, ultimately, it issues consolidated recommendations for action, so is expected to understand. The major weakness is that the Design Authority and project engineers are seldom consulted on technical matters. Here, the proposed actions addressed the *physical* safety of the strobes themselves, not the *functional safety of the system.* Nevertheless, there is evidence *someone* understood some of the issues because an article was published in Cockpit, the RN Flight Safety magazine:

'*Strobes are fitted to let everyone else know you're there. Recent practice of switching both to RED during the Pre-Landing Checks means that you may be deselecting your best visibility aid just before you enter the most congested airspace of your whole sortie. Unless there is a reason to deselect them, they should remain WHITE by day and both RED at night. Disembarked, both strobes should be ON before getting airborne and not switched OFF again until on the ground - standfast [except when conducting] operations in the vicinity of personnel. Embarked, both strobes should be selected ON once safely airborne, and OFF immediately prior to landing. The lower anti-col/strobe may only be turned OFF if it is causing actual disorientation to aircrew. If this is the case the crew must fully assess the Flight Safety implications and endeavour to reselect the anti-col/strobe ON at the earliest opportunity. Bottom line is to remember what they are there for and use them to your best advantage'.*

Whoever wrote this is to be praised. But, clearly, those with oversight should have been concerned the advice was necessary some 20 years after HISL was first fitted to Sea King.

12: Contributory Factors

The Board's report discussed three contributory factors:

1. High Intensity Strobe Lights switched off.
2. Poor aircraft/ship interoperability.
3. Lack of a Night Vision capability.

The RNFSAIC listed two:

1. High Intensity Strobe Lights switched off, as above.
2. XV650's mission critical systems being unavailable.

Each of the former was identified as a major risk by H/SK2 before contract award, and mitigation put in place. However, Mr Eason cancelled the HISL and interoperability mitigation work without taking alternative action, and the Director of Operational Requirements (Sea) rejected Night Vision Goggles (NVG). That is, both deemed the risks would never arise.

The Board's factors are discussed here, as they arose solely from violations. However, the unavailability of the Mission System is slightly more complicated - it had a violation at its root, but the final act was caused either by a technical fault or human error, perhaps both. The various events leading to this are discussed throughout. No criticism of aircrew or maintainers is implied, and should not be inferred, because the system was immature and full training had not yet been provided.

NVG

The Board stated:

'Ark Royal had a policy of reduced and deceptive lighting. An aircrew witness, supported by a conversation captured on the voice recording from XV704, stated this made Ark Royal difficult to see with the naked eye until viewed from close astern. This was in contrast with the perception of the Lynx aircrew, who wore night vision goggles and had no such difficulties. The experience between night flying with and without night vision goggles, as recorded by the Lynx pilot, is significant, and deserves following up. Consideration should be given to fitting all embarked aircraft with a night vision capability'.

It was seemingly unaware that DOR(Sea) endorsed retention of NVG in the AEW Mk2 in 1990, cancelled it in 1994, but in 2002 the RN issued a Release to Service acknowledging its use.

Interoperability

The Board stated (redactions reconstructed in **bold**):

*'The **XV650** rear seat crew did not contact **XV704** for a tactical handover at this point, as might be expected, suggesting some other pre-occupation: <u>probably a recurrence of the radar problem</u> encountered by XV650 on its previous sortie, which would have required a full recycling of the mission system. The logical conclusion is that it may not be possible in an ASaC Mk7 to navigate safely and maintain collision avoidance in the circumstances that the crews found themselves, although they were perfectly entitled by the rules and Standard Operating Procedures to do what they were doing. The rules were written when the Sea King was an ASW aircraft equipped with the **(Lightweight** or **Sea Searcher Radar;** or perhaps a reference to two pilots). The procedures that are employed at present are derived from a succession of adaptations of procedures that may no longer be matched to the systems employing them. The problem needs to be addressed from the bottom up, and not (by) applying iterative changes to procedures that were designed for earlier mission systems with different capabilities. <u>Some rules and procedures for night flying may no longer provide the requisite degree of safety'</u>.*

A basic principle applies. If the Standard Operating Procedures are followed, and a collision occurs, the procedures are inadequate. This precondition, whereby extant rules were based on Statements of Operating Intent and Usage, designs and capabilities of different aircraft, was recognised in 1996, is discussed in more detail in the next chapter.

*

The Board's assumption about XV650 (outbound) *'It can be assumed that JTIDS and Mode 4 IFF were both functioning: they are mission critical items without which the aircraft captain is unlikely to have launched'* has no technical basis. The precise status was unknown to the crew - except that they were unavailable, a fact admitted elsewhere by the Board.

The Board stated the crews were *'mistaken'* to use *'predominantly visual cues to guide their perception of events outside the cockpit'.* This ignored that XV704 had, as required, switched radar modes, limiting the radar returns received; and that XV650's sensors were not available. Also, Ark Royal's IFF was unserviceable and her radar limited. Defences in depth against collision were denied both crews. In darkness, what other cues were they meant to use? They were not *mistaken.* They were *let down.*

The Board ignored or did not grasp one fundamental fact. The Release to Service provided an INTERIM (Switch-on Only) clearance:

'The aircraft must not be operated in any way that places any reliance

whatsoever on the proper functioning of this equipment'.

Hence, the aircrew were criticised for not relying on equipment they were not permitted to rely on. This was known to all concerned, who were obliged to notify the Convening Authority. Not to criticise the Board for its errors, but to ensure the facts were known so as to prevent recurrence.

High Intensity Strobe Lights (HISL)

The immediate focus was on visibility, and a flight trial was conducted to assess HISL - the first in either an AEW Mk2 or Mk7. Correctly, it addressed both directly viewed and reflected light, and noted the lower forward strobe reflected off the sea, interfering with the pilot's vision. Also, that there was the potential for this strobe to be inadvertently left off, implying a warning system of some kind was necessary. (The Naval Service Modification was read across from other Sea Kings, locating the switches in the Overhead Console with no indication other than the actual switch position to advise the pilot of status. Therefore, the Board's comment also applied to these other aircraft, although to a different degree due to them being two-pilot aircraft).

The Board asked: *Why did both aircraft have the forward strobe light off?* The answer was it was directed, in Service Deviation 002/7. However, it could only speculate as to why HISL was fitted in the first place. It correctly implied a failure to appraise and trial the design properly, but did not address the key issue of the Naval Service Modification being rogue. The members would not understand such issues; rather, this is a reflection of the culture which discourages them from consulting with MoD's specialist staff who do. This can be seen in all Boards of Inquiry.

The Board continued:

'When the Sea King's rotating anti-collision lights were replaced by flashing HISLs, the reason for this appears to have been that HISL would provide an enhanced level of conspicuity because of their higher intensity'.

When asked this question in January 2004, <u>after</u> the Board's report was released, the IPT claimed to know nothing about HISL. Who did the Board ask, or was it just making an obvious deduction?

'When the associated Service Deviation was written, aircrew were instructed that the front HISL was to be switched off on entering cloud, when flying at or below 100 feet, in the hover and when taxying/on deck'.

While an accurate summary of the Service Deviation, the Board omitted it is incumbent upon MoD to provide a compliant and safe Navigation Light System (and other anti-collision defences) in the first place.

*'It is considered by the Board that the **HISL** is not fit for purpose and non-compliant with the requirement in Defence Standard 00-970 Volume 2 paragraph 2.1, in that the **forward strobe** should be located so that the emitted light shall not be detrimental to the crew's vision'.*

Having opined this, the Board did not ask why the design was approved. Self-evidently, this passage prompted the HISL investigation. The call for the forward (lower) strobe to be relocated is puzzling. By definition, it must be *forward*, to be visible by approaching aircraft. Also, it must be on the *underside* of the aircraft. When the aircraft was designed, with rotating beacons, their location was carefully determined. Other features, such as antennae location, worked around the lights. It was the selection of the type of light that needed addressing.

13: Background to contributory factors

Night vision

The Board recommended that, because Sea King aircrew were experiencing difficulty identifying other aircraft and ships, *'consideration should be given to fitting all embarked aircraft with a night vision capability'*. This does not necessarily mean Night Vision Goggles (NVG), which is but one type of night vision device. For example, Sea King crews had sought Forward Looking Infrared in 1994, following successful deployment in Canadian Sea Kings the previous year; but this was not pursued.

The Board confirmed NVG-equipped Lynx pilots had no such difficulty. It correctly stopped short of saying NVG would have prevented the collision, mainly because the decision to use it requires consideration of many factors - notably, the particulate matter in the air would have reduced the light energy reaching the device. Also, because few single-pilot aircraft use NVG, and seldom over sea at low level.

Notwithstanding, NVG was used unofficially in the AEW Mk2. Recognising this, and to maintain capability, a full Westland-designed modification was endorsed in January 1990; but cancelled in late 1994. Yet, in 2002 the Mk7 Release to Service acknowledged NVG operations were still conducted. Some years later NVG was formally approved in Mk7; but why issue such an approval if its use was already permitted? Perhaps MoD meant it had eventually satisfied regulatory requirements, long after claiming it had. The 1994 cancellation may have been for good reason (it was not stated, except that it would never be needed, which is inadequate when already used), but the problem was of not being able to revert to the *status quo*, for safety reasons. It did not save money - it just had to be spent on a different Build Standard. Procurers routinely face this scenario - *We don't want this, we're not telling you what we do want, and we want it next month.*

*

NVG is a tool for assisting flight under Visual Flight Rules, to increase safety, enhance situational awareness, and reduce pilot workload. It is not intended to enable additional capabilities in marginal Visual Meteorological Conditions. There is no set minimum height for NVG operations over water, as factors such as sea state, wind velocity, and availability of surface objects to provide contrast and maintain depth perception must be considered.

To provide for NVG operations is a major undertaking. A myth persists that all one need do is don goggles. However, a Night Vision Imaging System must include operational procedures, training and a compatible aircraft design; as well as the devices themselves. For example, all internal lighting, be it cabin, instrument or displays, must be NVG-compatible; meaning spectral wavelength, luminance level and uniformity must be set so the eye is not sub-consciously drawn away from important instruments, or the goggles bloom. Checking this balance, as part of lighting assessments on the ground with the interior blacked out by curtains, and during night flying trials, is a major design/safety milestone. To have numerous 'failures' requiring fine-tuning is common.

The first lighting assessment on Mk7 was carried out in August 1999, but as DOR(Sea) had stated NVG would no longer be used it was not assessed. An unauthorised NVG Attitude Indicator was then fitted to the trials aircraft by the support element of the Sea King Integrated Project Team at Yeovilton, negating the results. Further assessments followed at significant milestones - in March 2000, June 2000 and January 2001 - each resulting in minor changes.

Aircraft/Ship interoperability

While the Board of Inquiry did not mention 'interoperability' *per se*, many issues it raised were recognisable as such. What is it? In this context, the ability of military equipment or groups to operate effectively and safely with each other; the primary components being the Mk7, other aircraft, and ships.

To achieve interoperability, one must understand the interfaces completely, facilitated by preparing Interface Definition Documents; mentioned earlier in the Nimrod chapter. This cannot be done in a vacuum. It requires the active participation of all 'sides' - those managing the new system, and those responsible for what it interfaces with. The key factor here was that an aircraft with a different form, fit, function and use would be operating from ships, requiring new procedures to be developed. These differ depending on aircraft and ship capabilities. Ultimately, the aircraft Release to Service is complemented by a Ship-Air Release.

In late 1996, and noting the narrow scope of the Radar System Upgrade endorsement, H/SK2, sought a ruling on where the boundary of responsibility lay regarding the aircraft and host ships. Prior to Director

General Aircraft (Navy)'s restructuring in 1988, it had a section providing the focal point for this work - 'Ships and Bases'. Procedures and resources had not been updated to cater for its demise. The ship side was not knocking on doors demanding action, instead thinking the same aircraft would turn up with minor modifications. The programme creating a conflict must resolve it, or enter into a binding agreement with those who take on the task. (The 'agent of change' principle). This was doubly important due to the misconceptions about the programme's scope. Procedures, and mutual interference between ship and aircraft sensors, were the main concerns.

Dr Colbourne, Director of Helicopter Projects, directed H/SK2 not to concern himself with interoperability with ships; that this was the responsibility of Flag Officer Naval Aviation. A flawed argument, for the above reasons.

The Project Director, Kevin Thomas, agreed to a compromise. Racal would be tasked to conduct an Aircraft/Ship Interoperability Study. The primary output would be Interface Definition Documents; requiring interaction with the RN team who were, supposedly, working from the ship side towards the project teams. This would force the issue. That Mr Thomas felt compelled to ignore his line manager was a danger sign. Contract Change Proposal 038 was initiated.

In July 1998, data gathering began on AEW and ship emitters and receivers. The Comms System Design Authority (GEC-Marconi Secure Systems) was engaged, as the area of most risk was the Joint Tactical Information Distribution System (JTIDS) Low Volume Terminal. Its characteristics were unknown at the time; in particular its broadband noise output, which risked Electro-Magnetic Compatibility failure. Also, the Civil Aviation Authority was concerned about Secondary Surveillance Radars being blanked by JTIDS, with aircraft disappearing from Air Traffic Control screens. Other contacts were established and, while MoD had many resources on the subject, none had been approached to assist on Mk7. This, more than two years after being assured others were dealing with it. A major risk had materialised.

Mr Eason cancelled the task on 24 August 1998, and H/SK2 was instructed to take it no further. [45] That, the effect of high power transmissions from ships was now the responsibility of Flag Officer Naval Aviation (FONA) and Flag Officer Surface Fleet (FOSF), Mr Eason saying he had discussed it with them. But a 'discussion' is not a formal

---

45 Letter D/DHP/71/1/38/1, 24 August 1998.

agreement, especially to a Service HQ when chatting to someone who has no authority over, or knowledge of, the subject matter. This repeated Dr Colbourne's error from 1996. That is, the scope of any discussions ignored the Mk7 being different in form, fit, function and use. In fact, it must be doubted if any form of agreement existed, as one cannot imagine FONA and FOSF both making such a mistake; and in any case, they could not proceed without the aircraft office delivering Interface Definition Documents.

Decisions to cancel programme elements cannot be made in isolation. Compensatory provision is necessary. By September 2000, during the second phase of flight trials, the issue came to a head. However, ignoring H/SK2, Mr Eason and the new H/SK1 decided mitigation was unaffordable and simply let an enabling contract - a reactive device. Neither understood that a risk cannot be ignored on affordability grounds.

In summary, a management decision was taken to gamble that known certainties would cause no harm. This exposes a major organisational failure - the programme manager did not have authority commensurate with his responsibilities, compounded by constant overrules.

High Intensity Strobe Lights (HISL) installation

This section is more detailed because MoD believes it the main contributory factor. Significantly, upon release of the Board of Inquiry report an internal investigation was conducted into HISL, but not into interoperability or night vision. The key points are:

- Prior to HISL being fitted, the Mk7 Navigation Light System was safe.

- HISL was prohibited in the Mk7 until proven safe. This had not been demonstrated on 22 March 2003. Therefore, its status was that of a rogue Naval Service Modification. (One that does not comply with regulations).

- The Service Deviation governing HISL's use was therefore also rogue.

- It follows that the Safety Case was invalid in this safety critical area.

- When the Board conducted a flight trial, it declared HISL unairworthy.

*

Anti-collision lights bring to a viewer's attention that there is traffic in the vicinity. They must provide all-round visibility. Navigation lights allow the viewer to determine the direction of flight by the pattern of lights - red on port side, green on starboard, white at rear. Their angle of visibility is limited; for example, the rear light must not be visible to an approaching aircraft. Neither type of light is intended to provide illumination for passage, only to provide awareness for other aircraft.

HISLs emit red or white light, selectable by the pilot. Each strobe can be switched off separately. A switchable NVG-compatible Light Emitting Diode sub-ring may be installed. Also a dimmer unit, to allow the strobes to run at lower intensity. Mk7 had neither.

Once the installation design (power supply, wiring, controls, etc.) has been carried out and embodied, to fit a different variant takes 15 minutes for each light unit. While use of strobes is common, the combination of no dimmer and no NVG lights has been a known safety issue for many years.

There is no single 'HISL'. One cannot say HISL is safer without knowing the variant and how it is being used. And if an anti-collision system is disabled, it ceases to function as such. Before doing so, one must ask if the remaining defences are adequate. If not, the pilots face a dilemma. Improve their own visibility, or give themselves the best chance of being seen? I cannot offer a definitive answer, but that is the point. Aircrew must be permitted to assess each situation and the variables presented.

Background

MoD is often criticised for not procuring the correct kit, in sufficient quantity. It is seldom, if ever, asked if the Service quantified the requirement or provided funding - or even asked for it in the first place. Failure to appreciate these basic principles is widespread in MoD, as well as the media. As it was known a HISL Naval Service Modification (NSM) had been schemed for various other Sea Kings, H/SK2 sought a formal position at key points in the programme:

- 1995 - *HISL is not needed.* Defence Helicopter Support Authority (DHSA), when asked to state the Induction Build Standard. This was reflected in the contracted aircraft specification, endorsed by the RN.

- 1996-7 - *No Comment.* DHSA, after mooting the possibility of fitting HISL to AEW Mk2 and being asked to provide the data pack and trials results. This does not mean DHSA did not reply. At various meetings held to determine the Induction Build Standard, the NSM Manager stated *'No Comment'*, and asked for this to be recorded verbatim in the minutes.[46] Moreover, the RN delivered the Trials Installation aircraft (XV707) to Westland <u>without</u> HISL. A clear statement of intent, and contractually this constituted the RN's agreed Induction Build Standard against which development and trials proceeded.

- May 2000 (After completion of initial trials) - **We want to fit HISL to _Mk7_ by _Naval Service Modification_**. Same ex-DHSA staff, now in the Sea King Integrated Project Team (SKIPT). And again, **No Comment** when asked to provide data required to update the Safety Case.

- January 2004 - We know nothing about HISL; the programme manager alone decided it was needed in Mk7, procured and fitted it. SKIPT, to the post-Board of Inquiry HISL investigation.

In response to the May 2000 proposal, H/SK2 insisted HISL be appraised in Mk2, noting a false declaration had been made in 1997 that this had already taken place. The SKIPT support staff reluctantly agreed. He directed that, only upon successful appraisal could HISL be fitted to XV707 (the first trials aircraft). On 8 May 2000 Mr Eason overruled him and informed the support staff at Yeovilton that HISL could be fitted. (At the same time 'authorising' the fitting of the NVG Attitude Indicator). He had no authority to do so, and offered no justification or what it should be read across from.

This left Westland confused. They sought clarification and the following day H/SK2 wrote, directing that:

'If a satisfactory appraisal on AEW Mk2 is not received prior to planned embodiment, (HISL work) <u>shall be suspended</u>'.[47]

<u>Thus, the embodiment of HISL in Mk7 was predicated on the AEW Mk2 modification being airworthy</u>.

H/SK2's directive prevailed until, while absent following surgery, HISL was fitted to both trials aircraft in September 2000. Later, MoD claimed the Mk7s were <u>always</u> fitted with HISL. A January 2000 photograph of XV707, without it, refutes this...

---

46 *Inter alia*, minutes of Induction Planning Meeting, 21 October 1997.
47 D/DHP/24/4/93/29, 9 May 2000.

Figure 5 - Sea King AEW Mk7 XV707 - Maiden flight, without High
Intensity Strobes Lights *(Author)*

On 20 February 2001, Westland notified H/SK2 that HISL was still not
appraised or corrected in Mk7. (Remember, as a Naval Service
Modification the project office had no control over it). They were
concerned that the overrules required complementary actions, such as
contract amendments, alternate standards, and agreed design solutions.
Also, regression testing and additional trials. After conducting a safety
assessment they stated that, as the modification did not conform to
MoD's own standards, they would <u>not</u> take responsibility for the design
or its safety. That is, they made the same observation about non-
compliance as the Board did three years later.

On 21 February 2001, H/SK2 reiterated his requirement to Mr Eason for
flight trials to check aspects which could not be verified on the ground.
The response was to cancel the necessary contract. The intent was to
remove all project engineers from the loop altogether. Indeed, a few
weeks later, on 29 March 2001, a staff meeting was held and Mr Eason
stood the engineers down. (It remains unclear if the IPT Leader, Captain
Marks, knew of this, but he was certainly puzzled and concerned when
his experienced staff suddenly applied for other posts. It was left to one
of his officers at Yeovilton, Lt Cdr Mal Cochrane, to explain matters).

Henceforth, it was unclear who was responsible for the delivered Build
Standard and its safety. It could be nobody in the project teams, yet
Westland's contract did not permit them to heed anyone else. Yet again,
the 'solution' to verified risks was to cancel mitigation, without making
alternative arrangements. A conscious decision was made to retain the

rogue HISL installation. A status report was raised on 24 April 2001 noting the risk, and that it was an *'MoD liability'*. In June 2001, when H/SK2 left the programme because his role had (supposedly) been taken over by Mr Eason, HISL remained non-compliant.

*

By early 2002, Westland were having issues with the trials and contacted H/SK2 in his new post, seeking confirmation of past events and agreements. The latest Joint Trials and Evaluation Management Plan revealed why they were concerned. A typical example was paragraph 3.2.3 (repeated at 3.25.2):

> *'As a result of observed problems in the Enhanced Comms System caused by the anti-collision rotating light, the MoD has required the anti-collision light to be replaced with a High Intensity Strobe Light by Naval Service Modification'.*

This was wrong, and everyone concerned knew it. Development Event Note #9 of September 2000 had recorded that noise from HISL was present on UHF2 Homing. (This is what dates the fitting of HISL).

On 22 March 2003 HISL had still not been trialled in a representative environment, so its use was not reflected in the Safety Case. Instead, it was governed by Service Deviation 002/7, which told pilots when the lower strobe must be switched off. The Board was concerned over this practice and, post-accident, this Service Deviation was cancelled and 014/7 issued, allowing the pilots more scope to use their judgment and elect when to switch off. MoD misrepresented this as a minor amendment to 002/7.

Naval Service Modifications (NSMs)

Because the aircraft had to enter Westland airspace and land on their property, the company could demand the removal of unsafe equipment before flight, or remove it after landing. The main culprits on RN aircraft were always unappraised NSMs. HISL was one, so it is worth listing a few rules governing their use:

- The requirement must be essential, not merely desirable. HISL was not essential, and not treated as such, given it was schemed for AEW Mk2 in 1996 and still not embodied by mid-2000.

- It must not adversely affect other modifications under development. It did.

- It must have no adverse effect on the performance of the aircraft, or equipment or systems associated with it. It had.

119

- The Mobile Aircraft Servicing Unit must seek Aircraft Design Authority advice on the installation design. They did not.
- The Defence Helicopter Support Authority must seek aircraft project office advice on possible effects on the Aircraft Release. They did not.
- There must be a separate issue of the Safety Case. There was not.

Non-compliance with Design and Airworthiness Requirements

Defence Standard 00-970 states:

'Field of Coverage. The system shall consist of lights as will afford coverage of all areas around the rotorcraft'.

Also, an assessment must take place to ensure the navigation lights are still conspicuous when using HISL. On Sea King, while the upper aft strobe is obscured from dead ahead and below, and blurred from many other angles, an approaching aircraft (at or below the same flight level, or just above it) can see the lower forward strobe directly.

What the designer cannot take account of is pilots being instructed to switch off this lower strobe. This is why the Statement of Operating Intent and Usage (SOIU) is crucial. It informs the design, upon which the Safety Case is based. If the use changes, the SOIU, design and Safety Case must be revalidated. This was consciously ignored when scheming the HISL modification for Mk2, and when overruling the directive to abide by these regulations on Mk7.

Who had what authority?

Defence Standard 00-970, Part 7/2, Leaflet 110, opens:

'The navigation light system shall include anti-collision lights as well as side and tail lights or their equivalent, unless otherwise agreed with the Rotorcraft Project Director'.

This establishes his authority and responsibility, but who was he and how was this implemented in practice?

The Sea King Project Director was, at first, Assistant Director Helicopter Projects 2 (Kevin Thomas). On matters of design and airworthiness, formal delegation is necessary. This can only be afforded a 'Suitably Qualified and Experienced Person'; that is, an engineer of the relevant discipline(s). There are several ways of assuring this, the most obvious (for civilians, at the time) being the certifications in one's QC1 (or equivalent), following examination against MoD regulations and Civil Aviation Inspection Procedures. The disciplines one is deemed qualified in, and the levels of inspection and certification one is authorised to sign for, are set out. One can then be considered for higher airworthiness delegation (e.g. a Technical Agency appointment). Until the early 1990s, the criteria included proven ability and integrity, recognising one can be qualified and experienced, yet incompetent and a fraud. Today, the last two are considered irrelevant. Within the project teams, H/SK1 and H/SK2 held such approvals. Both were electrical/avionics engineers, but benefited from MoD's policy requiring its electrical specialists (but not those who join after external training, or direct entrant graduates) to be cross-trained on other disciplines.

MoD does not define experience. However, a Career Guidance Panel decision of 5 October 1998 set a reference point for avionic project management inexperience. Having only managed (not merely worked on) 125 projects, across all disciplines (radar, comms, navigation, sonics, electronic intelligence, electronic warfare, software), and in all phases of the procurement cycle, was too inexperienced for anyone above the most junior grade in MoD(PE) to be considered for promotion. Today, it is unclear how many, of any grade, come close to this figure.

Neither Mr Thomas nor Mr Eason had the necessary technical or financial approval delegation. This is not a criticism. Mr Thomas, in particular, had other important roles, not least management of the Queen's Flight replacement programme. (Requiring considerable tact and diplomacy when dealing with a family containing so many pilots).

Routine design and airworthiness issues, governed by clear regulations, were well below Dr Colbourne's pay grade. So, Mr Thomas delegated downwards, to H/SK2. However, this otherwise robust system of delegation does not cater for illegal overrules.

Emitted and reflected light

Both Board of Inquiry and Reviewing Officers noted the adverse effect of emitted and reflected light; and the programme manager, GEC-Marconi, Westland and Boscombe Down had assessed both.

However, FLEET rejected the Board's comments about reflected light, on 7 April 2010 stating to Mrs Lawrence:

'It is noteworthy that compliance with Defence Standard 00-970 requires the emitted light [MoD's emphasis] *of the HISL not to be detrimental to the crew - this was complied with by positioning the HISL outside the crew's direct line*

of sight. It is the opinion of the Subject Matter Experts tasked with considering the report that the Board of Inquiry had misinterpreted the Defence Standard (by referring to reflected light)'.

This conflated the HISL installation with the strobes themselves. However, in possibly the most asinine claim in this or any other case, FLEET claimed <u>reflected</u> light did not matter. This ignored that FLEET approved a Service Deviation requiring HISL to be switched off due to:

'<u>Reflections</u> causing distraction to the pilot and potential eye damage to groundcrew'.

FLEET's reasoning to Mrs Lawrence rejected its own Service Deviation.

*

Let us discuss Defence Standard 00-970. MoD quotes Part 7/2, Section 1, Leaflet 110 (Navigation and Anti-Collision Lights):

'The anti-collision light(s) shall be located so that the emitted light shall not be detrimental to the crews' vision and will not detract from the conspicuity of the navigation lights'.

This repeats Military Specification MIL-L-006730C(AS) (General Requirement for Aircraft Exterior Lighting Equipment). Mil Specs are of US origin, but are routinely invoked by MoD. The Sea King is based on a US Sikorsky design, so is directly traceable to them.

Defence Standard 00-970 does not say to ignore reflections - it just doesn't mention them. It is a case of the Technical Author not stating the obvious - a legacy of the days when MoD engineers were fully trained before being permitted to apply these standards. Therefore, one must drill down until mention is found - and that is in the Military Specification. No effort is required, as it is called up in 00-970, on the same page, at paragraph 3.1.7:

'Exterior lights shall be installed or shielded in such a manner as to prevent them from being a source of direct or <u>reflected</u> glare to the pilot or crew'.

Westland considered it normal to assess reflections. Military Flying Regulations mandate it. The Air Accidents Investigation Branch consider it vital, regularly quoting the work of the late Frank Hawkins (e.g. 'Human Factors in Flight'). Plainly, a design must take cognisance of them for it to be safe, because anything that impedes in-cockpit visibility is a serious hazard. No professional aviator or engineer would think otherwise.

Mrs Lawrence was lied to. (Are you beginning to discern a trend?)

Parliamentary Questions

On 26 March 2008, Bob Ainsworth MP replied to questions posed by Sir Roger Gale MP:

'The Mk2 to Mk7 conversion programme that was undertaken between 1999 and 2002 was conducted in two phases, giving rise to two different Build Standards of trials aircraft. The trial installation of HISL was undertaken during the first phase before the equipment was transferred to the second phase trials aircraft and re-tested, prior to release to service. This approach was agreed jointly between the MoD and the helicopter Design Organisation. The retro-fitting capability was introduced as a Service Modification, where design, test and installation is undertaken by MoD personnel. In all cases, the Department is required to seek independent safety advice before the modification is released to service. Additionally, MoD personnel are required to seek advice from the helicopter Design Organisation, as was the case for all Marks of HISL modification. For all Marks except Mark 5 and Mark 6 aircraft, the HISL modification has retrospectively been formally accepted onto the aircraft drawings by the helicopter manufacturer through a process called Cover Modification'.

Mr Ainsworth makes a positive statement that HISL was fitted to all Mk7 Build Standards. It was not. (See Figure 5). He talks of a *'trial installation'*. This does not mean a <u>flight</u> trial took place (and it did not). Nor does he mention that, as a result, Westland repeatedly rejected the RN's design.

It is disingenuous to associate Westland with the decision to release to service. Their testing was ground-based and ensured the installation was physically safe and functioned (i.e. could be switched on/off/between modes). This included initial Electro-Magnetic Compatibility testing - which it failed. But only flight trials in a representative environment could establish functional safety. As explained earlier, the Defence Helicopter Support Authority had consistently <u>refused</u> to provide any evidence of such trials in a Mk2, and Westland were not contracted to carry them out in a Mk7 (because HISL was not required).

Mr Ainsworth states, correctly: *'In all cases, the Department is required...'* He omits that these legal obligations were ignored; evidenced by the need for an appraisal in Mk2 <u>four years</u> after the Defence Helicopter Support Authority falsely declared it had already passed appraisal.

Only when the above is considered can the final statement *'the HISL modification has retrospectively been formally accepted...through a process called Cover Modification'* be placed in true context. If a Service Designed Modification is Cover Modified, it is subsumed within the drawing pack by the Design Authority but MoD retains liability for the design. Only if a Superseding Cover Modification is issued does the Design Authority assume this responsibility. Mr Ainsworth mentions the former, omitting the latter. Nor does this mean the HISL installation was functionally safe in either the Mk2 or Mk7. It means the engineering design deficiencies in the Mk2, and noted by Westland in 2000, were eventually corrected to their satisfaction. However, Westland were not responsible for how the RN used HISL. Nor for ensuring complementary Aircraft/Ship procedures were developed and implemented. Nor, for how the aircraft was operated. Westland had no input to this new use, and it was not reflected in the Safety Case.

*

Lacking electronic aids, in darkness, meant having both HISLs on was vital; but lower forwards were off and upper afts were dim and obscured. Having been denied other defences in depth, their last remaining defence was compromised. By permitting this - in fact directing it - MoD failed to ensure safe operations.

Capitulation and vindication

There was to be another twist.

On 8 February 2010, FLEET admitted the instruction in Service Deviation 002/7 to switch off HISL was *'unendorsed practice'* in any Sea King. [48] How can a formal instruction in the Master Airworthiness Reference be unendorsed? This proves the Service Deviation was improperly prepared and simply waived through, wrongly read across from another aircraft. It was rogue, like the Naval Service Modification itself.

This admission changes the entire complexion of the accident and subsequent investigations. H/SK2's directive not to fit HISL until proven safe was now fully vindicated. It warrants re-opening the Board of Inquiry and Coroner's Inquest.

---

48 Letter FLEET-DCS 48, 8 February 2010, to Mrs Ann Lawrence.

14: Overlooked factors

This chapter is intended to illustrate what was skimmed over by the Board of Inquiry. Some issues, like the stray Lynx helicopter, were mentioned, but not in detail. Others, such as missing safety modifications, not at all. Each of these six interrelated aspects of the accident can be seen as enlarged holes in the slices of cheese.

The impact of HMS Liverpool's stray Lynx

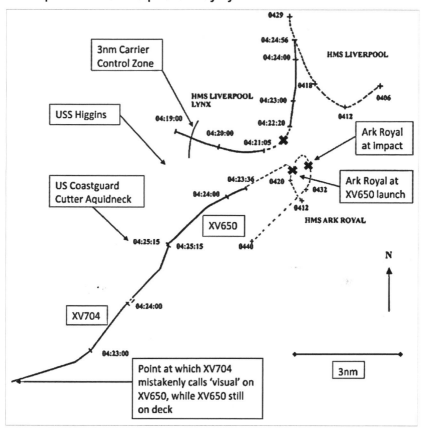

Figure 6 - Overview of aircraft and ship positions *(MoD, annotated)*

The Lynx experienced 'secure radio problems' shortly after launch, necessitating a return to ship. But first she was held within 3nm of HMS

Liverpool for 10-25 minutes (depending on which version one reads, and in any case wholly contradicted by Figure 6, issued by the Board) so she could attempt a fix of this mission critical equipment. This procedure was not used with XV650, who continued on *her* mission not knowing if *her* mission critical equipment was working. Unspecified *'problems'* (plural) is unhelpful, but it is not unusual to encounter crypto loading and synchronisation difficulties, similar to what occurred with XV650. Lynx was fitted with the same V/UHF multi-mode radios, UHF Homer and Secure Speech overlay as the Mk7, albeit at a much older Build Standard. (And different aircraft had different procedures - due to lack of maintainers, Sea King AEW/ASaC aircrew signed-out and loaded the crypto; in other Sea Kings it was correctly the maintainers).

A number among Liverpool's crew would have witnessed her landing. On Day 1 of the Inquest, the pilot stated he was <u>on deck</u> speaking to maintainers when impact occurred, but was not facing the area of collision. During RN Flight Safety and Accident Investigation Centre (RNFSAIC) evidence on Day 3, a radar trace (upon which the Board based Figure 6) was produced showing the Lynx <u>still in the air</u> at the time of collision. Richard Benson QC pointed this out, asking *'Am I wrong?'* The witness replied *'No'*.

If the pilot was correct - and one has to assume he was - the accuracy of MoD's timeline, based on Ark Royal's Type 996 radar, must be wrong. The Board left the conflict hanging but, again, GPS Time of Day is a major factor. The fact such an obvious line of inquiry *is* hanging suggests its conclusions were removed. The Coroner came close to postulating a general GPS system failure, which would explain many discrepancies. (Iraq was known to have a jamming capability, and in 2003 MoD's Anti-Jamming GPS programme had an In-Service Date of 2008).

*

XV650 took off looking north, turning left to the south-west. While returning to HMS Liverpool the Lynx crossed XV650's nose, left-to-right, ~0.7nm away. Whenever asked about this, MoD claims the Lynx's presence did not affect <u>inbound</u> XV704, but never mentions XV650. Except for an attempt by Mr Benson, this has never been questioned.

While returning to HMS Liverpool, the Lynx encroached into Ark Royal's 3nm Carrier Control Zone (CCZ) without permission. Minor under normal circumstances, but as the ship had no serviceable Identification Friend or Foe it was more serious on this occasion. There would be limited indications the Lynx was friendly, so she was a distraction to Ark Royal; who, in addition, could not positively identify (or initially see, electronically) XV650 once she launched. The two Sea Kings were the only aircraft authorised by Ark Royal to be within her CCZ. No other night flying was scheduled from the ship.

I mentioned earlier that the Board did not mention the Sea Kings' radar enhancement transponder, which enhances the conspicuity of the aircraft on the ship's radar. Lynx and Sea Harrier carried a similar system, with different coding; so the radar operator would know it was not a Sea King. While irrelevant here, RAF aircraft were not permitted to operate off carriers unless fitted with this RN equipment.

A point of fine detail. The Lynx radar had 180° scan. (A full 360° capability was approved and developed in the late-1980s, but cancelled). By reference to Figure 6, at her closest point of approach to Ark Royal, and thereafter, she would not have had XV650 on screen.

MoD's position is this: Lynx retained rotating beacon anti-collision lighting, so could not be mistaken for a Sea King. By omitting to say other (US) aircraft were airborne, with strobe lights, this diverted attention from XV704 misidentifying another strobe source. It also ignores the concept of the Lynx switching off her light on final approach, which may have deceived XV650's pilot. Distinguishing between a Sea King and Lynx was discussed by a FlyCo officer in written evidence:

'Given the right aspect, I can tell to 2-3nm from a fixed standpoint of being on the bridge. If I was on an aircraft doing landing checks, etc., I don't think I could visually identify it. I would identify it as an aircraft, and a helicopter from relative movement, but wouldn't be able to tell the difference between two aircraft'.

(FlyCo is a visual control room attached to the port side of the bridge, manned by aircrew and used to control the movements of aircraft within the vicinity of the ship).

This suggests XV650 would have had difficulty identifying the Lynx. While she switched off her light to prepare for landing, there is no evidence when. The Board and RNFSAIC offered opinions 30 seconds apart, an eternity given the timeframe under discussion. After this point, she would be showing only (much dimmer) navigation lights.

This raises the question of consistency in anti-collision light selection and use. Sea Kings had strobes, Lynx a rotating beacon. Why? There may be a reasonable explanation, but MoD could not say what it was. In fact, the Board recommended Sea King revert to beacons.

The Lynx's closest point of approach was at precisely the time XV650 launched (0422). MoD reports say encroachment lasted three minutes, but the radar trace shows five. A few minutes later, inbound (XV704) would have been in the same general position as the Lynx, on her final approach. That is, there was an <u>expectation</u> XV704 would be close by. This was not mentioned. By extension, it is entirely possible the crew of XV650 relaxed after turning away from the Lynx, because the risk of collision had apparently dissipated. After all, they had other pressing problems, such as their mission critical systems being unavailable.

*

The Board's report is heavily redacted on the above points, and difficult to follow. It notes the inconsistency between evidence; sometimes believing the radar, often rejecting it. Sometimes a judgment must be made as to which source is more reliable. But one cannot believe both, and that is what concerned Mr Benson and the families.

Both Board and Coroner glossed over this period, which would have been characterised by intense debate on Ark Royal. And there was no mention of the obvious - the aircraft trying to contact each other. Only Mr Richard Green, father of XV650's pilot, understood the significance of this and asked that it be discussed. The Coroner, by now more or less acting for MoD, and perhaps recognising the difficulty it now faced, told him to remain silent. Sadly, Mr Green passed away in May 2016.

*

During questioning of the Ark Royal FlyCo Officer on Day 2 by Mr Benson:

> *'You were very cross about the presence of the Lynx?'*

> *'Subjectively, yes Sir'.*

> *'What was irritating you?'*

> *'The Lynx had entered the Carrier Control Zone'.*

> *'Was it a potential hazard to aircraft taking off and landing?'*

> *'Yes Sir'.*

> *'XV650 launched at 0422. How many minutes before that did you first see the Lynx?'*

> *'I don't know'.*

Mr Green seeks to clarify this but is again shut down by the Coroner. Mr Benson asks good questions about communicating with the Lynx, inquiring why she was in the CCZ. The replies are non-committal. He

128

asks if there was any means of alerting the Lynx; receiving no definitive answer, only that the witness raised it with the Operations Room but does not know if they raised it with HMS Liverpool. No Ops Room witness is called.

*

The families are invited to ask questions. Mrs Sarah King, widow of Lt King (XV650 senior Observer and captain), is incisive and receives clearer, or at least more revealing, replies:

'Did you warn XV704 of the Lynx?'

'No. She was outside my zone, 12 miles away'.

'So it would be Air Traffic Control?'

'I think she was outside their zone too. I am not an expert, so can't say yes or no'.

'So, nobody is obliged to warn them?'

'Yes, if there is a conflicting interest, mentioned under Flight Information Service'.

'But you thought it was a conflicting interest because you told XV650?'

'Yes, but only because it was within my CCZ and on my frequency. 704 was 10-12 miles away and on a different frequency anyway'.

'So 704 wouldn't have needed to know the Lynx was there?'

'No, she didn't need to know'.

Mrs King moves on:

'Is it normal procedure for both aircraft to be coming towards each other at same height?'

'Perfectly normal'.

'What, to be coming towards each other at the same height?'

'It is, within close proximity of carrier'.

'If that's normal, does somebody warn them?' (A chorus from the families of *'Absolutely!'*)

'Under Flight Information Service, they were warned about each other, then reported visual. There is nothing to stop you flying close if visual. Under Flight Information Service, collision avoidance is the responsibility of the aircraft captain'.

(The Board did not say which frequencies he was monitoring; the implication being he did not hear these alleged calls, in which case his evidence is hearsay).

129

At this point, Mrs King is audibly upset and her father takes over:

'But XV650 was late and its radar not working. Would that affect the ability of XV650 to see XV704?'

(To Coroner) *'Sorry sir, I don't believe the radar was unserviceable. The problem was with other equipment. As far as I know, the radar was serviceable'.*

'In the report...' (Finished by Mr Green...) *'The radar switch was off'.*

'I don't know that'.

Mr Green: *'Somebody must know'.*

Coroner: *'Don't worry Mr Green, we shall be hearing about that'.*

The Coroner should have allowed this to be explored, given the Board had stated, not speculated, that the radar was <u>unavailable</u>, removing a defensive layer against the risk of collision. While he assures Mr Green the issue will be addressed later, it is not. Too often, a witness replies he does not know or recall, but no-one is called who does. This is frustrating, especially to Mr Green. As Mr Benson was neither party to pre-Inquest discussions nor provided with transcripts of interviews, only notes, it can be seen MoD, with the Coroner's assistance (unwitting or otherwise), engineered a situation whereby crucial evidence was concealed, and valid questions unanswered.

Mrs King, when asking about aircraft proximity at the same height, is fobbed off with *'perfectly normal'*. It may have been normal, but was it sensible? Some might think the airspace control plan was an accident waiting to happen. Especially if it assumed the sensors in both aircraft and Ark Royal were always fully working and presenting accurate and useful information to assist in collision avoidance. None were, and this point escapes the court entirely. The procedure didn't allow for any what-ifs; such as, what if the outbound aircraft is late and has unresolved equipment problems, leaving eyesight, in darkness, the only defence?

Visibility, and the alleged calls of 'visual'

MoD made much of alleged calls of *'visual'* by the pilots, presenting them as evidence of no other errors. Noting the source tape was not played in court or independently verified, the following is the totality of MoD's evidence:

- 04:21:24 XV704, on <u>Intercom</u>: *'Visual playmate'*, but it cannot be XV650 because she is still on deck, with her strobes <u>off</u> for safety reasons.

- 04:22:44: XV704, on <u>Intercom</u>: *'Visual playmate, <u>right</u> of nose'*. At this point, XV704 was on a heading well to the south (right) of Ark Royal. XV650 had only just taken off and was well to her <u>left</u>, out of visual range.

MoD claimed XV704 was advised, at 04:18:21, that XV650 was being delayed again (due to Lynx encroachment). Three minutes later (at 04:21:24), XV704 expected to see XV650 airborne; <u>but she was still on deck</u>. Self-evidently, at this later time XV704 had <u>not</u> been kept up to date on XV650's status.

Figure 7 - Sea King ASaC Mk7s operating at sea, illustrating how viewing angles change depending on aircraft aspect, and whether rotors are turning or at rest. *(Public domain)*

The important point is this. <u>XV704 saw something, and it was not XV650</u>. It would have to look like a strobe, not a rotating beacon or a light on a ship. There are three possibilities: the front crew saw a strobe on another, unidentified, aircraft; they were victim of a visual illusion; they saw a reflection of their own (rear) strobe. The Board mentioned illusion and reflection, but not the possible misidentification. Yet, it is just as likely.

It is probable other calls were made, but the only Air Traffic Control notes were jotted on a *'scrap piece of paper'* which *'did not survive'*. Ark Royal's Commanding Officer confirmed to the Coroner he was *'satisfied with the standards of Air Traffic Control on the ship'.* Really? A scrap of paper, that is destroyed, is an acceptable Air Traffic Control log? There is a resonance with the 1994 Mull of Kintyre Chinook crash, where Military Air Traffic Control in London destroyed all records, despite regulations requiring written logs to be retained for one year. The combination of this, AVRS tape damage, and poor recollection calls into question the accuracy of this evidence. But more disturbing are the attempts to divert attention from the effect the Lynx had on XV650, pointing to it being a key event.

It seems likely the XV704 cockpit crew saw, within a short period of time, HMS Ocean and an unidentified aircraft, both to the south (right) of Ark Royal; followed by US Coastguard Cutter Aquidneck and USS Higgins to the left. Then, <u>perhaps</u>, Ark Royal's and/or Liverpool's distant and deceptive lighting. What is certain is they were confused over the identity of these sightings; due, in part, to not knowing XV650's status.

*

The Board of Inquiry undertook a flight trial to assess visibility when using High Intensity Strobe Lights (HISL). Hitherto, the only night-time related requirement was to check cryptos for midnight rollover, which was part of ground testing. From the Board's report (reconstructions in **bold**):

'*The forward, lower, **HISL** was considerably brighter than the tail, higher **HISL** and that there was a significant <u>reflection</u> of the lower **HISL** from the sea surface. When the aircraft approached the ship with a near head-on aspect and switched the forward **HISL** light off, it became difficult to visually acquire the aircraft until it altered course and presented a front-quarter aspect, whereupon the tail light became visible again. The Board member who flew in the jump seat made the following observations;*

  *a. The forward **HISL** when switched on at **200 [?] feet** was distracting and disorientating in the cockpit:*

  *b. The deceptive lighting being employed by **Ark Royal** was effective and it was difficult to assess course and speed:*

  c. When flying in the Northern Arabian Gulf, oil rig burn-off torches are prevalent in many areas and made visual identification of aircraft lighting on the same plane of view difficult'.

Viewing a single light in these circumstances is similar to watching someone running through woods with a torch. The light disappears at irregular intervals, making it difficult to pinpoint its position, direction of travel and speed, especially when the viewer is himself moving quickly. The Board explained this well:

*'The importance of the aircraft navigation lights, and the interpretation of them by the front seat crews, became critical for collision avoidance. The lack of a visible **HISL** now became crucial. By their very nature navigation lights alone give limited angular and relative movement cues as each covers a wide angle of view. It is often only when one light disappears from view and another appears due to angular change that relative motion is measurable'.*

XV704 was slightly above XV650, and they impacted around the port cockpit areas. But further assessment is difficult lacking the precise altitude and attitude of each aircraft. The RNFSAIC made a good job of analysing this; but omitted each was viewing the other's HISL through rotor discs, which is akin to viewing a strobe through another strobe.

The unexplained 17° turn by XV704 (inbound)

In the rear of XV704, Lt Lawrence was confident and correct about Ark Royal's position, and called a heading change to 050°. But confusion reigned in the cockpit. Simultaneously, Air Traffic Control was on the radio to XV650 - the only suggestion of communication with XV650. The entirety of XV650's call was redacted by MoD. Ark Royal replied *'Playmate 12 o'clock 2.5nm'*, so one might assume the question was *Where is my playmate?* or something similar. But why redact what seems to be a simple request for XV704's range and bearing? Was something untoward said? If so, it must have been more robust than Lt West's (XV704 captain) comment about lighting being *'all guesswork'*, which MoD left in its report despite being a damning indictment. XV650's crew must also have been relying on guesswork; in fact more so, and this was causing increasing concern.

In response to Lt Lawrence's 050° call, the front seat Observer (Lt West) exclaimed *'not where I've been looking at all'*. It would appear he was looking well to the left towards the US ships, also running with deceptive lighting. Differentiation of light sources required other visual cues. But each aircraft had only one strobe on, and aircraft converging in darkness see little or no relative movement. (Detailed assessment is made more difficult if the aircraft were cocked off into the wind).

*

Approximately 0.4nm before impact, XV704 executed a 17° turn to the left, bringing the aircraft onto a collision course. Lacking a Cockpit Voice Recorder, the reason cannot be known. At the Inquest, Lt Cdr Dale (Air Traffic Control) stated this manoeuvre was not discernible on his radar. The hitherto parallel aircraft tracks were ~0.35nm apart. At 5nm range, the trace on his display was a blob ~0.25-0.75nm wide, depending on aspect. The ability to discern a turn is governed in part by the radar update rate. It took place just as the radar returns began to merge. Lt Cdr Dale's assertion was correct, emphasising the need for compensatory defences.

In Visual Meteorological Conditions, there are no set entry and exit routes to/from the ship. Procedures should be fail-safe, so deconfliction is assured. But they were not sufficiently robust to take into account operating at night with faulty or unavailable equipment on aircraft and/or ship. The procedures applied to a different concept of use. This is precisely what was recorded as a major risk in 1996.

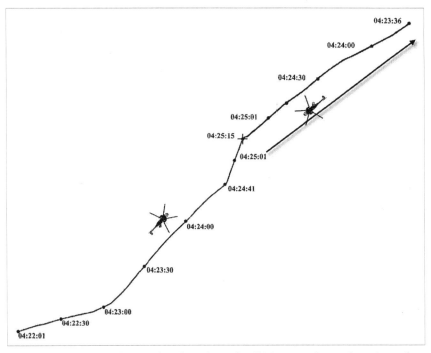

Figure 8 - HMS Ark Royal radar plot of collision tracks and projected course of XV704 (inbound) had she not turned 17° to port. *(MoD, annotated)*

The Board of Inquiry confirmed all aircrew, warfare and Air Traffic Control staff were fully conversant with, and practiced in, the

134

deconfliction procedures; and they were in force at the time of XV650 launch. It omitted they were inadequate, and in any case could not be implemented (which is the next step to being 'in force'). While Ark Royal offered (inaccurate) information in the horizontal plane (the radio message to XV650 that XV704 was dead ahead), the height restriction and lack of IFF made vertical deconfliction more difficult; although merely requiring radio calls, and tending to confirm a comms problem or more serious distraction. When trying to explain this at the Inquest, a witness was instructed by MoD's legal representative *'don't talk about those things'*. The Coroner allowed this, suggesting prior agreement.

What would the pilots have seen, or expected to see? To their left and right were the lights of ships, to be avoided by 2nm. (In the circumstances not always possible). XV704's front crew were uncertain *what* ships. Lt Lawrence in the rear knew, and was updating them; the RNFSAIC confirming he had *'a good understanding of the surface plot and his directions were accurate and logical'*. His opposite numbers in XV650 were constrained, as their radar was unavailable. By the time each crew assimilated what information they had, and realised (or thought) the other was <u>not</u> dead ahead, and commenced searching, they would be effectively invisible to each other. And very close. So, while the Board of Inquiry claimed both aircraft lost situational awareness, it is fairer to say this did not apply to Lt Lawrence in XV704 - and XV650 probably had none in the first place.

*

At this point, immediately before impact, the ability to see and avoid had been wholly compromised. The situation was:

- XV650 (outbound) had, unavoidably, been given an inaccurate range and bearing to XV704, and had no sensors available to appreciate this.

- XV704 (inbound) had, as required, changed range scale, and her radar was not displaying primary returns from XV650. Because of this, her IFF was restricted in effective range.

- XV704 was receiving no IFF returns from XV650. Nor from Ark Royal, whose IFF was not working.

- Ark Royal could not see either aircraft's pressure altitude, and they could not see each other's. (A function of the Height Encoding Altimeter, used by IFF).

- Both lower strobes were off, and neither aircraft had a clear view of the other's upper strobe, due to obscuration by aircraft structure.

In summary, Lt Wilson (XV704 pilot) was receiving conflicting information from four sources. (Lt Lawrence in the rear, Lt West beside him, Ark Royal, and his own observations). Only one was demonstrably accurate - Lt Lawrence. It is possible he followed Lt West's perception rather than electronic sensors, electing to turn left towards what Lt West thought was Ark Royal. The RNFSAIC discussed this in detail, confirming at the time of the turn Lt Wilson was looking directly down the stern of Ark Royal, and she would be difficult to identify. That, he may have turned to an intercept course with HMS Liverpool, which would have been more conspicuous as she was heading directly across him. (Figure 6).

*

What of the unasked questions? To appreciate questions needed asking, families would have to seek the Release to Service. Few, even in MoD, are aware such a document exists.

There was no mention of radio calls between aircraft, surprising given they were told they were heading towards each other. Moreover, upon changing radar mode XV704 was required by the Release to Service to execute 'at least' a 30° turn, so a comparison check could be made against heading and track markers, radar returns and individual console clocks; to be cross-checked for validity against the independent aircraft instruments. The Board stated the mode change took place at 04:07:14, and the descent from 1,500 feet commenced no later than 04:11. It also noted Tomahawk Land Attack Missile firings had been declared. This may have forced a re-prioritisation of tasks. Did Air Traffic Control ask XV704 to make a turn in order to identify her on radar?

Had XV704 not turned, the aircraft would have passed safely. But there was no mechanism to ensure they *did* pass safely. If they *had*, luck would have played a part. It is possible unreported near misses occurred frequently, with collision avoided only because one defensive layer remained effective; albeit hanging by a thread.

Active Noise Reduction (ANR) and the incorrect use of Socapex microphones

As neither the Board of Inquiry nor Inquest discussed the subject, on 12 January 2010 Mrs Lawrence sought details of what Build Standard helmet each of the deceased was wearing. Specifically, were they using ANR and what microphone was fitted?

FLEET replied on 20 January 2010, refusing to provide the information. Upon appeal, FLEET complied on 7 April 2010, confirming two crew in each aircraft had Socapex microphones, and one of those had no ANR. FLEET claimed the Socapex microphone was the *'only one used in Sea King Mk2'*. This was untrue.

Active Noise Reduction (ANR)

ANR was the engineering solution to an AEW Mk2 critical Health and Safety Constraint - hearing damage caused by excessive noise dose. (The RN rejected the option of in-ear devices). The prototype was initially trialled in a Sea King HAS Mk6 by Boscombe Down, on an opportunity basis during the 1995 deployment to BUTEC (British Underwater Test and Evaluation Centre) at Kyle of Lochalsh, Scotland; followed by sonar ranging trials at the Fleet Operational Readiness Accuracy Check Site (FORACS) near Stavanger, Norway. As an added benefit, the latter demonstrated a 78% increase in sonar audio detection range. An ANR modification set cost under £800, compared with ~£3M spent every 20 months or so squeezing low single figure gains via software. The Royal Canadian Navy showed most interest.

ANR addressed <u>damaging</u> noise, primarily from the main gearbox. Also, <u>annoying</u> noise, which is wearying and distracting; such as radar transmitter whine in the AEW Mk2 (situated immediately behind the Observers). To improve comfort and performance, especially when the operator wore spectacles, the helmet earshells were modified.

Thus, three programme elements (comms, ANR and helmets) were inextricably linked in design and performance terms. In isolation, each provided tangible benefits. Together, they were characterised by Boscombe Down's Rotary Wing Test Squadron as *'the greatest advance in aircrew safety since the ejection seat'*.

*

It is thought the ANR in use on 22 March 2003 was the AEW Mk2's analog system. Analog ANR is not generic - it is specific to aircraft types and, in some cases, Marks. This is because noise sources differ and certain audio cues must remain audible - so a broadband-type ANR, like those used by troops in an Armoured Personnel Carrier, is unsuitable and usually unsafe.

As Mk7 crews were to be exposed to a higher noise dose (because the Full Mission Trainer replicated noise, so counted as exposure), a programmable Digital ANR system had been developed. Laboratory trials were completed in January 2001, and full production was on schedule to commence in April 2002. Non-availability in March 2003 could only result from a decision to delay or cancel the programme.

The Board did not comment on this; perhaps understandably, given the question of litigation. (Due to this possibility, ANR and the cost/benefit of the programme was raised in Parliament in March 2000).

All on board with access to Intercom had to use ANR, or general audio degradation would occur. This reinforced the Full Fleet Fit policy, and sufficient systems were procured to equip all Boscombe Down crews, the entire 849NAS aircrew complement, plus spares for use by passengers (mainly squadron engineers). The modification set was fully reusable.

During testing and trials there were no ANR failures, indicating system reliability was good; although it was recognised 849NAS was a small statistical sample. If a failure did occur, the effect of the sudden increase in noise the wearer would experience was managed by including such a scenario in the Simulator and Full Mission Trainer specifications. It is unclear if these directives were implemented, or if crews received appropriate training prior to deployment. This would demand use of a correctly modified helmet, but the pilot of (outbound) XV650 did not have ANR fitted. Did he have a failure while deployed, in which case why was a spare ANR not embodied? Was his helmet a poor fit? This was immediately apparent because a gap in the passive attenuation (earshell padding) caused feedback (squealing) - hence the earshell re-design.

Crew discomfort can become a serious issue during long sorties requiring total concentration. During trials, several ill-fitting helmets were identified, a conscious decision by aircrew to improve comfort at the expense of their hearing. Forcing this decision is an abrogation of duty of care, which the ANR programme sought to overcome. Provision was made for any 849NAS aircrew who wanted, or needed, a made-to-measure helmet (something that should be routine) to visit the manufacturer and be fitted.

Racal and Socapex microphones

Socapex microphones were prohibited in the RN on safety grounds, a pilot having sustained a severe facial injury during a heavy landing. However, a concession was granted for 849NAS aircrew to use whichever they preferred. The primary difference is one of sensitivity - Racal is higher than Socapex, so provides a higher output for a given input. But no complementary action was taken to modify the Intercom; compounded by the AEW Mk2 Intercom being at a pre-1985, obsolescent, hybrid HAS Mk2/5 standard; further compromised by poorly designed Naval Service Modifications. The result was slightly reduced background noise, but poor audio quality.

One of the non-negotiable requirements of the new Enhanced Comms System was to remove the (perceived) need for this concession; the Directorate of Operational Requirements (Sea) and Flag Officer Naval Aviation <u>mandating</u> the Racal microphone. The specifications, prepared by H/SK2 in November 1994, reflected this. In 1995 ANR followed suit. Whichever entered service first, the new comms or ANR, would determine the stop date for using Socapex. In 1997, after deliveries had commenced, the RN asked that introduction of comms be delayed; now to be carried out during the Mk2 to Mk7 conversion - a consequence of having insufficient aircraft to bear overlapping modification programmes.

On 1 May 1998, the Directorate of Naval Air Staff issued a directive that the concession allowing Mk2 crews to use Socapex was cancelled upon introducing ANR.[49] This was achieved in March 1999.

<u>Thus, at the time of the accident, Socapex microphones had been actively banned in 849NAS for four years</u>. (Remember, FLEET claimed to Mrs Lawrence it was the only one used).

Yet, in 2002 the Mk7 Release to Service wrongly permitted their use:

'Using Socapex microphones, a satisfactory telephone level may only be maintained at maximum volume settings. Under emergency conditions, the telephone outputs may be unacceptably low'.

The setting referred to is in the operator's Station Box (Secure), which provides a switched volume control for each audio source (except warning tones, which must be unswitched). When using Socapex, turning this up would be accompanied by increased noise and distortion (signal level does not equate to quality). The practical effect was degraded speech intelligibility and, ultimately, situational awareness. This is particularly detrimental in an AEW/ASaC aircraft, so the comms programme set out to enhance this aspect, with new high-quality audio amplifiers, ANR, and use of Racal microphones the major contributors.

At the Inquest, the RN Flight Safety and Accident Investigation Centre, in an attempt to clarify why information was missing from the Airborne

---

49 Letter D/DNAS/901/001/001/C, 1 May 1998.

Video Recording System (AVRS) tape, stated one had to speak to activate a microphone. The phenomenon referred to is 'first syllable clipping' and, as it implies, refers to the loss of the first syllable only, not entire phrases. This was an undesirable feature of older designs (Merlin, Lynx, Sea King Mk6), so the noise tracking Voice Operated Switching (VOS) had been improved for Sea Kings Mk7 and Mk4. (Whereby only noise/speech above a certain threshold reaches the crew - the effect being to lower background noise and improve speech intelligibility). This threshold, and associated pre-set amplifier gain structure, was based on Racal microphones.

In XV704, whose Airborne Video Recording System recording is under discussion, the pilot and the senior Observer/aircraft captain, both sitting in the cockpit, had the wrong microphone. This might explain missing information, because the low sensitivity of their Socapex microphones may have delayed the VOS gates opening, or caused them to work intermittently.

However, the main concern must be this. Helmet modification HM080 covers the introduction of ANR and mandatory use of the Racal microphone. Why was it partially embodied in three helmets, and not at all in another? Why was HM080 not listed as an essential modification in the Release to Service? It is not even mentioned, meaning there is no warning of the effect of having the wrong helmet or microphone.

This issue encapsulates all the systemic failures noted herein. Safety directives were overruled. No-one spoke up and asked why this was withheld from both Board of Inquiry and Coroner. That silence is a fatal organisational and cultural failing.

*

All the above was posed to MoD by Mrs Lawrence on 2 June 2010. In his reply of 14 July 2010, FLEET's Deputy Command Secretary, Mr Simon Routh, acknowledged the serious nature of the issues.[50] It was therefore incumbent upon him to escalate, so they might be investigated and corrected. He did not.

On 20 October 2017, Sir Roger Gale MP wrote to the Minister for the Armed Forces asking if MoD's reports had been reviewed and amended. On 16 November 2017, Tobias Ellwood MP, Parliamentary Under-Secretary of State, replied stating MoD's position remained the same. Its state of denial is total, rejecting the existence of documented and

---

50 Letter FLEET DCS/NCE/2790/2003/8, 14 July 2010.

pictorial evidence. The issue has been swept under the carpet. FLEET may get lucky (if one can call seven dead lucky), but what aircraft do those who ignored the regulations go on to manage...?

Why did the UHF radios have no Time of Day input?

The Release to Service notes, in Section L:

'HaveQuick Time of Day: The present version of GPS used is not compatible with the ARC164 radios and will not provide satisfactory Time of Day input to them. Time of Day must be obtained from an alternative source'.

A second ARC164 radio was fitted in Mk7. The radio employs a pseudo-random frequency hopping algorithm, and the Mk7 was the first to encrypt a hopper and have secure Homing. Initialisation requires synchronisation in the time domain. This can be done on the ground using special test equipment, or over the ether from another aircraft. GPS brought an easier method - Time of Day, which is also required by the aircraft's encryption devices (e.g. Intercom, JTIDS, IFF) and the Airborne Video Recording System. Because the time references provided by these sources can differ, HaveQuick planners must establish time-distribution procedures that ensure the necessary synchronisation. Thus, Time of Day integration received particular attention. There are two entwined issues.

1. GPS incompatibility

The generic GPS specification only required it to handle two Time of Day loads; a quirk uncovered when it was decided to combine the hitherto separate GPS and Inertial Navigation System upgrades into a single Ring Laser Gyro/GPS unit. The United States determines this specification, and would not change it. In practice, many devices could only support one load, so Racal were contracted to design and build a Buffer Unit to provide sufficient Time of Day interfaces, to facilitate integration with other systems. As part of this process, in November 1996 they were directed to include an additional interface to accommodate a proposed third ARC164 radio (ultimately not endorsed).

This integration was to be effected without degrading the installed performance achieved under the comms programme; successfully demonstrated on the integration rigs in October 1998, and during flight trials in January 2000. At this time, the Ring Laser Gyro/GPS destined for the production Mk7 was not yet available, so a unit conforming to

141

the same GPS specification was provided by the GPS project office (who oversaw policy and general development, but did not procure the Mk7 system).

Having established this baseline, when the new RLG/GPS was first fitted in January 2001 the comms system was successfully re-tested. Whatever changed occurred later.

The Board did not go this far, or discuss the link between this and XV650's JTIDS software loading failure.

2. Configuration control of ARC164 radios

During preliminary risk reduction in 1994-6, GEC-Marconi Secure Systems expressed concern over out-of-date ARC164 publications and general lack of information from subsidiary Design Authorities. This confirmed a certainty - Post Design Services was not being funded or conducted properly, validating the reason for the risk reduction work.

The practical effects became apparent during rig testing. It was discovered that ARC164s with modification B1107 embodied in R1977A Main Receivers no longer worked when using the receiver's wideband facility in Di-Phase and Homing modes. This meant only 50% of the crypto variables were available. After some hours comparing drawings with actual radios, H/SK2a spotted a diode, costing 10p, had been removed by the US Design Authority. Drawings and documentation provided to the UK Design Custodian, Muirhead Avionics, reflected the wrong Build Standard.

Muirhead were quoted £1M to revert to the correct design. H/SK2 refused to succumb to what was, effectively, extortion. On 20 October 1998 SM46a(RAF) were requested to resolve what was their responsibility, as interchangeability was no longer assured. It is unclear if they did.

There is more to this. The RN's ARC164 repair rigs used a different variant radio (RT1505), so would have to be reconfigured to cater for Mk7's RT1504 – one of the tasks the Aircraft Support Executive had refused to carry out, and now fell to the Integrated Logistics Support Manager. If not completed, a radio at the wrong standard could easily find its way into a Mk7, and appear dead when the Intercom was in Di-Phase mode. If Boards of Inquiry listed the modification state of avionic kit, such issues would be readily identified.

Discussion

On 18 December 2000, H/SK2 had warned Mr Eason that:

> 'Performance of the Buffer Unit should be demonstrated first on the Mission System Rig against a specification and test schedule agreed between BAe, Thales, and Westland. The test schedule is that which already exists under Enhanced Comms, but which Thales must subsume within their own documentation'.[51]

(This and other warnings - and make no mistake, they were dire warnings - were based on concerns that systems integration and functional safety was being actively waived by Mr Eason).

Therefore, the statement in the Release to Service about Time of Day is inadequate and too simplistic. It worked to specification in January 2001, but later did not. This is why responsibility for installed performance is a vital aspect of contract negotiations. But one must be pragmatic. If the degradation described became unavoidable Racal would not be penalised, but it would still have to be dealt with.

At best, lack of Time of Day to the radios was a distraction. At worst, it might explain the failure to initiate systems that relied on it. Only one transmission from XV650 was admitted by MoD, the details of which were withheld; between her and Air Traffic Control, and which would not need an ARC164. The question is also important given the requirement to have two radios monitoring 243MHz, the International Distress Frequency.

In the context of XV650's initialisation failure, the start sequence included a check that GPS was present, viable and correct. It is *possible* excessive loads 'dragged down' the signal after this check. This *could* present itself as an intermittent fault. The effect would be variable across the fleet, because the degree of degradation would depend on other factors, such as antenna installation, quality of power supplies, etc. A faulty GPS, or defective, faulty or even missing Buffer Unit/distribution system is possible. In fact, nowhere is there a suggestion Time of Day was available *at all* in XV650.

Asked by Mrs Lawrence about this non-compliance, on 7 April 2010 FLEET simply stated what Time of Day was and why it was needed; not answering the question. The clue it knew of the failings. Who knows how many more remain hidden?

*

---

51 Loose Minute ES(Air)71/10/2/2, 18 December 2000.

143

There is much to consider here. Understanding system dependencies is important. The Release to Service stated the problem was in the GPS; but was it caused by the GPS module itself, or failure to correctly condition and distribute its Time of Day output? Either way, the correct directives were issued and there must be an associated Production Permit or Concession authorised by the technical programme manager.[52] Even then, these operate for a limited quantity or period. Certainly, H/SK2 did not grant one before leaving in June 2001. The limitation remained in the Release to Service in November 2009.

It would seem there was no technical oversight after engineering staff were stood down on 29 March 2001, Mr Eason advising them that henceforth *he* would manage all aspects of the comms system design and its integration. The consequential risks were obvious, and by MoD's own admission materialised and were not resolved.

Communications, handover and abort

Communications and handover are major contributors to situational awareness. In its reports, and at the Inquest, MoD made much of what was allegedly said. It did not mention what was (apparently) not said; for example, discussion about handover, deconfliction, and possible abort of XV650's mission. Nor did it reveal who heard what. Readers (MoD reports) and listeners (Inquest recordings) were given the false impression everything was normal, and everyone concerned heard everything on XV704's Airborne Video Recording System tape.

XV650 was held on Ark Royal's deck for 22 minutes while a Joint Tactical Information Distribution System (JTIDS) software loading problem was diagnosed. At the time of Board of Inquiry report release, and during the Inquest, this was characterised as a *'comms'* failure. Equally likely was a procedural error ('finger trouble'), but the knock-on effect would be the same - a significant delay in initialising and checking other systems. XV650's radar was recovered in STANDBY mode. JTIDS was in TOTAL mode, commensurate with on-deck software loading, and preventing transmission; not the expected NORMAL active airborne mode. This suggests the initialisation problem had not been resolved. Even if it was *thought* to have been resolved on deck, system interlocks prevented maintainers or crew confirming full functionality.

---

52 Defence Standard 05-61 (Part 1) 2.4.

At the inquest, the Coroner said:

'We know XV650 was delayed. I'm not concerned about what it was about because it wasn't anything to do with the condition of the helicopter. We've been told that'.

Wrongly, he equated the ability to take off and fly with serviceability and fitness for purpose. That is, and like MoD, he only looked at one small part of what contributes to safe flight. But when was he told this? Not in court, and both MoD and Coroner's Office claim no pre-Inquest discussions or meetings took place. On several occasions the Coroner contradicted this during the Inquest, referring to prior agreements with MoD. This misdirection masked MoD's omission of crucial evidence.

What actions were being taken to re-schedule the handover? 30 minutes had been allotted, but it had not commenced when the aircraft collided. Extensive discussions should have taken place onboard Ark Royal, between she and both aircraft, and between aircraft, on how XV650's delay would be managed. It would be understandable if any discussion was redacted from reports; but there is no such redaction, indicating the entire subject was either ignored, or deleted during review.

*

It is almost as if XV650 was on a training and familiarisation sortie, where such a problem might be ignored because other useful training remained possible. This would be consistent with the Mk7 still being in its training and familiarisation phase.

15: The Release to Service

The Release to Service is the Master Airworthiness Reference and the definitive document governing Service regulated flying. It must be reconcilable with the rest of the Aircraft Document Set. A natural administrative lag is permitted; but of weeks, not months or years. Here, over a decade after the accident, anomalies remain.

Note: 'Issue' is associated with a date, 'INTERIM' describes a type of release.

Status of the 'Mission System'

In October 2009 Mrs Lawrence sought the Release, including Service Deviations relating to High Intensity Strobe Lights (HISL) in other Sea Kings. MoD (as ever) refused, claiming the work would exceed 3.5 days. On 27 November 2009 she submitted an appeal:

'You state my original request would involve 3.5 working days. I understand the items form a single document which, at a working level (the Release to Service Authority), would be immediately available and readily copied'.

MoD replied on 21 December 2009, enclosing a partial copy of the Release at Issue 1, Amendment List 1. Also, Service Deviation 014/7 (HISL in Mk7, issued <u>after</u> the accident). It refused to release the older Service Deviations, and claimed a Defence Exemption for parts of the Release. Yet, it provided the most damning information...

The radar, JTIDS and the Mission System software (the Mission System Upgrade in its entirety), plus Orange Crop Electronic Support Measures and the Inertial Navigation System/GPS, had an INTERIM clearance.[53] That is, they were <u>not to be relied upon in any way whatsoever</u>. System dependencies meant this also applied to the comms system and IFF. Also:

'Inertial Navigation System/GPS derived navigation data is not to be relied upon and must be cross-checked against radar, stand-alone aircraft instruments, map and operator derived Dead Reckoning plot'.

In practice, the clearance restricted use to training and familiarisation, although it is clear limited operations were intended. In particular, the navigation system limitation complicated matters when aircraft were

---

53 Sea King ASaC Mk7 Release to Service, Section N (Mission Equipment) and Section O (Navigation Equipment).

placed in the same airspace, in darkness.

There is a redaction in the Environmental section. However, MoD forgot to redact other papers, which revealed a temperature limitation of −26° to +45°C for the Mission System. This remained extant in November 2009. Why redact this? The only reason can be concern that the limits were being breached and, possibly, this may be connected with equipment failures. Notably, the specification for other avionics was typically −40° to +55°C.[54]

Service Deviation 002/7, Issue 1, August 2002 - High Intensity Strobe Lights (HISL)

FLEET approves and issues the Release to Service and Category 1 Service Deviations. The latter are:

'Service Deviations giving clearances for Service regulated flying not within the envelope and other provisions of the Military Aircraft Release for the aircraft or equipment concerned'.

They are a short-term measure, subject to regular review. Engineering Service Deviations must be prepared by technical staff in the aircraft project office, although are still seen to be issued by FLEET. The project office was denied access to HISL design data, so by definition this mandate could not be met, and was not. Together with there being no endorsed requirement for HISL, this meant the Service Deviation was rogue.

SD002/7 states:

'The subject Naval Service Modification replaces the existing upper and lower anti-collision lamps with a two colour (red and white) HISL system'.

Thus, MoD acknowledges the baseline Mk7 Build Standard had rotating beacons; yet denied this to Mrs Lawrence when rejecting the photographic evidence. (Figure 5).

At the time of the accident HISL had not undergone the necessary trials and, therefore, would not have been considered in the Safety Case. Yet, by issuing the Release to Service, the Assistant Chief of Staff (Aviation) was stating there *was* an acceptable Safety Case; as laid down in JSP318B, Part 4.12 (Regulation of Ministry of Defence Aircraft).

Compounding the matter, it emerged in ministerial correspondence that the Naval Service Modification was read across from the

---

54 For example, Radio Installation Memorandum 144A, Appendix G.

Commando Role Mk6 (a stripped-out HAS Mk6); whose form, fit, function and use was entirely different to either a Mk2 or Mk7. This explains MoD's refusal to provide the Mk2/6 Service Deviations to Mrs Lawrence.

Summary

The Release to Service is dangerously flawed by it being a 'lazy' copy of the AEW Mk2 Release. It is usually wise for someone familiar with the programme to compile it, but this was not possible after 29 March 2001. The errors coincide with the main contributory factors and most likely cause of the accident.

16: Parliamentary Questions (2004-08)

Andrew George MP, Paul Tyler MP (now Lord Tyler) and Sir Roger Gale MP asked a series of questions after the Board of Inquiry report was released in 2004. The replies to Mr George were not made public at the time, only obtained from the House of Commons library in 2012 by Steve Webb MP. The Sea King base at RNAS Culdrose is in Mr George's St Ives constituency, and one can only surmise his remarkably well-informed questions emanated from there. Lord Tyler's interest stemmed from his involvement in the treatment of Gulf War veterans. Sir Roger continues to represent Mrs Ann Lawrence.

When briefing Ministers the Civil Service Code requires staff to:

- Conduct themselves with integrity, honesty, impartiality and objectivity.
- Endeavour to deal with the affairs of the public sympathetically, efficiently, promptly, and without bias or maladministration.
- Conduct themselves in such a way as to deserve and retain the confidence of Ministers, and be able to establish the same relationship with those whom they may have to serve in a future Administration.

The Code is closely linked to Covenant obligations. Breaching it is, in theory, an extremely serious matter. However, only serving civil servants may lodge a complaint.[55] An unlikely event, given the resources MoD commits to pursuing those who question wrongdoing.

As the questions all relate to the same issues and are discussed elsewhere, primarily 'see and be seen' and 'see and avoid', to avoid repetition here is a short selection of replies provided by Adam Ingram MP, Minister for the Armed Forces, and his successor Bob Ainsworth MP.

- 'Safety is provided by a variety of aids and by individual action. These include: operating procedures such as, air traffic control, awareness of hazards through radar detection, communications, lighting and lookout'. All these aids and actions were compromised or unavailable.
- *'The Board of Inquiry judged A Flight to be ready in all respects for the commencement of operations'*. This cannot be reconciled with the Board's confirmation that a crucial defence against collision was

---

55 Civil Service Commission letter AP000060, 1 May 2012.

unairworthy, or with the INTERIM clearance status of mission critical systems.

- 'Crews may request a Radar Advisory Service (RAS)'. Wrong.
- 'No formal report had been made by either of the crews about the flying conditions, restricted vision, restricted flight path or about any malfunction of equipment'. The crews died. How were they to make a report?

17: The Coroner's Inquest

The Inquest was convened in April 2003, immediately adjourned, and reconvened at Oxford Coroner's Court on 3 January 2007. The delay was caused by the belated publication of the RN Flight Safety and Accident Investigation Centre (RNFSAIC) report. The Coroner was Sir Richard Curtis, a retired judge.

The conduct of Inquests falls squarely within the scope of the Covenant. The positive duty to protect life and prevent recurrence means the Coroner must explore the broader circumstances of the death, including events leading up to it. This includes the effect of misconduct or neglect by those holding a duty of care. What questions are asked, and evidence presented, is vexed. Leeway is permitted, as the proceedings should set out as many facts as the public interest requires. Given MoD itself raised airworthiness failings, and the formal definition of airworthiness includes the safety of the public over whom the aircraft flies, by any reasonable interpretation the Coroner was required to consider airworthiness aspects. (His 'public assurance' obligation). Thus, there is more to the Inquest than *the crews died because the aircraft collided*, and the Coroner must determine the scope beforehand.

Families are at a distinct disadvantage unless they can afford to engage specialist advice. It is government policy <u>not</u> to provide assistance; which might be interpreted as a breach of the Covenant. This contrasts sharply with, for example, Australia, where legal representation is provided by the State. Matters are exacerbated if the other 'side' (MoD) is hostile. Doubly so if the Coroner sides with MoD.

As Inquests are conducted within the local authority area where the deceased are repatriated to, most in recent years have been in Oxfordshire (RAF Brize Norton) and, until closure of RAF Lyneham in 2012, Wiltshire. Costs are borne by the local authority, not central government. The increasing number of Inquests forced cuts elsewhere in the Oxfordshire budget; for example, there was no court stenographer. The Coroner was required to take his own, at times verbatim, notes; made more difficult by his unfamiliarity with military terminology, and being actively misled by MoD. This resulted in fragmented proceedings.

*

The Lawrence family expressed concern to Roger Gale MP (who was knighted in 2012) over MoD's conduct at, and the conduct of, the

Inquest. Questions were put to Ministers. Upon receipt of replies (but few answers), Mr Gale pressed. Obvious inconsistencies meant it became imperative a record be obtained. Mrs Lawrence had been told none existed. On 11 October 2011 she sought transcripts of proceedings - a courtesy extended previously to other families of deceased servicemen. The Coroner's Office replied five weeks later, advising *'this would be at your own expense'*, quoting £3,700.

Mrs Lawrence:

> *'I am being treated unfairly. I intend to take this forward because they clearly hope I will decline'.*

She lobbied Mr Gale:

> *'We feel a potential cost of several thousand pounds plus VAT is wholly disproportionate, unaffordable to many people and as such highly discriminatory. The cost is also, it seems to us, in stark contrast to the aims of the Military Covenant. We would ask that you raise a Parliamentary Question on our behalf. We do however feel a more public approach is to be preferred in view of the potential implications for other families in similar positions to our own. You will no doubt sense not only our frustration, but also our anger at being asked to subsidise the Coroner's Office when all we seek is, in our view, natural justice for one of the many servicemen who have made the ultimate sacrifice for their country'.*

On 28 November 2011 the Coroner's Office agreed to provide the recordings free of charge, but the necessary (bespoke) playback software would be in the order of £600. The upshot being a CD-ROM was provided, but not the software, Coroner's notes, or records of preliminary hearings (which must also be recorded). The audio recordings were in a non-standard, 4-channel format, encoded with a proprietary Audio Compression Manager. In layman's terms, a CD player could not play the files. The Coroner's Officer, sympathetic to Mrs Lawrence's plight, advised of a compatible software player, although it could only decode to two channels. An audio engineer was engaged to enhance the recordings, providing his services free of charge. The resultant files have the Coroner and witnesses in one channel, with the Coroner dominant; and the legal benches and families in the other channel, with the QC representing Mr Green slightly dominant, the families less so, and the MoD barrister low, distant and indistinct.

General observations

Within seconds, Mr Richard Benson QC, representing the family of

XV650's pilot Lt Philip Green, informed the Coroner that MoD has not yet provided any witness statements. It was similarly obstructive before and during the Chinook ZD576 Fatal Accident Inquiry in 1996, denying even the Sheriff, Sir Stephen Young, relevant documents. And again, during the subsequent Mull of Kintyre Review in 2010/11. Each occurrence is excused as an isolated administrative oversight, but this contempt, and breach of the Covenant, is routine. Why did Mr Benson not ask for an adjournment so he could prepare? The answer lies in cost to the families. MoD knows this, and takes advantage by drawing out the process.

The Coroner instructed MoD to provide specific evidence. It did not. Frequently, he referred to prior meetings and agreements. Yet, both Coroner's Office and MoD now deny a Pre-Inquest Hearing, meetings or discussions took place. Coroners are obliged to invite families to formal hearings, but none received any invitation. It can only be assumed he, or his Officers, met or corresponded with MoD privately to agree who would appear, and what evidence would be given.

The evidence of some witnesses was factually challenged. Each mistake or omission seemed designed to divert attention from the contributory factors. The Coroner antagonised the families; especially Mr Green, telling him to keep quiet when seeking to ask valid questions. Also, he instructed MoD witnesses not to reply to key questions, permitting them to obfuscate and mislead.

No attempt was made to reconcile contradictory evidence. Some errors can be excused due to the 'fog of war' and receding memory. However, each witness would have been encouraged to re-read, at least, the Board of Inquiry report. Plainly, some were briefed on what line to take, to the point of dissembling - the most obvious example being denial of Super FIS. Once, when a witness tried to reply, he was interrupted by MoD Counsel and told not to. There was no challenge, no question from the Coroner.

The witnesses were rehearsed - some candid, others stuck steadfastly to the party line. When uncomfortable, voices lowered to the point of unintelligibility. Whenever a question inconvenient to MoD was asked, a fit of coughing erupted from its benches - clearly a pre-arranged signal.

There was a failure to focus on the important points. Blatant deceptions were allowed to pass. Lacking information, Mr Benson was often unable to step in and challenge. In fact, he did extremely well in the circumstances.

The plight of Lt Cdr Alastair Dale RN, HMS Ark Royal Air Traffic Control officer, engendered sympathy. Events beyond his control hindered him. He came on watch at precisely the time XV650 was due to depart. The aircraft was being prepared for some time beforehand, trying to clear initialisation failures; yet no witnesses were called to discuss these critical events or the decision to launch. Nor was he informed that someone else had been blamed by MoD for what it deemed the main contributory factor. And, as all MoD witnesses discover sooner or later, the Crown legal team was there to represent MoD, not its employees or servicemen.

*

The proceedings quickly became hostile, often obstructed by witnesses not answering the question. For example, under questioning by the Coroner:

'Tell me the drill if the radar is not working'.

'XV650 had flown earlier that evening and I was captain'.

The Coroner let this go. Thus, the vital question of when the decision to abort is made, and by whom, was not addressed.

Replies were frequently vague or the witness professed not to remember. This time, under questioning by Mr Benson:

'Have you been issued with Night Vision Goggles since or were you issued (at the time)?'

'I have since changed squadrons and type of Sea King'.

And so the prior use of NVG within the AEW fleet was avoided.

On Day 1, contradictory evidence was presented about where HMS Liverpool's Lynx was at the time of the collision. The witness was instructed by the Coroner not to answer Mr Green. This line of questioning continued on Day 2, when the Coroner again rejected any attempt to reconcile the evidence. An exasperated Mr Green exclaimed **'What a fix!'** He was instructed to sit down and not *'make speeches'*. No-one else was inclined to see that the aims of the Inquest were satisfied.

Compounding matters, the Coroner asked about the impact of HMS Liverpool's Lynx on the <u>inbound</u> Sea King, assisting MoD's strategy of studiously avoiding the impact on <u>outbound</u>. In effect, he acted for MoD against the families. And, strangely, the whereabouts of the Lynx pilot's logbook was unknown. Is the RN content a logbook cannot be found?

Both Coroner and QC questioned one witness at length about events on Ark Royal. He presented as knowledgeable and competent. (He is). Then, a family member asked where he was during the events he described so well. *'Actually, I was in bed'.* Would it not have been better to call someone who was awake and at his post? And who provided the information that prompted the question? And why?

*

The Coroner referred to the Airborne Video Recording System (AVRS) as a *'Cockpit Voice Recorder'*. Such a basic mistake is alarming, and he was forcefully corrected by a witness, one of the investigators.

His assertion that the AVRS timings are wrong by a *'minute or two'* called into question how much heed he paid to this main source of evidence. He appeared to decide the AVRS tape, and hence the Board of Inquiry and RNFSAIC reports, had less value than verbal evidence; much of which was hearsay. No-one challenged him.

Elsewhere, many anomalies were noted that could be explained by Time of Day being absent, making this statement even more significant. Was he repeating something discussed at the meetings he said took place, but MoD says did not? The Board of Inquiry into Tornado ZG710 (shot down the following day) encountered the same problem, saying timings were out by over a minute. Does no-one in MoD look at these reports and say *wait a minute...*? Perhaps they do, but don't want to admit how such an irregularity can occur.

The one person with a detailed grasp of the issues was Mr Green, but the Coroner did not allow them to be developed because he made statements (of truth) rather than asking questions. However, the event best illustrating MoD's anxiety occurred when its Counsel interrupted and complained to the Coroner that Mr Green *'is represented'*, so shouldn't be allowed to ask (awkward) questions. To be blunt, so what? Under Coroner's Rules, he was permitted to ask questions, because the Coroner invited him to. The Coroner chastised Mr Green. For pity's sake, the man lost his son. But MoD Counsel was merciless in his disdain for both the deceased and their families. (And who was sitting behind Counsel prodding him to object?)

Quite the worst aspect was that the Coroner was oblivious to the fact this was the first opportunity for families to speak to MoD witnesses. Even if initially unfamiliar with military proceedings, this is unforgivable; compounded by there being no opportunity for the families to explain this. One could argue this is grounds for reconvening the Inquest. Who spoke for the dead? Mr Green tried, but he must have felt very lonely.

Aircraft status / serviceability

MoD commonly equates airworthiness with serviceability. (The former facilitates the latter). Before the Inquest commenced, families were told both aircraft were airworthy, serviceable and fit for purpose. The Coroner accepted this, which he confirmed in court.

In reply to a request to discuss <u>avionic faults</u>, the Coroner stated:

> *'As I've said all along, no-one is suggesting a <u>mechanical defect</u> caused the accident'.*

In fact, he said such matters are *'irrelevant'*, which any competent accident investigator might argue with. And *defect* is meaningless when the subject is *faults* - one assumes he understood the difference. And, he forgot he had <u>not</u> mentioned this at the Inquest. It had clearly been decided beforehand that such matters would <u>not</u> be discussed. Mr Benson demurred, asking if evidence relating to navigation system unserviceabilities in XV704 (inbound) might be discussed. The Coroner replied *'later'*, but at no point was the issue raised again. (*'Later'* seems to be Coroner code for *sit down and shut up*).

*

In its report, MoD had made a firm statement - outbound XV650's mission system was <u>not</u> functioning. This rendered XV704 invisible (electronically) to XV650, and unable to receive data from XV650. When the father of Mrs Sarah King (widow of Lt Tony King, XV650 captain) tried to raise this, he was met with obfuscation and received no answer.

A statement by Ark Royal's Air Engineering Officer was read. He was happy with the training of his engineers and they were capable on the mission system; which he then contradicted by saying he had to rely on Observers to solve problems. No criticism should be inferred here, given the aircraft was still in its training and familiarisation phase. But, he went unchallenged.

Outrageously, the Coroner stated there were no previous technical arisings pertinent to the accident, and no history of recurring unserviceability, despite both being admitted by the Board of Inquiry. He could only be repeating a line fed to him by MoD. In fact, there was no indication he understood or had even read the Board's report at all, despite claiming otherwise on the final day - *'I think we know enough about that'*. (No we don't, you haven't allowed it to be discussed). And so all technical discussion was shut down.

Evidence of Rear Admiral Alan Massey RN, Commanding Officer HMS Ark Royal

Admiral Massey appeared on the afternoon of Day 2. It was clear from the Coroner's comments that his evidence had been agreed beforehand. Much of it was a monologue which the Coroner, deep in conversation with an unidentified person, was not listening to. With the Coroner dominant on the recording, the Admiral was often drowned out.

A feature of his evidence was that he suggested <u>both</u> mission systems were fully serviceable and not limited in any way; also omitting that Ark Royal's Identification Friend or Foe was unserviceable. He used this to imply pilot error.

When discussing Visual Flight Rules, he stated the eyes of two pilots are better than depending on the quality of technology (radar, IFF, comms, etc.). This ignored that Mk7 is flown single-pilot, and for the most part he is alone in the cockpit. Also, that the electronic systems he was so dismissive of serve to provide layered defences against the risk of collision. This diverted attention from the fact these systems were not available to XV650. His evidence directly contradicted the Board of Inquiry and his own FLEET HQ, who had confirmed that lack of electronic cues placed the aircraft at serious risk. At no point was this internal MoD argument discussed, or even pointed out. Like the Coroner, he seemed completely ignorant of the content of the Board's report and the Release to Service. And the way in which the aircraft on his ship operated.

*

Mr Benson asked whether scenarios such as flying towards each other were practiced. (A better question might have been: *Were the deconfliction procedures tested adequately to <u>prevent</u> flying against each other?*). Admiral Massey conceded this may not have occurred; but doing so in close proximity was - by 849NAS <u>B Flight</u> during Exercise Destined Glory in *'October/November 2002'*.

This implied the exercise lasted up to two months. The media reported at the time: *'Destined Glory runs from October 5-15...'*. Eleven days, which may or may not have included sailing time to and from the Mediterranean. Confusingly, the Board of Inquiry stated this autumn 2002 deployment was 'Exercise Strong Resolve'. NATO records show *that* exercise ran from 1-15 March 2002.

More importantly, it was <u>A Flight</u> deployed on Ark Royal. Lt Lawrence (Observer in XV704) first flew in a Mk7 on 21 November 2002. His previous flight, on 10 October 2002, was in a Mk2; perhaps indicating he underwent conversion training during this 6-week hiatus. His logbook shows that on 7 October, during Destined Glory, he undertook a transit from Leeuwarden in the Netherlands to RNAS Culdrose. His father made this point to the court, but was ignored.

The relevant section of the Board's report is heavily redacted; probably because it is crucial to understanding (im)maturity of training and knowledge. What remains confirms A Flight did not undertake Operational Sea Training. That is, a risk control measure was omitted.

*

On the matter of HMS Liverpool's Lynx, Admiral Massey overlooked that it encroached into his Carrier Control Zone. He declined to comment on the potential for misidentification because he had not *'seen the geometry'* or *'heard the tone'* of voices on the tape. But <u>what</u> tape? There is no mention of Lynx in the AVRS transcript provided to families. Had he just let slip MoD possessed other unreleased recordings?

He claimed the aircraft had *'big flashing HISLs'*, ignoring that their forward strobes were off and rears obscured. Mr Benson challenged this, and the Admiral admitted his evidence was gleaned from US witnesses (who were viewing the aircraft from the side and had direct line of sight to both strobes). Strange that he read the US witness statements, but didn't bother watching or listening to UK recordings.

*

At this point, the Coroner finished his chat and returned to rustling papers, masking much of the Admiral's remaining testimony. But the reason he was there had been made clear. MoD was nervous about the Lynx, High Intensity Strobe Lights, the availability of mission critical systems, and the risks associated with single-pilot operation. The court had been misled on every point.

The concept of single-pilot maritime operation at night under Visual Flight Rules, with no Night Vision systems

Admiral Massey's mention of two-pilot operation is deserving of further comment and analysis. To recap, MoD confirmed this was a night-time flight under Visual Flight Rules (VFR).

Operating Environment

A moonless night at sea can be very dark. With virtually no ambient light it is almost impossible to see the surface or, indeed, any unilluminated object from any height. Consequently, even when the meteorological visibility is good, the handling pilot needs to fly the aircraft exclusively on instruments. So much so, in the Anti-Submarine Warfare (ASW) Sea King variants (Mks 1, 2, 5 & 6), over-water night flying at 200' and below was logged as instrument flying regardless of the visibility, because it was considered dangerous for the handling pilot to look away from the instruments. This provides much needed context, and an indication of what the pilots would be focussing on.

Under such circumstances, pilot disorientation, distraction or inattention can lead to a sudden and catastrophic accident. Consequently, safe flight at low-level (i.e. 500' and below) under night-time VFR is not truly possible without a properly-trained second cockpit occupant. Increasing the challenge during military operations, Emission Control (EMCON) might preclude the use of external lighting, radios and radars. For operational reasons, the aircraft's landing lamps and hover-flood lights are almost never used except in the Search and Rescue role. This hazardous environment has claimed many UK military helicopters and their crews.

Extended operations mean long and monotonous hours in the air. During a North or South Atlantic winter, much flying would be at night and/or in poor weather. This, combined with disrupted sleep patterns, could result in crews flying in an under-aroused state. In such circumstances, it is all too easy to pay insufficient attention to flying the aircraft or even to fall asleep at the controls. Returning to a darkened ship in radio and radar silence, perhaps with low-fuel captions flashing, demands a level of care and attention that a single pilot might be ill-placed to deliver. This applies equally to all aircraft.

Given the Sea King's operating environment, extended endurance, lack of systems redundancy, and the physical strength required to fly it with a failed auxiliary hydraulic system, the presence of two pilots is a significant operational and safety requirement.

Operational flexibility

In addition to its Primary Role, the Sea King has numerous Secondary and even Tertiary Roles. Amongst these were Search and Rescue, load-lifting and passenger transfer. The Sea King has a wide cockpit and, sometimes, the visual references required to provide an accurate hover during winching or load-lifting are only visible from the left-hand side of the aircraft.

With only one pilot, in the right-hand seat, a compromise must be made regarding relative wind and/or degraded hover accuracy, which risks impacting upon the safety and effectiveness of the operation. At night the references are further degraded, accentuating the problem. While the Sea King is fitted with an automatic hover facility, its sensors (Radar Altimeter and Doppler) tended to lock on to obstructions such as vessel superstructure or terrain, which renders the system unusable over anything other than open sea. (Not a criticism - it is how such systems work, and aircrew must be aware of their limitations).

Flying the ASW Sea King at night

Under normal circumstances, the Sea King is an easy aircraft to fly; its 'classic' instrument panel is well designed and its auto-stabiliser, though simplex, works reliably. However, routine operation at very low heights carry an ever-present risk. Adding to this problem is the lack of a low height audio/voice warning; indeed, the only attention getter is a small yellow 'LOW' light on the Radar Altimeter Indicators, and all too easy to miss. (Dim attention getters is a common observation by Boscombe Down, including Chinook HC Mk2 in 1993).

The Low Level warning bug can be set to illuminate at a specified height. On ASW, the pilot's will usually be at 35', because the aircraft normally hovers at 40'. The setting remains unchanged throughout the sortie. In higher sea states, the warning light flashes as waves pass beneath the aircraft, and some pilots obscure it with chinagraph to prevent distraction. With the advent of an audio alert and better Indicators, 'bug discipline' has improved. I explored this aspect in detail in *Their Greatest Disgrace'* (2016). The bug settings played a crucial part in the Chinook ZD576 investigation, the RAF report revealing an alarming lack of knowledge about the system. This raises a further point; what was the AEW Observer trained to set *his* bug at? Did the instruction come from the pilot, or was he left to make his own decision?

In cruise flight, the Sea King is normally flown manually. The only available autopilot facility is the Height Hold, which operates in two modes - Barometric Altitude Hold or Radar Altitude Hold. Routine ASW 'active' (i.e. dipping sonar) profiles are normally flown at 200' with the Radar Altimeter Hold engaged. It is a single system with no back-up; consequently, it needs to be constantly monitored for any divergence from the set height. Sea King is also fitted with a Heading Hold system which operates whenever the auto-stabiliser is engaged; however, this has limited capability. Unlike more modern systems, it does not offer automatic turn coordination, and balanced flight needs to be maintained manually.[56]

The AEW Sea King

If we accept that flying with a single pilot almost always carries a greater degree of risk, and that the risk is further increased for a maritime helicopter operating at night, then why was it considered acceptable to operate the AEW Sea King with only one pilot?

There were a number of factors: the nature of the AEW role, pilot motivation, Fleet Air Arm culture, and cost. Also, flying with a single pilot saved mass, increasing the allowable fuel load and hence mission duration - one of the key requirements of the Mk7 programme being to extend mission duration to 4.25 hours.

Let us expand on these points:

- Compared with ASW, an AEW flight profile is much less hazardous. Normally, the aircraft will be operated at heights above 500' and at endurance speed (60-70 knots). This provides more time to react to malfunctions, and it is relatively easy to maintain height should an engine fail. Of course, the aircraft has to launch and recover from the ship which, by definition, involves operating below 500'; however, the time spent in this configuration is only a small proportion of the overall mission time. But, as explained, flight at or below 200' was prolonged in this case due to Tomahawk missile firings. During launch and recovery, the senior Observer would move to the cockpit to provide lookout; however, as a non-pilot, he would neither have taken control of the aircraft nor monitored the instruments as effectively as a pilot. This clearly posed an additional risk, but one that the RN clearly considered tolerable. But the legal requirement is tolerable <u>and</u> As Low As Reasonably Practicable

---

56 All Sea King Releases to Service contain two WARNINGS related to Rad Alt Hold. Press to Test is not to be used while in Rad Alt Hold; and Rad Alt Hold is not to be engaged at low altitudes over snow when recirculation is anticipated. There are also two CAUTIONS. Height indications will be disturbed if No.1 Generator fails, resulting in sudden uncommanded movements of the Collective (thrust) lever, resulting in an inadvertent over-torque if not contained. Also, there will be disturbances to the Flight Control System if transmitting on the HF radio between 3-7MHz while Rad Alt Hold is engaged.

(noting affordability is not an allowable factor).

- In the ASW Sea King, the co-pilot's job is considered tedious. However, he has a distinct role. Throughout the sortie, the non-handling pilot normally operates the autopilot, maintains a dead-reckoning navigation plot and, most importantly at low-level, monitors the aircraft's flight path. (And, as I mooted earlier, Lt King in outbound XV650 would in all probability have been distracted by the ongoing failure to initiate the Mission System, and head down in his Intercom). In the AEW, once the aircraft is on-station a non-handling pilot has almost nothing to do. The question of continuation training arises, and the RN admitted that Operational Sea Training had not been conducted. Can it be honestly said that the Observers were adequately trained to assist during prolonged flight at 200', when normally the aircraft would have quickly transitioned to a higher altitude? Especially in the prevailing conditions of post-sandstorm darkness.

- In 1982, when the decisions regarding the manning of the AEW Sea King were made, the new fleet <u>supplemented</u> the existing ASW and Commando fleets. That is, Reserve aircraft were brought forward and converted, resulting in an immediate pressure on aircrew numbers. Single-pilot operation may have been a compromise to maintain ASW capability, and unlikely to have been challenged within the Command Chain. Thereafter, normalisation of deviance set it, whereby an unsafe practice came to be considered normal as it did not immediately cause a catastrophe. This is a recurring feature in MoD accidents.

Impact on Mk7 programme

The associated hazards were identified during an initial 4-phase risk reduction programme, an activity led by the main pre-requisite programme, the Enhanced Comms System. The RN confirmed it wished to retain single-pilot. But the *status quo* could not remain, because the AEW Mk2 comms system contained unappraised Naval Service Modifications, meaning *(inter alia)* the concept of an Observer moving forward during launch and recovery was not addressed in the Mk2 Safety Case. This would change for Mk7.

The initial question was - *Must the Observer remain connected to his Intercom while moving forward and back?* Yes, as it was unacceptable for the aircraft captain to be out of contact with his crew. The obvious solution was a long wander lead, fixed and stowable at his Observer Station, and long enough to allow him to sit in the left-hand pilot seat. This sounds simple, but two issues arose. First, the Mk7 Intercom/Helmet cables were heavier, as they were now 6-core to provide power for Active Noise Reduction (ANR), as well as mic/tels, and had extra screening. Neck strain and, critically, emergency egress, had to be reassessed. (A maximum pull weight to disconnect helmet connectors must not be exceeded, again made more difficult by the new ANR and the RN's requirement to retain the standard NATO mic/tels jack plug and socket). The correct engineering solution was a 'snatch' connector, but the RN rejected this. A compromise was reached, each core being 26swg (thinner and therefore lighter), and a concession granted to fit a 5A circuit breaker, as anything less caused nuisance trips.

Of greater impact was Westland, correctly, classifying the wander lead as a snagging hazard, saying it would/could not approve the concept. This was not the company being awkward. From their viewpoint, the aircraft was designed for two-pilot operation, reflecting the original (ASW) Statement of Operating Intent and Usage. The practical problems were the length of the lead, the potential for snagging, and the fact the walkway between the starboard mission console and cooling equipment, and cockpit, was very narrow and difficult to negotiate, especially in darkness. The installation design was approved without the wander lead; which was then added by Naval Service Modification - MoD being seen to accept the risk. And, like single-pilot operation, the risk may have been tolerable, but it was not ALARP.

Summary

Plainly, two-pilot operation enhanced safety in the Sea King's challenging operating environment. During initial training, pilots were told the reason was to enable the mission to continue should an engine need to be taken into manual control. This particular malfunction needed an extra pair of qualified hands in the cockpit solely dedicated to that task. By definition, therefore, this applied to all Sea Kings.

This was reinforced by the Sea King being a two-pilot design. A simple example of this is the location of the Ice Accretion Meter (which looks like a small blade antenna). It is located outside the cockpit on the left side, below the level of the pilots' feet, and intended to be monitored by the co-pilot. It is almost impossible to see from the right-hand seat, the angle of view too oblique to make an accurate interpretation.

Immediately, there is a conflict between the Build Standard and Concept of Use. The Release to Service offers the following:

'The minimum crew for the aircraft is one pilot and a suitably trained aircrew member to carry out the left-hand seat cockpit duties as required; and other such personnel as are required for the role. It is mandatory that the left-hand seat is occupied when an aircraft, fitted with a FOD Shield, is flown in airframe/rotor icing conditions.

Certain operational circumstances may demand that the left-hand seat be occupied at all times or that a second pilot may be required. These may include NVG operations, certain sorties of prolonged duration, use of the FCS for automatic transitions, and hovering in adverse weather conditions or at night. The responsibility for ensuring crew composition is appropriate for the operational circumstances rests with the authorising authority'.

This is unhelpful, especially to the *'authorising authority'*. Here, one aircraft was authorised by the A Flight Commanding Officer, the other self-authorised by the aircraft captain.[57] However, if the squadron is not manned to allow for two-pilot occupancy, a decision taken many ranks above them, then it is a *fait accompli*, the only option being to risk already fatigued aircrew. (Also noting that AEW Mk2 had 3-aircraft flights, but ASaC Mk7 had four). The wording in the Release is wholly inadequate. One can surmise, therefore, that the Safety Case did not reflect the Build Standard.

---

57 Board of Inquiry report, paragraph 12.

18: Post-Inquest

On 16 November 2009 Mrs Lawrence brought some of the emerging evidence to the attention of the now retired Board of Inquiry President, Commodore Richard Hawkins RN. He declined to comment, citing lack of involvement. A strange claim. Nevertheless, he retains an enduring duty to report fresh information which would have influenced the conduct and conclusions of his Board. Perhaps his position was directed, as he copied his reply to FLEET and a legal advisor; which could be his way of meeting his obligation.

Mrs Lawrence pursued matters through FLEET. Here is a self-explanatory extract from her letter of 18 February 2010:

'I acknowledge receipt of your letter dated 8 February 2010. I am concerned that it contains a number of factual errors. The purpose of this letter is to correct them and seek responses to my valid questions.

In your paragraph 2, discussing High Intensity Strobe Lights (HISL) in the ASaC Mk7, you state the "form, fit and location remained identical to the original anti-collision lights". This is complete nonsense. The form of a high intensity strobe is not the same as that of a rotating anti-collision light. The internal fit of HISL is also completely different. Also in paragraph 2 you state "... in other words it was the same in all respects except brighter. This means, therefore, that HISL was more effective in providing an enhanced level of visibility, due to its higher intensity". This view was not shared by your Board of Inquiry. This higher intensity required aircrew to switch off the lower HISL in various conditions.

You seek to justify HISL on the grounds that civil commercial and light aircraft worlds have adopted it. I doubt many in these worlds habitually take off from and land on a carrier at night, or routinely fly at only a few hundred feet without full radar or Air Traffic Control coverage. I have no doubt HISL is effective in most uses, but the point is that this particular use (ASaC Mk7) was not properly assessed and trialled.

Turning to the programme manager's report of 25 February 2004, I note the Integrated Project Team (IPT) denies any knowledge of it. I find this astonishing given it was addressed to its Requirements Manager, and copied to the IPT Leader and three others. I have seen this report and it reaffirms the introduction of HISL was the responsibility of the IPT, who had claimed unverified "read across" from the Mk2 (demonstrating their claim of no prior knowledge is entirely false). As the IPT refused to adhere to the regulations, it was left to the programme manager to ensure the proposed installation (in Mk2) was safe. The record shows he instructed that HISL should not be fitted (to Mk7) until proven so. He was overruled and, according to previous correspondence from the RN, read across was granted even though deemed wholly inappropriate by both he and Westland.

I am content that, at this point (mid-2000), the regulations were being applied properly by the Mk7 programme manager, but not by the IPT. It is what happened after this that continues to concern me. That IPT staff have been party to a catalogue of untruths and misleading statements (which it would seem from your letter is still ongoing) naturally makes me think they have something to hide. The evidence shows this to be their failure to implement the airworthiness regulations - precisely the point made by the Board of Inquiry.

I agree with you that these problems with HISL were probably not the sole cause. However, I suspect the Board of Inquiry and Coroner would have been most interested in the truth. I am therefore copying this to the current Coroner and my MP. I am sure the above verifiable facts will both interest and concern you, the latter because you have been misled. I am sure you will seek to correct this and look forward to your reply, in which I would ask you to confirm, or deny, what I have said'.

FLEET replied on 7 April 2010. Extracts are discussed below. Some of this is mentioned elsewhere, but bears repeating because it is revealing of MoD's intransigence and obfuscation, even after being confronted with the truth.

'Regarding the reason for fitting the HISL to the Mk2 and Mk7 Sea King, the decisions date back to 1994 at the Naval Air Command Flight Safety meeting, which decided that the fitment of HISLs across the RN aircraft should be pursued'.

The *'decision'* of such a meeting is not a formal endorsement. It constitutes tacit approval to prepare a case for fleet-wide HISL. This is the first of many steps in a lengthy process, which can be halted at any stage, on many grounds. Within months the recommendation was rejected, because the Operational Requirements branch, Flag Officer Naval Aviation, and Director General Aircraft (Navy) all endorsed the Mk7 aircraft specification <u>without</u> HISL.

'HISL was introduced to the Sea King Mk2/7 by Naval Service Modification 3642. The modification was submitted to GKN Westland for appraisal, their reply ED/JB/2888 dated 15 March 2000 states: "The proposed Naval Service Engineered modification has been appraised in accordance with Defence Standard 05-123 Chapter 213 paragraph 4.1. The Design Authority would

166

however like to make a __significant__ number of observations which will need resolution prior to subsequent cover mod action being taken by the Defence Helicopter Support Authority (DHSA)"'.

In quoting a Westland appraisal of 2000, FLEET omits to mention the false declaration of 1997 that this appraisal had already taken place. Also, that it was the Mk2 being appraised, not the *'Sea King Mk2/7'*. Westland's reference to DHSA is an important subtlety. In March 2000, DHSA had not existed for a year. The company is making the point that the proposed modification originated from DHSA in 1996, but was only submitted for appraisal in 2000, after their demise. Importantly, their comments relate to the physical safety of the installation, not the functional safety when put to use (e.g. when flown at night, at low level, off a carrier, with the lower strobe off) - something that would need to be assessed during flight trials. No Design Authority can be responsible for Service Designed Modifications schemed and introduced by MoD without appraisal. Ultimately, FLEET's claim lacks credibility because 15 months later Westland still refused to underwrite the design.

'At two subsequent meetings chaired by the SKIPT project manager SKPE1 on 22 May 2000 and 9 June 2000...the work required to read across from the Mk2 to the Mk7 was agreed, as was an implementation strategy for introduction of Design changes and the Trial Installation'.

(SKPE1 was H/SK2's new post title in the Sea King Integrated Project Team). The aim of the meetings was to progress the appraisal and rectification of the Mk2 design, to establish a baseline for Mk7. FLEET neglects that there were two separate tasks. That of the IPT's support element on AEW Mk2; and H/SK2's on Mk7, to understand the impact on *his* aircraft and facilitate a proper Design Authority modification. Westland confirmed that, because the NSM did not satisfy design and airworthiness regulations in the Mk2, by definition it did not in Mk7. What is more - and this is what FLEET avoids entirely - even if corrected in Mk2 the modification would still be unsuitable for Mk7, due mainly to wiring clashes and power supply location. Crucially, FLEET omits that the *'work required'* was to implement mandated airworthiness regulations, and MoD did not carry it out. The key question here is why the Naval Service Modification Manager was not chairing the meeting. The reason is, he and his superiors had made false record that the work had already been done.

This kills FLEET's argument stone dead.

*

On 14 August 2013, as a follow-on from FLEET's refusal to answer, Andrew Robathan MP (Minister of State for the Armed Forces) was asked:

1. *Was the Board of Inquiry, Coroner or families informed of the HISL investigation; and that MoD named and blamed the programme manager, knowing this to be false?*

2. *Was the programme manager's letter report, detailing the actual events, made known to the Board or Coroner?*

3. *Was one free to quote from this report in order to correct statements made to Mrs Lawrence by MoD?*

4. *At what point, and by whom, was it decided neither the programme manager nor the HISL investigator would be called as witnesses?*

5. *Was this evidence relating to the contributory factors advised to the court, families or their legal representatives?*

6. *At the Inquest, the Coroner agreed several detailed questions could be answered 'later' by witnesses/MoD. Is there a record of these later answers and could it be supplied?*

7. *Several contradictory and incorrect statements were made in court under oath. Did MoD seek to correct these statements?*

8. *Given the evidence that emerged in the RN Flight Safety and Accident Investigation Centre report and the HISL investigation, was consideration given to reconvening the Board of Inquiry?*

Mr Robathan replied on 4 September 2013:[58]

Q1, 5, 7 & 8 - Not addressed. All relate to breaches of regulations and the Covenant.

Q2 - MoD is *'not able to determine exactly what documentation was provided to the Coroner'.*

Q3 - He suggests the programme manager's report be sought under Freedom of Information. Whether it was submitted to the Board of Inquiry is not addressed.

Q4 - He notes Pre-Inquest Hearings determine what evidence will be heard and from whom, but omits to say both MoD and Coroner's Office claim no hearing took place.

Q6 - *'There is no record of the detailed questions that you state the Coroner*

---

58 Letter D/Min(AF)/AR MC03390/2013, 4 September 2013.

agreed could be answered later'. There is a record - the court recordings.

Six refusals to answer, one risible claim, and one outright lie. Par for the course and venal beyond measure.

Design decisions were overruled and legal obligations overlooked. This knowingly increased risk to life, constituting culpable negligence. In practice, policy became: *We know it's unsafe. Let's leave it at that and hope for the best.*

*

On 25 August 1997, H/SK2 wrote in a briefing to Director Helicopter Projects, Dr David Colbourne:

'Repeated warnings are going unheeded. You are standing into danger'.[59]

He did not reply, although Kevin Thomas was asked what the phrase meant. He replied:

*'It's a naval term. It means you've ****** up'.*

Quite.

---

59 Risk briefing D/DHP/24/1/8, 25 August 1997.

PART 3: OTHER CASE STUDIES

Chinook HC Mk1 ZA721 - Falkland Islands, 27 February 1987

Chinook HC Mk2 ZD576 - Mull of Kintyre, 2 June 1994

Tornado GR4A ZG710 - Iraq, 22 March 2003

The death of Corporal Mark Wright GC - Afghanistan, 6 September 2006

Hercules C-130K XV179 - Iraq, 30 January 2005

The grounding of Air Cadet Glider fleets (2014-on)

19: Chinook HC Mk1 ZA721 - Falkland Islands, 27 February 1987

Chief Technician David Chitty

Sergeant Andrew Johns

Corporal Jeremy Marshall

Corporal Karl Minshull

Flight Lieutenant Anthony Moffat

Flight Lieutenant Stephen Newman

Corporal Peter Whitwell

During an air test, without warning the aircraft pitched nose down until almost vertical, and dived into the ground. All onboard were killed. The Board of Inquiry deemed the aircraft unserviceable. Officially, cause was unknown. The evidence said otherwise.

Flight Lieutenant (later Air Commodore) Carl Scott offered this, under oath, to the Chinook ZD576 (Mull of Kintyre) Fatal Accident Inquiry in January 1996:

'Boeing have a vested interest in deterring any report which leaves them liable. The company has shown a determination in the past to influence the outcome of Inquiries. When Wing Commander Malcolm Pledger took command of 78 Squadron in the Falkland Islands in February 1988, I asked him to brief the Chinook Flight on the findings of the Board of Inquiry, as this had not then been published. [It was signed off on 16 May 1988]. *As chairman of the Board he briefed two findings: the first his own most probable cause (failure of a hydraulic jack due to poor quality control at Boeing Vertol) and then that which would actually be published due to the failure of MoD to face pressure brought to bear by Boeing Vertol (cause unknown)'.*

That is, the finding was directed. (Note: Wing Commander Pledger, as Air Chief Marshal Sir, was later unfairly named and shamed by the Nimrod Review; discussed later).

Flight Lieutenant Scott's evidence was in many ways the most damning heard at the Inquiry, given the Chinook HC Mk2 being unairworthy was concealed. In 2009 Mr Haddon-Cave QC agreed there were savings at the expense of safety. But what of pandering to a contractor to preserve relations, knowing this places aircrew lives at risk?

The Air Accidents Investigation Branch (AAIB)

With a civil accident, the AAIB will look into the airworthiness background in detail, including consideration of type certification, previous incidents and accidents, maintenance standards and practices. The Engineering, Operations and Flight Recorder Inspectors will then analyse all the evidence and try to reach conclusions about <u>events</u> and <u>factors</u> that possibly or probably contributed to the <u>cause</u>. With military accidents, the AAIB's brief is to provide the Board with a factual statement on the evidence found at the scene. Its report forms an Annex to the Board's report. Airworthiness and organisational aspects are covered by the Board. Both were robust in their criticism of Boeing. The Board was *'disappointed'* with the company, saying some information was *'parochial, contradictory, misleading* and *unacceptable'.*

This reflected the experiences of the AAIB:

*'Evidence of a number of **pre-impact defects** (in actuators) was found. Co-operation from Boeing Vertol was generally good, but **little in-depth knowledge** of the actuators was apparent in the responsible Design Groups.*

Forward-Swivelling Upper Boost Actuator

***No upper roll pin or locking wire was present** and the clevis attaching rod had **not been drilled** to accept the pin. These were clearly **assembly omissions**. Relatively deep witness marks were found on the rod, indicative of it having been **carelessly clamped** in a vice or grips prior to final assembly.*

Aft-Pivoting Upper Boost Actuator

*Examination revealed that some of the seals in the head housing assembly had been **incorrectly installed**. One head housing back-up ring on System 1 and two on System 2 were found with bevelled ends **crossed over**. In addition, it was found that **incorrect** back-up rings had been fitted in the 1.5" diameter seal between the piston bearing sleeve and the outer cylinder in **both** Systems 1 and 2. Continuous back-rings should have been used, but scarf cut rings were fitted. (This same defect was discovered in the Aft-Swivelling Upper Boost Actuator). It was found that the outer seal in System 2 between the core of the head housing assembly and the piston assembly was **incorrectly assembled and had suffered a gross failure**. The inner back-up ring was **missing**, and the evidence clearly indicated it had **not been installed** at assembly. A 0.5" circumferential length of the O-Ring and the outer back-up ring was **missing**, providing a large overboard **leakage path** for System 2 fluid'.*

You do not have to be an engineer to grasp something is very wrong here. Vital parts were missing or wrongly installed. Not drilling a hole for the roll pin is scandalous, and *'made possible the potentially catastrophic jam or runaway of the Forward-Swivelling Upper Boost Actuator'*. Perhaps even worse was failing to pick this up on the many visual and physical inspections before the component, and the aircraft itself, were delivered.

Aftermath

The Board stated the most likely cause was a jammed Forward-Swivelling Upper Boost Actuator (see above), with an Aft Longitudinal Cyclic Trim Actuator (LCTA) malfunction a likely contributory factor.

Experienced Chinook pilots prepared a short paper with their own thoughts, submitted to superiors. It was not included in MoD reports. They concluded three interrelated factors forced the aircraft into its nose-down attitude and fatal plunge:

- Differential Airspeed Hold (DASH) actuator motor stall.
- Aft LCTA clutch slippage (compounded by the above Aft-Pivoting Upper Boost Actuator problem).
- Forward and Aft Rotor Head lift imbalance.

The first two were logical deductions based on physical evidence, and had been experienced before - especially DASH failures. The last was alluded to by the Board, without explanation. It relates to incorrect adjustment of the Pitch Links. One effect would be to reduce the authority of the DASH actuator, ultimately preventing any further reduction of, for example, aft pitch. Consequently, the apportionment of lift between the forward and aft rotors is wrong, with the aft rotor wanting to overtake the forward, causing a nose down attitude.

In each scenario normal control is lost; and had occurred before to Squadron Leader Robert Burke, the RAF Odiham Unit Test Pilot. He considers himself lucky to have survived, mainly because he had sufficient height. This experience enabled him to contribute to the above report.

Separately, the Flight Safety Cell at HQ Strike Command was so unhappy with the official version, Squadron Leader Burke was sent a complete <u>original</u> copy of the Board's report and allocated simulator time at Mannheim with the US Army to verify his findings. He wrote a test schedule and the Chinook Flight Commander on the Operational Conversion Unit was able to repeatedly replicate the crash. The only way to avoid the accident was to take off all power by lowering the collective (thrust) lever completely, thus slowing the aircraft down. This is counter intuitive. Given the directive to find 'cause unknown', MoD would not wish this to be made public.

Burke's experiences had also led him to develop the necessary training to recover from DASH and LCTA failures; which is again contrary to that taught in non-tandemrotor helicopters. Neither pilot had been given this extra training. They would have been taken by surprise and need time to react. With only 700 feet of height available, the crash became inevitable.

Additionally, an air test schedule had been developed by Burke, which was approved and issued by the RAF Handling Squadron at Boscombe Down. This included, at about 85 knots, a check on the action of the LCTAs against the cockpit indicators. This must be done before transitioning to fast forward flight. If there is an LCTA problem it will show up here, as will unusual fore and aft stick positioning. The Board's timeline reveals this check was not carried out, probably due to ZA721 being asked by Air Traffic Control to expedite clearing the approach path because of a TriStar returning to the dispersal area. Thus, the aircraft accelerated with, certainly, a faulty aft LCTA, and a handling pilot who was unaware of the correct recovery procedures.

Following Flight Lieutenant Scott's evidence, families will have suspected they were misled. More so, because MoD did not investigate known events and factors. The uncertainty eats away relentlessly. The motive behind the directive to find cause unknown is likely to be a much higher political decision not to upset the US Department of Defense. Our political masters might think this acceptable. Others might consider it wiser to prevent avoidable deaths of our servicemen.

There is evidence of lasting concern. In August 1992, the RAF Director of Flight Safety called into question Boeing's ability to act as a Design Authority for the MoD.[60] The failure to act upon the ZA721 report meant systemic airworthiness failings were allowed to fester, leading to...

---

60 Chinook Airworthiness Review Team report, issued under cover of Loose Minute D/IFS(RAF)/125/30/2/1, 14 August 1992.

20: Chinook HC Mk2 ZD576 - Mull of Kintyre, 2 June 1994

Major Richard Allen
Colonel Christopher Biles
Detective Inspector Dennis Bunting
Detective Chief Superintendent Desmond Conroy
Flight Lieutenant Richard Cook
Martin Dalton
Detective Superintendent Phillip Davidson
Detective Inspector Stephen Davidson
John Deverell
Major Christopher Dockerty
Assistant Chief Constable Brian Fitzsimons
Master Airloadmaster Graham Forbes
Detective Superintendent Robert Foster
Lieutenant Colonel Richard Gregory-Smith
Detective Superintendent William Gwilliam
Sergeant Kevin Hardie
John Haynes
Major Antony Hornby
Anne James
Detective Inspector Kevin Magee
Michael Maltby
Detective Chief Superintendent Maurice Neilly
Detective Superintendent Ian Phoenix
Major Roy Pugh
Stephen Rickard
Major Gary Paul Sparks
Flight Lieutenant Jonathan Tapper
Lieutenant Colonel John Tobias
Lieutenant Colonel George Williams

'My mother has been lied to by the MoD. It treated my family with utter contempt following the crash and despicably tried to enact the Warsaw Air Carriage Act to limit payouts to the widows and families. Hardly the actions of a moral outfit. Even after we overturned this obscene effort they forced my mother to produce receipts for the clothes my father wore on the day of his death, and list how many potatoes he would eat in an average year as part of their quest to limit compensation. The callousness was breathtaking and displayed a complete lack of integrity. Quite frankly we were treated like Irish peasants by uncaring, absentee feudal landlords and the disdain was palpable'.
Captain Niven Phoenix, son of Detective Superintendent Ian Phoenix, RUC (late Parachute Regiment)

The aircraft struck a gently sloping hillside, bounced twice, inverted, and disintegrated. Twenty-five of Northern Ireland's most important counter-terrorism agents and the RAF crew of four were killed.

Lacking a Flight Data Recorder or Cockpit Voice Recorder, the RAF Board of Inquiry was *'unable to determine a definite cause'*. The senior Reviewing Officers replaced this finding with their own opinion - that the pilots were negligent to a gross degree. The standard of proof required was *no doubt whatsoever*. Here, there was no positive, verifiable evidence; but there were huge doubts.

There followed a 17-year public and at times bitter campaign to clear the pilots. In 2010, Lord Alexander Philip was asked to set up the Mull of Kintyre Review. His recommendations were accepted by Secretary of State for Defence Dr Liam Fox MP, who set aside (quashed) the findings in July 2011.

The central points are:

- The Controller Aircraft Release provided an INTERIM clearance. This prohibited operation of the aircraft *'in any way that places any reliance whatsoever on the proper functioning of this equipment'*. This was mandated upon the RAF, as it was the RN in the Sea King ASaC Mk7 case.

- By signing the Release to Service, the Assistant Chief of the Air Staff made a false declaration that the aircraft satisfied airworthiness regulations.

- Knowing this, and disregarding regulations, senior Reviewing Officers applied their own legal test and blamed the pilots.

After Dr Fox's decision, some retired senior RAF officers continued to denigrate the deceased pilots - one of the worst breaches of the Covenant imaginable. This prompted me to write a book: *Their Greatest Disgrace - The campaign to clear the Chinook ZD576 pilots*. Still they continued, and I later published a prequel *'The Inconvenient Truth - Chinook ZD576 Cause & Culpability'*. Both detail sustained misconduct. MoD continues to make the same errors and mistakes, and commit the same offences. It refuses to learn.

21: Tornado GR4A ZG710 - Kuwait, 23 March 2003

Flight Lieutenant Kevin Main
Flight Lieutenant David Williams

At 0248 hours local time on 23 March 2003, Tornado GR4A ZG710 was lost over Kuwait while returning to the Ali Al Salem Air Base. It was shot down by a US PATRIOT Battery; a long range, mobile, ground-based air defence missile system. The Battery had arrived in theatre without its equipment and was allocated a partial set of spares. It did not have voice or data links with its Command HQ or other Batteries, and was not part of the integrated air defence network; meaning it was forced to act autonomously. It was not fit for purpose.

Flying at around 18,000 feet, in congested airspace, ZG710 was mistaken for an Iraqi Anti-Radiation Missile. (One designed to detect and home in on radio frequency emissions). The Battery had interrogated the target with Identification Friend or Foe (IFF) but received no response. The extant (US) Rules of Engagement allowed it to engage the target in self-defence, but did not provide adequate defence against the possibility of friendly fire.

Board of Inquiry

The Board noted many contributory factors. Primarily: firing doctrine, crew training and IFF procedures. Also, aircraft routing and airspace control measures. Many of these were US liabilities, but the Board did not record what actions the US Inquiry had recommended. However, it did criticise the criteria programmed into PATRIOT, which did not include the possibility of an airborne IFF being unserviceable or unavailable. Much was implied - in the vernacular, US training encouraged a trigger-happy approach.

Worryingly, the Board stated:

'IFF is a system designed to identify automatically whether or not a particular asset, such as an aircraft, is a friend or foe'.

This is misleading. IFF can identify a friend, but cannot positively identify a foe. Such an incorrect assumption about one defensive layer might result in other layers being omitted, and a potentially fatal over-confidence developing.

In his remarks, the Station Commander, Group Captain (later Air Commodore) Robert McAlpine said:

'The reality dawned only after the event, destroying a valuable aircraft and costing two aircrew their lives'.

He was not informed the *'reality'* was well-known long beforehand.

The Air Officer Commanding, the late Air Chief Marshal Sir Christopher Moran (then an Air Vice Marshal) stated:

'Thus prevention of a fratricide relied almost entirely on IFF interrogation, which in the case of ZG710 had failed. They correctly followed the IFF procedures but, tragically, were unaware that their IFF equipment was not responding to any interrogations during the crucial recovery phase of the flight. Furthermore, to my mind it is unacceptable for the Tornado IFF to be able to fail without any warning being provided to the operating crew. This situation applies equally to all operational air platforms'.

Unwittingly, he repeated the concerns of MoD civilian engineers.

The senior Reviewing Officer, Commander-in-Chief Strike Command Air Chief Marshal Sir Brian Burridge stated:

'I therefore <u>direct</u> that urgent work be undertaken to <u>modify the Mk12 IFF installation to ensure that the cockpit warning is triggered in all failure modes</u>. The Board's findings revealed a number of failings in these areas that form a chain leading to the loss of Tornado ZG710 and its crew. <u>Had any one of the failings been identified and corrected, ZG710 would almost certainly not have been shot down'</u>.

Please note this direct order - we will return to it later.

*

With reference to the Reason Model, a number of defensive barriers had been removed. Neither the Board nor Reviewing Officers were told that senior staff had condoned improperly integrated and functionally unsafe IFF systems. That, the increased probability of occurrence had been identified in 1998, only for the mitigation to be rejected.

Boards of Inquiry tend not to criticise poor decisions. They do not say *bring me the head of the idiot who approved this modification*, because the signatory is a superior. But everyone knew precisely what was being said. *This was avoidable had the regulations been followed.* But too many use the omission as an excuse to do nothing. This cultural reticence (in fact, gross negligence and dereliction of duty) is a significant barrier to basic safety.

ZG710's Identification Friend or Foe system

A design feature within the IFF detects failures and routes a signal to the warning system. The logic is simple. For example: *I have been interrogated. Have I responded correctly? Yes. (Okay). No. (Warn crew, who take action).* As this can be an audio warning and/or visual cue, the output from the IFF itself is generally a simple switching signal requiring integration with other aircraft systems. In Tornado GR4A there are both audio and visual warnings, although the Board noted crews preferred visual because the audio could be *'confused with other Intercom signals'*; itself a systems integration failing typical of Service Designed Modifications, and an utterly damning indictment.

This potential hazard is well understood, and was the subject of a task placed on DRA Farnborough on 24 March 1999, to study the new tones in both Sea King Mk4 and Mk7; specifically the Mk7's IFF warning tone clashed with that of JTIDS and the GPS Time of Day update tone. It was cancelled as a waste of money by the same official who cancelled the Mk7 risk mitigation tasks. The point, however, is that once again a recommendation arising from a fatal accident came as no surprise.

*

Correct integration facilitates the demonstration of functional safety, as opposed to stand alone performance on a test bench. It is a pre-requisite to a valid Release to Service. Plainly, if a specified safety feature has not been integrated properly, the installation does not meet the required performance or airworthiness standards. Nor can the risk it is designed to mitigate be tolerable and As Low As Reasonably Practicable. We have seen it was common practice in MoD <u>not</u> to effect this integration correctly, rendering the aircraft vulnerable to friendly fire, and increasingly so to collision. None of this is discussed in the Board's report, which stops at the point it decides the IFF failed.

The Board reported a ground check in IFF Mode 4 (encrypted military mode) was conducted prior to engine start. This involves pointing a test set at the upper antenna and interrogating the system. If the reply is valid, this is deemed a successful test. However, it is not an end-to-end test, because only a small part of the system is checked. It does not check practical use in any way (interrogations while airborne, from the ground, sea, or other air assets).

The Board revealed an RAF Rapier Missile System that *'regularly'* checked the IFF of departing aircraft did not report the aircraft or log a fault. There is a difference between *regularly* and *routinely* - this was an *ad hoc* arrangement, not part of formal pre-mission checks. To reinforce this, Air Chief Marshal Burridge recommended a positive challenge and response check be completed after take-off between every aircraft and an appropriate control authority.

It was noted there was no firm evidence the IFF had worked at any time during the mission. But there *was* evidence (from data recorders) that the navigator had carried out his appropriate checks. No conclusion could be drawn on *when* any failure occurred, only that his check did not reveal the fault. This offered a clue where to begin - integration of failure warnings.

It was mooted at the Inquest in October 2006 that the most likely failure was a *'blown fuse'*, but this was not evidence-based and in any case is too simplistic. Even if correct, this *should* have resulted in a failure warning to crew - explaining Air Chief Marshal Burridge's order to conduct further research into failure modes. This means one of two things. The Failure Modes, Effects and Criticality Analysis (FMECA) was flawed, or it was not conducted.

Crucially, neither the Board nor Reviewing Officers were made aware Boscombe Down had reported such failures on previous occasions - but were ignored. The casual reader might think, good, you've done something positive. However, to any engineer or project manager the very need for this order cries prior negligence. Aircrew have every right to assume failure warnings will work.

Significant questions arise, the most obvious being:

- Why did the Board not discuss or investigate poor installation design of this Service Designed Modification?
- Were the failings mentioned in Boscombe Down's Military Aircraft Release Recommendations report? Or did the RAF ignore its obligation to have the Aircraft Project Director, Boscombe Down and the Design Authorities appraise the modification?
- Was the simulator modified and training updated before the IFF entered service, including immediate action in the event of IFF failure warnings?
- Were the Aircraft or Air System Safety Cases valid?

In other words, the same systemic failings that arose on the Sea King mid-air collision.

Warnings to senior staff

To briefly recap, Boscombe and the Sea King programme manager had identified the <u>refusal</u> to integrate IFF failure warnings in Sea King AEW Mk2 as a safety critical issue. But, false declarations were made that the aircraft was safe, knowing it was functionally unsafe. The programme manager was able to fix *his* aircraft (ASaC Mk7), but how to deal with a systemic failure? The proper answer is escalation through one's line management chain, to a member of the Executive Board (as it is a corporate level risk). In practice, this should take about five minutes. When his line manager refused to act, he then had several options:

1. Advise the equipment (IFF) project office. As explained before, Military Communications Projects (MCP) also refused to act.

2. Advise the aircraft project offices. This requires knowledge of what aircraft a particular equipment is fitted to. The reference document, the Avionics List, was by this time no longer maintained by Air Member Logistics.

3. Advise the IFF Design Authority, via the project office to whom it is under contract - in this case MCP21. See above.

4. Advise one's own Aircraft Design Authority.

Given the failure was identified by his Sea King programme, the route taken was (4), and Westland were informed by letter on 25 January 1999. By taking this action (1) and (3) were also satisfied, with Westland's Statement of Work stipulating they must make provision to engage affected parties. This ensured the resultant modification proposal would include, at least, MCP21, who would be <u>obliged</u> to respond and notify aircraft offices, including Tornado; closing all loops. What neither the programme manager nor Westland could ensure, however, was that others fulfilled their obligations. Nor was there independent oversight, as the HQ Modifications Committee had been disbanded in June 1991.

The above solved the immediate Sea King problem, and satisfied the programme manager's legal obligations, but he knew others would continue to abrogate their responsibilities. What to do next? There was no point escalating (again) to his line manager, as he would bury it as before. His only recourse was to go straight to Executive Director level.

He recommended to XD1 (Mr Ian Fauset) and, later, XD5 (Mr Stan Porter) that all aircraft IFF installations be inspected for correct failure warning integration. XD5 ignored the recommendation without comment. (Assuming his dismissive laugh was not a comment, as such).

For his part, on 15 December 2000 and 10 January 2001 XD1 ruled it was acceptable to:

- Deliver an aircraft with the IFF failure warnings not integrated.
- In the knowledge it was unsafe, falsely declare it safe.
- Permit a non-engineer to overrule the engineering design/safety decisions of the person holding airworthiness and technical delegation.

The Chief of Defence Procurement, Sir Robert Walmsley, upheld XD1's rulings, twice. When escalated to the Permanent Under-Secretary of State on 10 June 2002, he did not reply. It can be seen all reasonable steps were taken to highlight the precise failures, long before the loss of ZG710. Also, that the systemic failings were all well-known many years before the Nimrod Review presented them as revelations in 2009.

Thus, the opportunity to prevent the deaths of the crew was lost.

The above is a litany of monumental incompetence, maladministration, and misconduct in public office.

The Board expressed itself:

'Surprised that an aircraft without an apparently serviceable IFF was allowed to enter hostile airspace'.

But it did not consider there to be aggravating factors. Had it known fleet inspections of IFF systems and their installation designs had been rejected, it would have come to a different conclusion.

*

Interestingly, in 2007 Defence News reported:

'The final Puma helicopter to be fitted with an improved and secure means of identifying friendly aircraft has returned to service. Successor Identification Friend or Foe has been fitted to 33 aircraft, reducing the risk of friendly fire incident'.

One of the civilian staff named in the article (co-incidentally, a recipient of the High Intensity Strobe Light report of 2004) is on record as regarding the need for systems integration as good reason to cancel programmes due to excessive risk. (See next chapter). Undoubtedly, this change of tack was due to the adverse publicity received on internet forums, such as...

http://www.pprune.org/military-aircrew/85355-raf-aircraft-hit-us-missile-6.html.

This forum has, for many years, been MoD's main source of corporate knowledge.

Postscript - August 2012

Returning to the words of Air Chief Marshal Burridge:

'Had any one of the failings been identified and corrected, ZG710 would almost certainly not have been shot down. I therefore direct that urgent work be undertaken to modify the Mk12 IFF installation to ensure that the cockpit warning is triggered in all failure modes'.

What would he say if he knew the failings <u>had</u> been identified, but those responsible had <u>refused</u> to act? Worse, that others had conspired to conceal the systemic nature of the failures? We now know, because what you are reading was sent to him in June 2012 (six years after his retirement) by a Fellow of the Royal Aeronautical Society, the late Captain Ralph Kohn. He replied:

'The Successor IFF upgrade of two years ago has addressed the compatibility problems that you cite'.

Is this not an odd reply? On 1 March 2004, as Commander-in-Chief Strike Command, he had <u>directed</u> that urgent work be undertaken to make IFF installations safe. Yet, seemingly, he is content his directive was ignored and the design not corrected for some six years. Surely if a subordinate had disobeyed his direct order he would not have replied as he did? Who has the authority to overrule a Commander-in-Chief and carry such a risk to life for six years, or dictate such a response to him? And why would someone do that? Regardless, as the Senior Reviewing Officer it was his enduring duty to now advise MoD and Ministers that he was misled (by omission), and recommend the facts be placed on record. Perhaps he did, but his advice was rejected? Yet again, we have been there before.

22: The death of Corporal Mark Wright GC - Kajaki Dam, Afghanistan, 6 September 2006

Figure 9 - Map of Helmand Province *(Public domain)*

The Parachute Regiment's 3rd Battalion had moved into Sangin, in Helmand Province, Afghanistan on 2 June 2006. A key role was to prevent Taliban occupation of the strategically important Kajaki Dam area, 24 miles to the north-east, which provided water for irrigation in the Helmand Valley and power for the whole province via its hydro-electric installations. A permanent British presence was established at the dam, one among many remote outstations across Northern Helmand that attracted sustained, intensive attacks, and remained under siege for long periods. The Task Force's limited resources became dangerously stretched, and the terrain made communications difficult.

On 6 September 2006, a patrol entered an unmarked Russian minefield near the dam. One soldier stepped on a mine and was seriously injured. Corporal Wright and colleagues from his mortar platoon went to give aid and radioed an Observation Post for assistance (who would then contact main base). Further landmines detonated as a landing space was cleared for a helicopter evacuation attempt, inflicting severe injuries upon several others. Corporal Wright ordered his men out of the minefield, while he remained to tend the injured.

Back at main base their Commanding Officer, Lieutenant Colonel Stuart Tootal, was thwarted by bureaucracy in his attempts to have US Combat Search and Rescue helicopters deployed. The US aircrews were keen to go, but because the landing site was deemed insecure permission had to be sought from their HQ in Florida; which was not forthcoming after some hours. The Board of Inquiry later put this down to *'mechanical problems'*.

The RAF Chinooks in theatre did not have rescue hoists. Landing would risk setting off more mines. Corporal Wright had foreseen this, specifically requesting an aircraft fitted with a hoist. Faced with an impossible dilemma, Colonel Tootal chose to deploy a Chinook. Upon arrival, it set down on its rear undercarriage, nose up. Recognising the danger the troops signalled the aircraft to take off, but (it is believed) its downwash set off another mine, gravely injuring Corporal Wright.

Eventually, two US HH-60G Pave Hawk helicopters were authorised, arriving some five hours after the first explosion. The casualties were winched on board and ferried to a waiting Chinook. The bravery of the US crews was such that they were recognised with a Queen's Commendation for Bravery in the Air.

But the medical 'golden hour' was long gone. Corporal Wright died of his wounds during the flight to Camp Bastion, 58 miles to the south-west. He was posthumously awarded the George Cross. Like the Victoria Cross it is a Tier 1 award, for gallantry not in the face of the enemy. Somewhat moot, when in a minefield.

*

At the Inquest on 17 October 2008, Coroner Andrew Walker said:

*'To reach the position where soldiers stationed at two important observation posts, through a **shortage of radio batteries and re-chargers**, had to resort to firing shots into the air to attract their colleagues' attention to the presence of a threat, simply beggars belief. In fact the battery situation was so dire that a radio communication channel between the two outposts at Athens and Normandy* [Observation Posts, overlooking the Kajaki Dam] *that should*

*have been open all the time could be opened for **only one minute every two hours**. In my judgment it was the downwash of the Chinook that was directly responsible for the explosion that injured Corporal Wright. What was needed was a medium-frame helicopter with a winch. The actions of the US personnel who flew into the minefield is without doubt heroism of the highest order, by the specialist rescue and recovery team. Those who survived owe their lives to the Americans. **It is lamentable that the UK is not able to provide dedicated helicopters for the same service.** Corporal Wright died of haemorrhagic shock on his way to hospital. He would have survived if he had been taken sooner. **You are courageous and utterly fearless.** I have nothing but admiration for you and your fellow soldiers'.*

Mr Walker directly challenged MoD, who claimed Corporal Wright could not have survived. He has been MoD's nemesis, the only man in authority to consistently speak for the dead. I want to discuss three aspects of his summing up, all largely ignored - radio communications, batteries/charging, and lack of dedicated Combat Search and Rescue.

Communications

For understandable reasons, MoD has not revealed the communications protocols. It is unclear precisely what radios the troops had. Who is issued with what is a doctrinal matter. Possibilities include the new BOWMAN (tactical communications) system, or more modern and capable radios delivered some years earlier. (Think about that).

Everyone within a patrol or infantry section is issued with a UHF Personal Role Radio. They have limited range (hundreds of yards), and are used for <u>intra</u>-section comms. Powered by two AA batteries, they are not the radios/batteries referred to by Mr Walker.

Each patrol or section would typically have two low-power VHF radios, with an effective range of about three miles. These are for <u>inter</u>-section comms. At platoon level, and in some vehicles, a higher power variant is used, with a range of around 18 miles in ideal conditions. But VHF and UHF comms are limited to line-of-sight. Establishing a relay is common, using Forward Operating Bases, Observation Posts or Patrol Bases.

To a foot or vehicle patrol, especially in mountainous terrain, longer range is achieved by High Frequency (HF) communications, which 'bounces' the signal off the ionosphere (sky-wave propagation). (Satellite communication is a possibility, but in practice access was limited and assets scarce). Again, there are low and high-power versions. The practical difficulty is finding a working frequency, as good HF frequencies tend to last 10-15 minutes due to ever-changing atmospheric conditions. Hence, every military employs a frequency prediction methodology, and signallers are given around 20-30 predicted frequencies, often a month in advance. These are pre-programmed into (e.g.) the BOWMAN HF radio, which 'polls' and ranks them. By definition, this requires the radio to transmit, which eats up battery power and lets the enemy know where you are. The difficulty faced by users is obvious, especially if restricted to one minute every two hours - or if none of the predicted frequencies work.

*

BOWMAN was contracted in September 2003. In September 2006 it was still in its test and evaluation phase. The Infantry did not want it. To much acclaim from his men, Director of Infantry Brigadier Jamie Balfour had stated:

'All the rumours. It is as bad as you've heard. But we have been told that, politically, we have got to make it work. Now you guys will have to go out and find a way of making it work. Hang on to your cell phones'.

Perhaps more fundamentally, BOWMAN did not truly cater for sky-wave propagation, so would be limited in theatres such as Afghanistan unless a decision was made to procure the correct antennae. HF typically requires at least six types, for different situations. And the correct antenna permits lower power consumption.

In 1999 a programme had been initiated to replace or enhance BOWMAN HF with a Low Probability of Intercept/Low Probability of Detection system, providing real-time frequency acquisition. That is, to reduce or eliminate the need to poll, and guarantee the message would get through first time.

It cannot be overemphasised how extraordinary this was - a formal requirement based on the premise BOWMAN (a £2.5Bn+ programme) would not be good enough was political dynamite.

Worse, BOWMAN was delayed by many years, so this replacement programme became an embarrassment. Even when due to arrive *after* BOWMAN, it was such a hot potato the BOWMAN project team refused to touch or even acknowledge it. As it was at first intended for 'specialist' units, it was given to a 'specialist' team. However, again, everyone gave it a body swerve, because it would bring one into immediate conflict with superiors, who would be furious if it was delivered *before* BOWMAN. The increasing casualty rate was overlooked.

*

No progress had been made in four years. In April 2003, the new Communications, Intelligence, Surveillance and Reconnaissance Integrated Project Team Leader, a Special Forces Colonel, decided he needed someone with nothing to lose, and approached an experienced engineer who was working part-time due to critical health issues. Asked if he knew how to proceed, he replied the solution was already in service with both RN and RAF, and would speak to Marlborough Communications Ltd (MCL) and seek a loan. This was duly arranged; and it would be remiss not to mention their military marketing director, former Royal Signals Captain Shane Knight, now Managing Director.

So important was the capability to the users, a Warrant Officer was extracted from theatre and flown back to the UK for the trials, which were successful. Fifteen sets (ample for the unit involved, which must remain unnamed) were loaned free of charge and deployed to Afghanistan in September 2003 - three weeks before the main BOWMAN contract was let. And, bearing in mind the antenna issue mentioned above, the unit's Rhode and Schwartz broadband antenna had been bought at a boot sale from mess funds, for £2k (a bargain). This is by no means unique. The unit who later relieved them in theatre were 'sponsored' by a small firm in Yorkshire, supplying them with specialist antennae stitched into their clothing, used to communicate while conducting High Altitude High Opening parachute insertions.

At a January 2005 press briefing, the General Officer Commanding called this *'the comms system of choice in Afghanistan'* - another swipe at BOWMAN. Nobody asked why there was a choice. The reason was, there were least three separate project teams buying radios to meet the same requirement. One had already delivered the best solution. Another was delivering something two generations older that the Infantry didn't want. And a third had specified something the Infantry couldn't use.

*

Having delivered, the project manager now had to seek approval to initiate the programme. (Something else to think about). At the time (2003), MoD had abandoned its previous efficient delegation and approvals system, and 15 people now had to read and approve his plans. Fourteen were reasonably quick, most admitting that, as they were non-technical and didn't understand the issues, they simply rubber-stamped. (You might well ask why they had this role). However, the last was on extended leave and due back in five weeks. When he returned, his only comment was the project manager had typed a double full-stop (..), which must be corrected. This, on a programme whose sole aim was to improve communications and situational awareness, reducing casualties. (You might well ask why he was employed).

This one example exposes many of the day-to-day problems encountered by MoD's procurers.

*

There is a linkage to the Identification Friend or Foe (IFF) and Sea King ASaC Mk7 sagas outlined earlier. A civilian recipient of the High Intensity Strobe Light report issued instructions this comms programme was to be cancelled, as it necessitated a small degree of systems integration. He deemed such a risk intolerable, even after the equipment was deployed successfully in-theatre - a not dissimilar attitude to that adopted by his old project team in 1998-99, when they refused to integrate IFF failure warnings. (You might well ask why his post was necessary, if the project manager could just ignore him and do the right thing).

The real issue, of course, is what capability servicemen are doing without due to this approach. What if *they* said, *too much hassle, let's give up.*

Batteries

Power, in general, is termed a 'critical enabling technology'; for obvious reasons. Without it, much equipment won't work.

What MoD concealed from families and Coroner was the background to Mr Walker's comment about battery shortages. At the time (2006) BOWMAN Lithium-Ion radio batteries had been the subject of a recall and destruction order, due to what MoD euphemistically called *'flaming events'*. (That is, Lithium-Ion cells igniting). Replacement began the following year. Other project offices had long regarded this recall as inevitable.

The battery specification called for internal electronics (state of charge sensing and indication) to be potted (encapsulated with a waterproof compound) and the case fully welded, to prevent water ingress. Anecdotally, they were unpotted and crimped; leading to electrical short circuits and the batteries violently igniting. The effect is like a large Roman Candle and lasts many minutes. As the batteries are in the radio, in a pouch, and not easily removed, the operator can be severely burned. The recall critically depleted battery supplies, at a time when military demands had the world's factories at full capacity.

When a Freedom of Information request about these flaming events was submitted in August 2006, a Brigadier replied. [61] This was extraordinary, as requests are usually dealt with at the lowest level possible. The only inference one can draw is he wanted to ensure the truth, as far as he was able to reveal it, was out there.

*

Turning to charging, the batteries were specified to be charged 500 times, which meant designing a compatible charger. When a battery is recharged it will not go back to full charge, and over time this results in reduced capacity. Typically, one would seek x recharging cycles to 80% of original charge. If a battery is exhausted, safety circuitry kicks in to safeguard its cells; so, the charger will indicate a fault condition and reject it. The BOWMAN batteries failed after only a few attempts at charging, and could not be recovered from deep discharge.

There are two main types of charger; one portable and using direct current (e.g. mounted in a vehicle), the other alternating current and used in buildings. Here, the batteries and chargers were not designed as an integrated system. The sudden demand for replacement batteries could not be met. Worse, directives were issued that procurers continue using the same supplier, when other UK-based suppliers had proven systems at a fraction of the price.

*

At the same time (2005-6) a requirement was being put out to tender by the Dismounted Close Combat team (DCC), to develop a Portable Power System for infantrymen. Bidders were to propose a method of maturing existing technologies, in a word-capped submission. There were many possibilities (batteries, fuel cells, hybrids, micro-generators, etc.), using many chemistries. The cap meant each could only be addressed in broad terms.

However, one supplier (as above) was given access to a 2004 Defence Scientific Advisory Council (DSAC) report, which set out MoD's preferred technology.[62] (The DSAC reports directly to the Secretary of State for Defence). That is, they had the exam answers. Moreover, they alone were given briefings by DCC. MoD and DSAC refused to provide

---

61 Letter Defence Procurement Agency BLD/3/10, 5 September 2006.
62 Report D/DSAC/65/2, 4 March 2004. 'Portable Power Sources and Energy Storage for Future Soldier and similar Land Battle Technology'.

the report to other bidders, or under Freedom of Information.[63] The advantage was clear, and a 3-year Research and Development contract was awarded; despite another bidder undertaking to satisfy the first of three phases with an off-the-shelf product (not the technical paper or prototype requested by MoD), and complete the entire programme within one year.

So, MoD chose to ignore a bid from a reputable supplier, which promised a <u>faster, cheaper and better</u> capability, in favour of one who did not. These are (were) the three strands of MoD's 'Smart Procurement' initiative. Senior endorsement would be needed to ignore such a bid. Hansard is revealing, offering clues such as favourable parliamentary statements and, later, Executive Directorships for a former Defence Minister.

This losing bidder notified DCC their bid would realise savings of over £100M if MoD would consider specifying the same working voltage across several equipment programmes. The company had spotted that Portable Power System, BOWMAN and Future Integrated Soldier Technology (FIST) specified different voltages. This was particularly inept, as FIST was also a DCC programme. DCC did not reply, although changed specifications without crediting the company.

DCC's commercial manager declined to meet the company, but did write saying their bid had been marked down for assuming Portable Power System was to work with BOWMAN and FIST. In fact, the Invitation to Tender, issued in her name, said:

'Item 17 - The programme shall address the requirements for interfacing the portable power systems with other power consuming systems, including connectivity, power control circuits, etc. for FIST, BOWMAN and Special Projects systems'.

Moreover, her tender assessment scheme allocated 20 of 100 available points to agreeing Terms & Conditions and Intellectual Property Rights - which are mostly statements of fact and acceptance. But, only <u>one</u> point to safety - at a time when troops were being injured and killed due to defective and unsafe batteries.

The company appealed to the Defence Procurement Agency's Commercial Director (Mr Stan Porter who, in 2002, had failed to act on advice that Tornado should be made safe - discussed earlier), copying the appeal letter to the Minister for Defence Procurement, Lord

---

63 Letter D/CST/06/01/10/04, 17 November 2005.

Drayson. It was rejected. MoD's Codes of Commercial Practice were ignored.[64]

Today, 13 years on, it is unclear when this 3-year programme will be delivered.

Combat Search and Rescue (CSAR)

What differentiates CSAR from 'ordinary' SAR? Rescue is largely down to a suitable aircraft and trained aircrew, important features being endurance and night flying capability. Combat describes the environment - the enemy will be close by, so by definition it is a military role and requires an ability to protect and survive; typical features being Kevlar flooring/seats and Defensive Aids Suites. All this is well understood and easy to achieve, given resources, political will, and a sense of duty of care. Search is where matters become slightly complex. CSAR will often be a task force, requiring fixed wing ground attack, air-to-air refuelling, and airborne command and control.

Let us concentrate on the physical rescue. Military SAR was conducted by RN Sea King HAR Mk5 and RAF Sea King HAR Mk3/3A, with rescue of fast jet ejectees their primary role. Chinook was unsuitable as none had rescue hoists. One reason why is because they couldn't. Problems, including variations in wiring, and performance of hydraulic pumps, meant a hoist simply wouldn't work. In fact, the RAF had no stated requirement for hoists in Chinooks. [65] MoD claimed the lack of capability was because all hoists had been returned to the UK for servicing.

Even in tertiary role hoists are fitted to other aircraft, emphasising Chinook should be regarded as the last, and quite limited, resort. But such is the abrogation of duty, and dearth of capability, it is now the primary SAR asset; the Sea King SAR Force having been disbanded in February 2016. There remains no dedicated CSAR capability.

Therefore, the UK had to rely on the US. But over five hours were wasted trying to persuade senior commanders to authorise deployment, suggesting the US did not sign up to the UK's assumptions.

*

---

64 MoD/Industry Commercial Policy Group, Guideline Number 5, Defence Acquisition - The Commercial Framework, Best Codes of Practice, September 2001.

65https://publications.parliament.uk/pa/cm200708/cmhansrd/cm080623/text/80623w0 011.htm.

What the Board of Inquiry did not mention, and the media did not ask about, was MoD's official policy on CSAR.

In the early 1980s, all three Services were continuing to press for a dedicated capability. By 1985 the decision had been made to proceed. Detailed plans were drawn up that would see the first aircraft converted in the UK by Westland Helicopters, the remainder in Cyprus by a Westland working party.

In early 1986, the annual Search and Rescue policy meeting was convened in Empress State Building, London, chaired by an Air Commodore. Progress was reported as satisfactory, when a 'beancounter' entered the room. He opened a flipchart showing a map of the UK (a typical BBC weather map, with Orkney and Shetland in a box off the Northumberland coast). He announced the range of a helicopter (he didn't differentiate between Wessex and Sea King) was 400 miles (not particularly accurate for either), so had drawn circles of 200 miles radius (200 out, 200 back) around each SAR station. Where there was overlap, one station was to close; his assumption being that one simply flew to the single victim, winched him on board and turned for home (bypassing the 'search' part).

Faced with such jaw-dropping stupidity, those present were rendered speechless. As he stood to leave, attendees finally found their voice - *'Time on task!'* He walked out. Fighting this base closure policy immediately became the highest SAR priority, and CSAR was forgotten (doubtless part of the plan). The fight was lost and capability further reduced.

Analysis

This case illustrates many of the issues discussed:

- It is not general MoD policy for our Services to be interoperable with each other, never mind allies.
- The lack of, or the wrong, equipment and capability, is often caused by poorly stated requirements, not lack of funding.
- The insistence on savings and shortcuts at the expense of safety, when it is invariably faster, cheaper and better to follow the regulations.
- The need for better programmatic integration, instead of parallel programmes with the same aim, or new teams formed to develop a capability that has been in service for years.

The Board of Inquiry report has never been released to the public, although an advance copy given to families was shown to The Guardian, and extracts reported. Senior Reviewing Officer General Andrew Farquhar, General Officer Commanding 5 Division, remarked:

'I find it disturbing that, in an area of operations where there is such a marked mine threat, there are no UK-equipped rotary wing airframes that can provide guaranteed availability and an immediate casualty extraction capability'.

In 2007 Colonel Paul Parker, an experienced combat surgeon, wrote in the Royal Army Medical Corps Journal:

'In Vietnam, wounded soldiers arrived in hospital within 25 minutes of injury. In Iraq in 2005, that figure was 110 minutes, on Operation Herrick IV [Afghanistan 2006] the average pre-hospital time was seven hours. A casualty evacuation request has to go through too many layers of command. There seems little point in providing high-technology in-hospital care when our patients still take several hours to travel a few miles to us'.

What did the threat assessment say? The existence of the minefield was well-known, but not marked on the maps given to UK troops; which is perhaps the primary mitigation if the resources aren't available to clear it. Comment is difficult, because MoD simply avoids the issue.

But a conscious decision was made, many times, not to provide a viable CSAR capability, suitable batteries or the correct radios. What little capability available was not fit for purpose. Who was most at risk if the threat materialised? The foot soldier. But he was not represented when any of these decisions were made.

23: Hercules C-130K XV179 - Iraq, 30 January 2005

Chief Technician Richard Brown
Flight Sergeant Mark Gibson
Lance Corporal Steven Jones, Royal Signals
Squadron Leader Patrick Marshall
Master Aircraftsman Gary Nicholson
Sergeant Robert O'Connor
Flight Lieutenant Paul Pardoel, Royal Australian Air Force
Flight Lieutenant Andrew Smith
Flight Lieutenant David Stead
Corporal David Williams

At 1620 local time on 30 January 2005, Hercules C-130K XV179 took off from Baghdad. It was to fly at low level to Balad, 50 miles to the north, to deliver freight and two passengers. Twenty-five miles out the aircraft was shot down, probably by Sunni insurgents, killing all 10 on board. At the time, it was the largest single loss of life suffered by the British military during Operation Telic.

US Apache helicopters located the crash site 45 minutes after the distress call. As the site was in a hostile area, the priority was to recover human remains, personal effects and classified material. By 3 February the site had been looted. It was decided not to attempt further recovery.

The Board of Inquiry was convened on 31 January 2005, and reported in August. It concluded the aircraft had been shot down by ground fire. An inert projectile had penetrated the starboard wing fuel tank, causing a fire. The subsequent explosion, leading to the loss of 23 feet of wing, including the aileron, rendered the aircraft uncontrollable. The Board found there were contributory factors; primarily, lack of fire retarding technology in the fuel tanks.

Explosion Suppressant Foam (ESF)
The Lockheed C-130 was developed in the 1950s. ESF has been standard fit since the late 1960s. It is a reticulated polyurethane foam, enabling fuel to pass through readily while preventing flames spreading, confining ignition to the immediate area of the ignition source if the

tank is ruptured. At MoD's insistence, no RAF C-130s had ESF. The known risk had not been reduced to tolerable and As Low As Reasonably Practicable.

*

As the Coroner's Inquest loomed, Bernard Collaery QC, representing the widow of Flight Lieutenant Paul Pardoel, RAAF, made himself known to, and sought advice from, various campaigners who were working on Nimrod XV230 and Chinook ZD576. Two significant events followed.

First, and despite MoD claims it was only made aware of ESF after the accident, Mr Collaery was provided with two MoD specifications, DTD5627 and DTD5624; clear evidence the general vulnerability had been recognised by MoD and mitigation developed. Each were so old they had been superseded in 1982. Coroners tend to take heed of actual documents over claims they don't exist.

Second, on 6 May 2008 Mr Collaery and the Coroner's Special Investigator were provided with an analysis, including a brief extract from Defence Standard 00-970, Part 1/5, Section 9, Vulnerability to Battle Damage:

> 'The Chief Designer SHALL consult with the Integrated Project Team Leader and establish whether, and how, the vulnerability of the aeroplane Defined and Specified Threat Effects will be assessed and consider how subsequent design changes, if any, will be introduced'.

The Table of Defined Threat Effects includes inert bullets, inert fragments and incendiary bullets. That is, one does not have to think too hard. Having identified the threat and effect there must be a mitigation plan (e.g. fit ESF). The decision whether or not to implement it, and the rationale underpinning the decision, must be recorded. To aid the decision, 00-970 calls up the above specifications.

It transpired a 2002 Tactical Analysis Team report had reiterated the need for ESF. Shortly before the Iraq war, in 2003 another report repeated this, but was again ignored. RAF crews were not told of the extent of the risk, information that might have helped formulate alternative tactics. MoD denied all knowledge of the reports, until retired witnesses such as Squadron Leader Chris Seal and Flight Lieutenant Nigel Gilbert came forward, forcing it to back down. In fact, the latter was detained by MoD security forces on the steps of the court building, to prevent him giving evidence. A clear case of witness intimidation.

197

After sitting for 16 days, upon receiving this undermining evidence the Wiltshire and Swindon Coroner, David Masters, adjourned the Inquest on 25 April 2008 to allow MoD to consider its position. When it reconvened on 30 September 2008, MoD submitted a brief paper unconditionally admitting liability. It had been caught lying - in itself never a concern to MoD, so there had to be another reason. By this time it was well-known Nimrod XV230 had suffered from the same shortcomings - the only difference was the failure to implement a different paragraph in the same section of the regulations.

Mr Masters ruled the 10 servicemen were unlawfully killed and *'serious systemic failures'* in the RAF had robbed them of *'their opportunity for survival'*. He said the Hercules community felt *'it had let itself down'* and (a named officer) felt *'ashamed'* he didn't know of this vulnerability or appreciate the threat. Seasoned observers knew he took the hit for his superiors, who did not appear in court. A familiar story. Those present would think a Group Captain 'senior' and 'in command', but in 2008 he could not be held responsible for decisions made many years previously.

Allies or associates?

Mr Masters expressed frustration with the US military, saying their reluctance to co-operate with the inquest was *'difficult to comprehend'*. Besides an Iraqi man who gave varying accounts of the plane coming down, US servicemen were the only eyewitnesses. Their authorities refused to authorise interviews, and they were not permitted to attend the inquest. Mr Masters:

> *'I just wonder, as an aside, what if the boot had been on the other foot - if a US aircraft had come down with the loss of 10 lives and the only eyewitnesses had been British forces'.*

The detailed background to these general concerns is set out in the Chilcot Report (2016). But it was the Oxford Coroner, Andrew Walker, who pushed the issue. Prior to the Inquest into the 'friendly fire' death of Lance Corporal Matty Hull, killed on 28 March 2003, he ruled that a heavily redacted US report was inadmissible in evidence, because no US representative would be in court to explain it. This forced the government to press the US, to no avail.

Mr Walker then stated he wanted to use a video recording of the incident, taken by a US A-10 Thunderbolt aircraft, which he had been provided with as part of the Board of Inquiry data. MoD had told the family that no video existed.

On 4 February 2007, Harriet Harman MP stated:

'My letters haven't proved successful, phone calls haven't proved successful, requests from the coroners haven't. It's just not fair on the relatives to sit in on an inquest and to know that they can't ask questions. They're entitled to know the truth from our allies'.

Intriguingly, the tape was leaked to The Guardian the following day. Only then did the US gave permission for it to be viewed; but only by the family, the Coroner and MoD.

Mr Walker ruled Matty Hull was unlawfully killed.

Evidence of the Hercules Integrated Project Team Leader (IPTL), Coroner's Inquest, 15 October 2008

It would be unfair to name this RAF officer. It was clear from his tone and manner he was genuinely distraught over the deaths, and answered the questions as honestly as possible. However, he was unable to describe relevant processes or procedures. This was not a personal failing. MoD will not tolerate anyone who knows the answers appearing in court.

The following are abridged contemporaneous notes taken in shorthand by Sean Maffett, a highly respected aviation journalist.

Coroner - *'Does the IPT have a strong airworthiness and safety culture, with risk management system and hazard log?'*

IPTL - *'We identify what can go wrong, look at results, and put in place responses that will stop that causing loss of life. eCassandra is used to keep those hazards to an acceptable level. We used to deal with safety in more absolute way. Now we look at likelihood of risk happening'.*

Perhaps not expressed well, but a belief that eCassandra (a database for hosting Hazard Log data) is used to keep those hazards to an acceptable level is dangerously close to the notion, taught to MoD staff from the mid-1990s, that it is sufficient to populate the Risk Register, but actual risk mitigation can be ignored. The likelihood of risk occurring is <u>always</u> assessed. This comes across as an attempt to persuade the court MoD is doing things better. In fact, he is saying he now implements policy, whereas *his predecessors did not.*

Coroner - *'Fitness for purpose concept. Knowing what we know now, would the aircraft have been tasked to do that job?'*

IPTL - *'I have responsibility to ensure the aircraft is airworthy. Fitness for purpose resides with operators, not us. We kind of misused the fitness for purpose ideas when we approached industry to provide our aircraft with the Safety Case'.*

The team leader divorces himself from a large part of the process, ignoring the requirement for continuous feedback, review, assurance and improvement. *'Approached industry'* to provide a Safety Case is odd phraseology. Unbroken contractual cover is required, to maintain the Build Standard and Safety Case.

Bernard Collaery QC, for Mrs Kellie Merritt - *'Why didn't the Safety Case include Explosion Suppressant Foam until after 2005?'*

IPTL - *'The Safety Case doesn't include fit for purpose. It's not part of our consideration'.*

This is wrong. The Safety Case must address <u>all</u> uses and the associated Build Standards. Only if the Operational Commander makes an in-theatre, first-time decision to operate outside the Release to Service can there be no expectation the Safety Case will cover the use. In such cases the Commander must state his reasoning, and the 'system' catches up when the team leader is informed. In-theatre one does what is necessary to succeed, but the more mundane act of reporting and feedback is nonetheless vital. But this does not apply in this case, as ESF was consciously rejected by MoD. It is unlikely Lockheed would omit mention of the residual risk in Safety Case Reports. Misunderstanding this concept taints much of his evidence.

Bernard Collaery QC - *'How is the Vulnerability Assessment done?'*

IPTL - *'Responsibility for vulnerability is for front line command and Director of Equipment Capability. They come to us to ensure it. My role is airworthiness. I don't know what they do, nor where they do it. That's their responsibility'.*

This is wrong. Vulnerability is a basic component of airworthiness, and Defence Standard 00-970 <u>requires</u> the team leader to initiate the Vulnerability Assessment with the aircraft's Chief Designer. If a new threat or vulnerability is identified, the Safety Case is reviewed.

Bernard Collaery QC - *'If you had known what you now know, would you have done something?'*

IPTL - *'I'm not allowed to do that'.*

This is wrong. Not only is he allowed, he is obliged. However, in practice a Group Captain would have had no exposure to such routine matters. This is a job for his junior civil servants.

Bernard Collaery QC - *'How do you reconcile your evidence with the requirement for you to consult with the Design Authority over survivability issues?'*

Jonathan Glasson QC, for MoD - *'This is not a question for the team leader'.*

This is wrong. It is a fundamental part of the team leader's job. That MoD briefed Mr Glasson to interject at this specific question reveals Mr Collaery has got to the nub of the issue. It is unclear if Mr Glasson knew he had seriously misled the court. His client did.

Bernard Collaery QC - *'The IPT had no role in knowing what the flight profile is?'*

IPTL - *'No, I am only interested in flight profile for fatigue purposes. But not where it goes. In airworthiness terms, low level across Afghan mountains is same as low level in Welsh mountains'.*

This is wrong. *'Where it goes'* is part of the Statement of Operating Intent and Usage, and the Release to Service includes sections on what environmental conditions (cold, snow, ice, precipitation, heat, etc.) the aircraft is cleared for. The team leader must maintain the integrity of those clearances, requiring his constant involvement. Most obviously, the sandy conditions of Afghanistan are more detrimental to the aircraft (through abrasion) than the temperate maritime climate of Wales. He must understand these effects and make provision for increased maintenance costs (although, again, this is a task for his most junior civil servant engineer).

Bernard Collaery QC - *'Who is working with operators monitoring vulnerability of aircraft to threats?'*

IPTL - *'2 Group would go to QinetiQ, the Defence Science and Technology Laboratory, or other users, to get understanding of vulnerability. They would not talk to engineers - it's an operator thing'.*

Again, this is wrong. Defence Standard 00-970 places the onus on the team leader to lead on this subject with the Chief Designer, and conduct continuous through-life assessment to ensure the Safety Case remains valid. In a more basic sense, he is wrong because airworthiness is an engineering discipline. There is seemingly no understanding airworthiness facilitates fitness for purpose. That is, if airworthiness has not been attained, or a process is not in place for it to be maintained, the aircraft cannot be declared airworthy and should not be in theatre for a fitness for purpose decision to be made.

John Cooper QC, for some other families - *'At the January 2002 meeting, we see who was there, but shouldn't the IPT have been there?'*

IPTL - *'No, the sponsor knew the subject was survivability and vulnerability, so wouldn't have invited the IPT. I believe the right people were there (not us, though)'.*

As above, he is wrong to say his team should not have been at a meeting discussing vulnerability and survivability. Any decision would require re-assessment of the Safety Case, which he is responsible for. Seldom, if ever, would the team leader himself attend such meetings. Again, it is a routine task for his junior staff. In fact, so routine it is possible he was oblivious to the entire process. Whether he had the necessary staff was not mentioned.

*

On 30 October 2008 Mr Masters wrote to Bob Ainsworth MP, Minister for the Armed Forces, setting out his recommendations; most of which amounted to *implement regulations*. One was:

'No scientifically legitimate and consistent recommendation on a safety issue such as the fitting of Explosion Suppressant Foam should be ignored or not acted upon'.

He reminded Mr Ainsworth he was obliged to reply within 56 days, in which he should detail *'action that has been taken or which is proposed should be taken'*. After a reasonable time, on 10 June 2009 Steve Webb MP asked what progress was being made. On 25 June 2009 Mr Ainsworth's successor, Bill Rammell MP, replied:

'There are currently 14 Hercules C-130K aircraft in service with the RAF. All of these are airworthy and safe to fly'.

He did not mention the newer, larger C-130J fleet, or whether this meant the C-130Ks were now fitted with ESF, or they were just not being exposed to this risk any more. They were removed from service in 2013.

Summary

Here we are, at an Inquest in 2008, discussing systemic failings notified by civilian staff from 1988-on; and by the Director of Flight Safety in a series of airworthiness reviews between 1992 and 1998.

It is inconceivable Lockheed did not submit a proposal to retro-fit ESF. As the base C-130 design included ESF, their Safety Case could not be reconciled with the RAF's. They would highlight this regularly, and pester MoD to meet its own regulations. It would be seriously remiss not to.

Mr Masters:

'I believe that the ability to retrieve and view documents that record key

202

decisions as not just important, but essential - equally important is the rationale behind them. This Inquest has been plagued by an inability to retrieve documents'.

Two years later, Lord Philip encountered the same problem during his Mull of Kintyre Review. Like Mr Masters, he was helped by (the same) members of the public providing documents MoD had denied the existence of. Most, including the ESF specifications, were downloaded from MoD's own website - raising serious questions about the competence of MoD's investigations, and its intent when lying to the court and families.

Despite being exposed so many times, MoD continues to act in the same vein. This denial of evidence is not a one-off that can be dismissed as an error. It is constantly repeated. At what point does this become perverting the course of justice or even perjury? The judiciary, Crown Prosecution Service, Crown Office, police and Ministry of Justice are aware of all this, and condone it.

*

It is little known that, after the Inquest, bereaved families sued MoD. A multi-million pound settlement was reached. This cost, and that of the lost aircraft, far exceeded that of fitting ESF.

The cost in human lives was immeasurable.

Annex to Chapter 23: The Hercules Airworthiness Review Team (1997)

The Hercules Airworthiness Review Team (HEART) was one of a series conducted by the Inspectorate of Flight Safety (RAF) in the 1990s. On 8 November 2011 MoD denied the existence of HEART, only providing its report upon appeal. In it, the Director of Flight Safety <u>again</u> warned the RAF Chief Engineer and the Assistant Chief of the Air Staff of systemic failures.

HEART characterised the Cloud and Collision Warning Radar (CCWR) as the *'principle airworthiness hazard to the routine operation of the aircraft'*, criticising its reliability. In fact, the evidence cited below demonstrates it met MoD's reliability requirements, comparing favourably with other airborne radars. The problem was <u>availability</u> and <u>maintainability</u>, brought about by the Air Member Supply and Organisation policies mentioned earlier.

Extracts from HEART report relating to CCWR

'The Hercules' Ecko [sic - EKCO, Eric Kirkham Cole Limited] *E290 radar has been a <u>long-standing flight safety concern</u>. The Hercules has been cleared to operate in conditions of only light to moderate icing. There is a clear need for a reliable radar to enable crews to identify and avoid heavy cumulus type cloud formations. <u>This requirement is essential to flight safety</u>.*

Over a two-year period up to March 1997, a Mean Time Between Arisings (MTBA) rate of only 61 hours had been recorded. Moreover, many failures either could not be reproduced on the ground or were intermittent.

The HEART understood that there had been various poorly orchestrated efforts since as long ago as 1986 to justify the procurement of a replacement system on ill-founded "spend to save" reliability and maintainability grounds.

Ecko 290 CCWR is used satisfactorily on other aircraft types. The HEART considers that a thorough investigation should be undertaken to determine whether environmental improvements could be made to the Hercules installation which would improve the reliability of the present CCWR'.

What HEART termed CCWR is two distinct radars, each with numerous variants. Hercules was fitted with ARI 23175/1, commonly known as EKCO 290 or E290. The other version was ARI 23116 (EKCO 190 or E190). The essential difference being E290 was designated 'high power'.

The five-digit ARI (Airborne Radio Installation) number commencing with a '2' indicates equipment whose Intellectual Property Rights (IPR) reside with the manufacturer. By contrast, equipment originating from an MoD specification, and funded by MoD, would have a four or, latterly, five-digit number commencing with '5'. Today, equipments still have ARI numbers but they are simply sequential; the underlying meaning has been lost. Failure to understand this often leads to significant delays while attempts are made to compete work that should be single-tender due to IPR ownership.

The design was 38 years old at the time of HEART. It originally used Germanium technology, resulting in susceptibility to heat stresses. In 1961 a major modification saw the introduction of Silicon technology, but in the 1990s MoD still retained both standards. Care was needed to match technology with aircraft cooling arrangements.

Maintenance Policy

In the early 1980s, MEL (originally Mullard Equipment Ltd) advised the MoD project manager they no longer wanted to undertake CCWR repairs. They retained the IPR and remained Design Authority, providing advice and assistance (primarily technical bulletins) to the new contractor, Air Transport Charter (Ltd), Heathrow, who ran three repair lines; one for MoD, two for commercial users.

The Post Design Services contract still lay with MEL, but in 1991 the RAF commenced its rundown of airworthiness management in earnest. This was preceded by the 1987 policy not to provide spares to Fourth Line ('DM87', outlined earlier).

These policies are crucial to understanding HEART's concerns. Equipment shortages meant CCWR needed a one week Turn Round Time on its repair contract. Most stipulated six months. To achieve this, vast quantities of spares had to be on hand - over £3M worth at ATC (Ltd) alone (over £7M at today's prices). By denying the company these spares from January 1988-on, the contracted Turn Round Time could not be achieved. Pressure mounted on air stations to repair the kit themselves. But they, too, lacked spares; and in any case did not have the necessary tools, test equipment or training. (And a repair is not complete until verified using this test equipment). Nevertheless, they felt compelled to try, and throughout the 1990s many unauthorised and, in some cases, manifestly unsafe repairs were carried out.

Why not buy more kit? The answer lies in HEART's statement about seeking a replacement. Funding could not be made available for both. As soon as this intent was declared, any attempt to buy more CCWR would fail scrutiny, as one had to demonstrate five years useful life. The situation was partly eased by airlines agreeing MoD could 'borrow' their spares held at ATC (Ltd). But this was only a short-term agreement, as no small company could tolerate a situation whereby it was acting as MoD's procurer and intermediary with major airlines.

Issues raised by HEART

Perceived Unreliability

By the early 1990s, the RAF had a severe shortfall of E290 Transmitter Receivers (high power model M3051A). RAF Lyneham were advised by HQ Support Command they could fit a low power model, of which there was a surplus. However, this required two changes to the aircraft configuration, which were not always embodied. The low power variant required a different circuit breaker (to protect the aircraft wiring), and it was four inches shorter so the Mounting Tray required different anti-vibration mounts. With the wrong ones fitted the Transmitter Receiver could, eventually, shake itself to bits.

The approved aircraft fit was ARI 23175/1, but the actual fit was now a hybrid ARI 23116/23175, which was not reflected in drawings, publications or Safety Case. HEART noted many failures could not be reproduced on the ground. If, for example, the failure was induced by excessive vibration or heat, a static test on a bench could not replicate the airborne environment.

HEART noted the system Mean Time Between Arisings (MTBA) as 61 hours, implying this was low (poor). It did not explain what MTBA is, how it is calculated, or how this compared to other similar equipments using similar technology. Put simply, all avionic equipment provisioning starts with a baseline reliability assumption of 500 hours MTBA for a Line Replaceable Unit (LRU). However, the Provisioning Authority (the owner of the equipment) may offset the generally higher reliability of relatively simple systems like navigation or communications, with more susceptible systems such as radar; so is permitted to buy more of any LRU that falls short of 500 (which, for example, most radar transmitters do).

CCWR has eight LRUs, so a system MTBA of around 61 hours would be deemed fully acceptable. Justifying expenditure on a reliability programme would be difficult. For comparison, in 1989 the Sea Harrier radar (Blue Fox) had a system MTBA of 29 hours, considered first-rate by the FLEET Air Arm. At this time, the RAF Buccaneer radar (Blue Parrot) was four hours, and the subject of a multi-million pound reliability improvement programme to achieve seven. The latter is a good benchmark for radars of CCWR's vintage and technology; although Blue Parrot was more complex and one would expect CCWR to be better.

Maintenance at RAF Lyneham

Following the instruction to Engineering Authorities to curtail requests for Fault Investigations (part of the airworthiness rundown), Technical Agencies saw only omnibus requests. Serious fault notifications were saved up and only submitted for investigation when there were 20 or so similar arisings. One event sums up the situation...

In February 1990 the radar project manager received such an omnibus request on CCWR Scanner Gearboxes, a result of severe cracking discovered at RAF Lyneham. Immediate investigation was required. RAF suppliers, with their self-delegated engineering authority, refused. The project manager challenged this, but in turn they blamed him for this apparent decrease in reliability.[66][67] Quite how they thought he had achieved this was unclear. The situation was highly dangerous; resolved by ignoring them and suspending lower priority contracts to fund the work. (Not the first time I have noted this). However, this fire-fighting could not address the wider systemic failings and maladministration.

Environmental improvements to Hercules

HEART implied criticism of the aircraft installation design. But one must differentiate between the responsibilities of the Equipment/Aircraft Design Authorities and MoD, who must have them under suitable contract.

The key document is the Radio Installation Memorandum (RIM), maintained under Post Design Services. It provides the Aircraft Design Authority with the information required to design the installation and interfaces, listing all Line Replaceable Units and their cooling requirements, wiring considerations, limitations on proximity to

---

66 Letter Directorate of Air Radio 30/18/4/24, 10 April 1990.
67 Letters D/DDSM 13(RAF)/302/204/8 (various).

magnetic fields, etc.

When MoD issues a Statement of Operating Intent and Usage, it is the responsibility of bidders and project office to ensure the proposed equipment, the aircraft design, and RIMs can be reconciled. In other words, what is suitable in one aircraft may not be in another. HEART touches on this briefly when noting CCWR was fitted to other aircraft, apparently without the levels of problems faced in Hercules. But the comment lacks context, and omits that by 1992 the RAF had ceased maintaining RIMs. By the time of HEART, the C-130 installation could not be reconciled with the RIM or Safety Case.

Attempts to replace CCWR

HEART was correct to say such attempts were made. But, in practice, when subjected to Requirement Scrutiny they would be rejected because the scrutineer would have access to the information outlined above. That is, the RAF claimed CCWR was unreliable but the facts proved otherwise. If, however, a case were made to 'spend to save' it would be more likely to succeed; primarily because equipment numbers had been allowed to fall and the Build Standard needed stabilising. But that would require admitting why the Build Standard had lapsed, revealing culpability for airworthiness failures and deaths.

Post-HEART actions

As ever, most of HEART's 85 recommendations can be summarised *implement mandated policy*. However, there is a record, albeit partial, of action being taken. On 14 January 1998 the RAF Director of Flight Safety wrote to the MoD(PE) aircraft project office (Directorate of Military Aircraft Projects) and various RAF Deputy Directors of Support Management outlining an action plan.

This was a positive step, as the recently retired RAF Chief Engineer, Air Chief Marshal Michael Alcock, had pointedly excluded these staff when issuing the first ART's terms of reference. (The Chinook Airworthiness Review Team, which reported the same systemic failings in August 1992).

Now, the Director of Flight Safety reminded the Assistant Chief of the Air Staff (ACAS) that he must mitigate or accept the CCWR risks. This was a key aspect of the Mull of Kintyre case, where the previous ACAS simply ignored the 1992 Chinook ART report and the fact the aircraft was not airworthy. Were these actions taken with the Mull of Kintyre tragedy in mind? At the very least, it seems likely the Director of Flight Safety saw Alcock's retirement as an overdue opportunity to meet legal obligations.

*

It is important not to view HEART in isolation. It was the latest in a series of reports by concerned Directors of Flight Safety - Chinook, Wessex, Tornado, Harrier, Nimrod, Puma (twice). Their increasing irritation at lack of action is evident, which would have been more vociferous had they known of the policy to run down airworthiness. And, that MoD(PE) staff had been voicing precisely the same concerns, and making the same recommendations, for nearly 10 years.

24: The grounding of Air Cadet glider fleets (2014-on)

The Military Aviation Authority (MAA) was created in April 2010, consolidating several remaining airworthiness functions but not resurrecting important disbanded posts, so was immediately constrained. While it initiated audits of aircraft offices, malpractice was overlooked or just not recognised. Much trumpeted, these audits missed the point that the assurance they were meant to provide must be continuous, not a reluctant response to problems identified by members of the public.

No lessons were learned, and on 17 April 2014 the Glider Delivery Duty Holder issued an Advice Note acknowledging the glider fleets (powered and conventional), providing flying experience to civilian Air Cadets aged 13-18, were not airworthy. [68] It listed *'significant'* airworthiness issues, but was otherwise remarkably thin on detail. Important questions arose:

- It did not mention the Aircraft Design Authority. Were they not involved?

- Why were unauthorised maintenance and modification activities, and lack of independent inspections, not picked up by routine audits; not to mention day-to-day supervision?

- Who did not progress Special Instructions (Technical) and Unsatisfactory Feature Reports effectively?

- What were the 'other contributing factors' of which there were a 'significant number'?

- The Regulator had failed in its duty. Who regulates the Regulator?

The Delivery Duty Holder said it was *'pleasing'* the airworthiness process had *'proven its design utility'*. Did he not appreciate all that had happened was people had been compelled to carry out their legal obligations? He proposed two *'courses of action'*. Pause flying (a euphemism for grounding) or continue flying. How about - *those responsible should never again be put in charge of anything remotely connected with aviation.*

*

In early 2017 an MAA report became available revealing a full-blown audit was conducted in December 2013. No.2 Flying Training School

---

68 Duty Holder Advice Note 20140417 - DHAN/86.

failed - miserably.[69] The positive spin in the 2014 Advice Note was exposed as an attempted cover-up.

It seems this 2013 audit was prompted by a December 2012 study 'Review of Air Cadet Organisation Flying and Gliding'. Primarily discussing the future of gliding, it also provided warnings of serious engineering deficiencies going back many years. (The two are linked. If the engineering problems are not fixed, there can be no future). In isolation bad enough. But when viewed with the Director of Flight Safety's airworthiness reports of 1992-98, it becomes inexcusable dereliction of duty.

Officer Commanding No.2 Flying Training School's response was to blame *'lack of resources'*. He proposed *'obtain more resources'* and to set up offices of people dedicated to producing the *'airworthiness assurance'* documentation required by the MAA regulations. This type of response is unhelpful, and overlooked two things. This assurance was required long before the MAA was formed; and all the assurance in the world won't make an organisation do the right thing if it is not led properly. Lack of resources wasn't the root cause. It was a failure to carry out duty.

MoD dithered. The internet was rife with comments such as *gliders are simple, how difficult is it to get them flying* - the usual mistake of thinking serviceability and airworthiness are the same thing. Fingers pointed at the company contracted to carry out repairs. Few understood that, to make them serviceable, first the airworthiness baseline had to be stabilised after decades of neglect. That was MoD's responsibility.

Glider flying resumed in 2017, but with only a handful of aircraft. Three years had passed, illustrating how long such a resurrection can take. One can imagine the pain if a front line fleet had to be grounded. Better to do the job properly in the first place. But this was a token gesture by MoD. There was to be no long-term future, as further reductions were planned for 2019. MoD had been preparing the aircraft for sale, while misleading the cadets into thinking gliding would return to its former glory.

*

Unbelievably, matters got even worse, and on 6 May 2018 the RAF finally admitted defeat:

'The 2016 relaunch of Air Cadet Gliding stated we would operate up to 15

---

69 20160511 MAA 15 CAMO 0051 1 - Gliders Continuing Airworthiness Management Organisation Initial Approval Audit Report.

Vigilant powered gliders with an Out of Service Date (OSD) of October 2019, six having been recovered already. The recovery of remaining nine relied on an innovative recovery proposal from Grob Aircraft SE. This is no longer an option. The removal of this option, challenging technical support for two fleets, and low Vigilant availability mean that continued operation of Vigilant is no longer considered viable. Consequently, we will withdraw the Vigilant glider fleet from service immediately, bringing forward its planned OSD'.

To the uninitiated the blame was being heaped on the original manufacturer, Grob. In fact, they were not the appointed Design Authority for MoD's aircraft, so if their recovery plan was to be successful they would require access to engineering records from both MoD and the company it had employed to do some of the work of a Design Authority. But there were no such records, meaning there was no verifiable airworthiness audit trail. (For example, verifying the provenance of spare parts is always a concern). The task was no longer simple stabilisation and recovery, but major re-certification. MoD was not prepared to admit that for many years false declarations had been made that this work had been carried out and the data retained, so the aircraft had to go.

The important issue here is who holds and controls the Master Drawing Set. As Grob owned Intellectual Property Rights (IPR) on Vigilant motorgliders, if MoD did not want to contract them as Design Authority, or Grob did not want to be contracted, then either MoD had to purchase the IPR, or appoint a Design Custodian who would be directed to sub-contract Grob to provide a set of Secondary Masters and continued support. The latter is common on very old equipment, where the original manufacturer retains only a minimal support capability. (Cloud and Collision Warning Radar, in the previous chapter, is a good example). In this case, Grob refused to release proprietary information (which is their right, and again common, because the gliders remain a major source of business). They were not contracted, so by definition there was neither a Design Authority nor Design Custodian. It follows there could be no valid Safety Case reflecting the In-Use Build Standard.

Another aircraft fleet the victim of systemic airworthiness failings, negligence and maladministration. But why the immediate cessation of flying? First and foremost, this was another grounding. And, as ever, MoD tried to hide the real reason - that it had thrown in the towel, unwilling and unable to implement its own regulations.

But, yet again, the admission hid even worse failings. Many of the deficiencies were centralised functions. That is, they affect all MoD aircraft. Gliding was to be the sacrificial lamb to hide the fact that, <u>eight</u> years after being instructed to implement the recommendations of the Nimrod Review, MoD had failed to make any progress on the central point - the failure to implement mandated airworthiness regulations.

*

Regardless of motivation, the 2014 decision to ground was a good one. The Duty Holder had no choice. He was, and remains, much maligned by the Air Cadet fraternity, who never ask why his predecessors left him in this position.

In November 2011 Red Arrows pilot Flight Lieutenant Sean Cunningham was killed because orders had been issued not to service ejections seats in accordance with manufacturer's instructions, meaning his had not been checked for functionality. It inadvertently fired on the ground, and the main parachute did not deploy.

His Hawk shared the same Type Airworthiness Authority as gliders. Neither had a valid Safety Case, so neither had a valid Release to Service. Once again, years of prior negligence, and the fact these are systemic failings, has been overlooked. The Cunningham case was a recurrence, and so too is the glider grounding as it was the same regulations that were disregarded. The true culprits were protected, making further recurrence more likely.[70]

*

The truth is, MoD has been caught out. If a Hawk pilot dies because of this negligence then that is containable, with the help of government and legal authorities. But MoD knows there would be an outcry if <u>more</u> Air Cadets died.[71]

The upshot is Air Cadet gliding (and arguably the Air Cadet organisation itself) has been decimated, due to the same failings and violations reported in 1988 by MoD's civilian engineers, and throughout the 1990s by the RAF Director of Flight Safety. It is understood to be the RAF's longest ever grounding.

The cause, contributory factors and solution are not new. Like every Inquiry report mentioned herein, the solution can be summarised - *implement mandated regulations*. Almost two-thirds of the Volunteer

---

70 The death of Flight Lieutenant Sean Cunningham is the subject of *'Red 5'* (2019) by the author.

71 On 11 February 2009, two Cadets and two Instructors were killed in a mid-air collision over South Wales.

Gliding Schools were closed in 2016. There are none in Northern Ireland or Wales, one in Scotland, and nine in England. Most Air Cadets must now travel huge distances to gain experience. Yet, and for obvious reasons relating to the vagaries of the UK weather, gliding needs to be, as far as possible, a local activity. What can be more disheartening to a 13-year old than a long trudge home having wasted a week-end?

There is one positive. RAF leadership no longer has the appetite for placing thousands of schoolchildren at risk in sub-airworthy aircraft. Good - but brought about by self-interest, not a sense of duty. The glider fleets have been picked on, deemed the path of least pain. That is MoD at its worst. A decision designed to hide systemic failings. Almost any fleet could have been grounded for precisely the same reasons.

Supplement (2020)

It was announced in early 2020 that disability charity Aerobility had purchased 63 Vigilant motor gliders, aided by a Department for Transport grant.

'Despite the fleet being grounded in 2014 as part of the infamous Air Cadet flying 'pause' and subsequently deemed irrecoverable, it now seems that the aircraft can be recovered.

The first batch of ten aircraft is being modified and refurbished by German company Grob Aircraft SE - the original manufacturer and Design Authority - to meet civil certification standards. [Which MoD's standards must reflect]. The remaining aircraft will be engineered and recertified in the UK by Southern Sailplanes.

Aerobility is a UK charity that "helps all disabled people to experience the thrill of flying an aeroplane as a pilot, an experience that often proves profoundly transformative for the people involved". The purchase of the Vigilants, which will be helped by a grant from the Department for Transport [DfT], means that Aerobility will now be able to help about 2,600 people into the air every year, compared to 1,000 currently.

Modifications to allow the aircraft to achieve civil certification will include a new engine and propeller [the Rotax 912iS3] and the installation of the latest Garmin avionics to create a modern "glass cockpit". [Another way of saying they could not have been certified by MoD without undergoing similar work, raising further serious questions about its Continuing Airworthiness management obligation].

The refurbished Vigilants will be called the "Grob 109 Able", and the charity hopes the first aircraft will be ready to fly in the summer of 2021.

Aircraft that aren't required by Aerobility will be refurbished and sold to generate revenue for the charity and help them branch out into other parts of the British Isles. The machines to be sold on will also be fully refurbished, finished to the customer's specification and will be supported by a manufacturer's warranty.

The sale agreement will create four full-time engineering jobs, one project management role and one administration position at the charity'. [72]

This is the perfect job for an Apprentice Training Centre, and management of the work a typical task for a junior member of the project team to get his teeth into. No labour costs, no pressure to show a profit, and all the resources one needs immediately to hand. Today's staff in MoD will think this mad, but slightly older readers may recall the famed Embassy powerboat racing team of the 1970s. Much was made of their craft being fitted with aircraft jet engines. It was little known that these engines were life-expired (unsuitable for flight), but refurbished by teenage RN civilian apprentices and gifted to the team. But then reality sets in. The workshops have been privatised. The expertise is long gone, as is the imagination to think of something like that, or the long-term value of such an immensely satisfying task - both to the apprentices and MoD itself.

But the more obvious question is this. If MoD made no progress in six years, why is it these gliders can now be flying again in little more than a year? The answer is simple: Grob have been appointed Design Authority, and the new owners have accepted that the Vigilants must be re-certified. MoD could not afford to admit this, due to the inevitable knock-on effect on other aircraft fleets; initially those (e.g. Hawk) under the same Type Airworthiness Authority; and then the remainder, under the oversight of the Military Aviation Authority.

The clue to this thinking is the involvement of the Department for Transport. They are being used as a front, to isolate and protect MoD. MoD could not ask for money, because (a) it had already been provided and misspent, and (b) it would mean revealing the sheer scale of the problems caused by the decisions of senior officers. In any case, new money doesn't just appear; the process takes a minimum of two years. It would have to come from existing funds, which are needed to protect Hawks from the same fate, while hoping no-one complains about something as trivial as Air Cadets losing their capability. A gross naivety

---

72 https://ukga.com/news/view?contentId=48392

in today's internet age.

*

On 1 June 2020 a complaint was submitted to the Health and Safety Executive that, by permitting the above breaches of Military Airworthiness Regulations, MoD had endangered the lives of schoolchildren; and asked that an investigation be carried out.

On 4 June 2020 the Health and Safety Executive's Concerns Handling Officer, Mr Alan McGovern, replied:

> 'HSE does not regulate on matters of airworthiness, any concerns should be directed to - in this case of military owned and operated aircraft - the Military Aviation Authority or to the Defence Safety Authority - who are the independent defence safety regulator and investigators'.73

He had not been asked to regulate. He had been asked to investigate a failure to regulate. MoD was to continue as judge and jury in its own case.

---

73 E-mail 4 June 2020 14:37, from Health and Safety Executive.

PART 4: BEFORE IT GETS TOO LATE

'If, after attempting unsuccessfully to persuade those in power of their needs, the defence chiefs of staff are to remain silent, this would entail a serious breach of one of the cardinal principles of leadership; namely, the integrity of command. Most officers understand that, in any military organisation, the man at the top must remain loyal to the men at the bottom if he is to command their respect; if he cannot do that with a clear conscience, he should resign'.

Rear Admiral Ron Holley RN, CB

25: It's all about (the type of) people

In human nature there is a predisposition to regard others' statements as truthful. When perpetuated in the media, the public is quickly sucked in. In the cases outlined here, if the truth were heard in court families would be asking why the same old failings have not been corrected. But the judiciary routinely accepts being misled. It wants, perhaps even needs, to believe government officials will not deceive the court. MoD is emboldened in its contempt for legal obligations. It relies on the fact few are able to identify the lie. It wheels out a retired senior officer who appears credible, when in fact it is his rank and knighthood splashed on the screen that is persuasive to the average viewer. Few appreciate these officers are defending themselves, desperate to avoid the witness stand. They refuse to engage one-on-one. Invariably, the media declines to publish rebuttals.

This is such a complex and obscure scandal that, in truth, few can truly grasp its depth and extent. Concealing the offence is made easy. That is not just a breach of the Military Covenant. It is a full-frontal assault.

*

I have explained systematic breaches of the Covenant and how they are directly linked to avoidable deaths. The common denominator is refusal to carry out duty. That is nothing to do with experience or qualifications. It is about people and attitude. More specifically, it is about the type of person MoD eulogises. As so many deaths have been caused by these people flouting regulations, I suggest we look at the underlying ethos that permits this.

One reason I explored the Sea King ASaC Mk7 programme in detail was to illustrate the day-to-day obstacles faced by MoD staff. Conscious decisions were made, repeatedly, and by the same few, to abrogate responsibilities and ignore legal obligations. Let me be clear where I stand. These people should have been dismissed, and in some cases prosecuted. Failure to do so leaves servicemen at risk. In the commercial world their actions would not be tolerated. What would Rolls Royce do if, like the RN's Aircraft Support Executive, its main technical support department told its own programme manager for a new engine to push off, do it yourself? Sackings would follow, and any tribunal would uphold them. Similarly, what if the company falsely certified there had been successful testing and trials? Prison time would beckon.

An error can be rectified but flat refusal is more difficult, especially if the culture permits it. Irrefutably, those responsible cultivated this climate. When told of the inevitable outcome, they shut down dissenting voices and lied to cover it up. Their actions have been exposed in courts and by legal reviews, yet MoD glories in them and legal authorities remain indifferent. That is repugnant to the moral sense. Why act as they do? It is a form of madness. What sane person would place in writing that false declarations may be made that airworthiness regulations have been met? What kind of man sneers in the face of the person who tells him deaths have resulted?

As Sir Malcolm Rifkind MP, former Secretary of State for Defence, said:

'There is a culture of resentment at others seeking to second-guess RAF expertise. To acknowledge a mistake would hurt, and might reopen many policy questions. I am sure there are many who wish this whole issue would just go away. Yet it will not. There are basic issues of natural justice at stake. It is, in any event, no longer for the RAF or for the officials in the Ministry of Defence to decide. This sort of issue is exactly why we have ministers; why ministers are accountable to parliament and to the public for the actions of those under them'.[74]

He was speaking of the refusal of senior officers to acknowledge the truth in the Mull of Kintyre case. His words remain relevant. This type of person and their behaviour is readily identified. Do away with them.

But Sir Malcolm is a rarity. Ministers seldom understand their departments or stay in post long enough to make a difference. Continuity, and understanding of detail, is provided by the Civil Service - but with that comes the ability to hide the truth. Together with senior officers, all must share the blame - because they have colluded. Contemptuously, they continue to protect the guilty. They must be publicly held to account.

*

Today, MoD has changed beyond (my) recognition. At the most basic level its workshops have been privatised, so the main recruitment pool for trained engineering staff is gone forever. New recruits now typically skip five grades. Few realise this, so cannot appreciate what is not being done. I learned most of what I've written about here in these five grades. Even MoD doesn't take someone straight from school, give him a

---

74 Sunday Herald, 10 February 2002. 'Why the MoD must pardon the Chinook pilots', Malcolm Rifkind, Secretary of State For Defence 1992-1995.

helmet, and tell him to fly a fast jet. So why do the equivalent on procurement and safety management?

Competence and integrity are no longer welcomed. In the 1980s I could count on my Admiral (to whom this book is dedicated) backing me to the hilt against anyone, of any rank or grade, contemplating a breach of regulations governing airworthiness or financial probity. In those days it wasn't called the Military Covenant, it was simply your duty. By end-1992, senior RAF officers deemed it a dismissible offence to refuse to obey an order to commit these offences. The inevitable happened. Chinook, Nimrod, Hercules, Tornado, Sea King... Denials. Lies. The innocent blamed. Ministerial support. Carry on as before.

*

Concepts such as oversight and peer review are important. There are two key aspects to oversight - monitoring progress, and maintaining the integrity of the four pillars (Safety Management System, Standards, Independence and Compliance). In MoD this is seldom effective. If one looks down and can't recognise what's going on, even when set out in detail (for example, by the Director of Flight Safety), that is not oversight. It is navel-gazing. Peer review (evaluation of work by others in the same field) is encouraged within MoD. In practice, finding peers is often difficult. Defence aviation is a small world. Were you wanting some aviation work reviewed, who would you ask? The Military Aviation Authority? Perhaps at first, but having read this book are you confident it would understand the question? In fact, the best advice (and constructive criticism) always comes from Chief Design Engineers at the Design Authorities. In my experience they care little about commercial matters - their interest is a safe design that meets the customer's requirement. Hence, providing 'advice and assistance' is one of the core components of maintaining the Build Standard.

But what if the peer review conflicts with management directives? A demonstrably fatal example was Executive Director 1's ruling that IFF systems need not be functionally safe. My peers, both civilian and serving, agreed the aircraft should be made safe, but would not place this in writing or offer any support, for fear of upsetting superiors. That rendered the review pointless. Aircrew died as a direct result. Can those who did nothing look the families of their dead friends in the eye? When your turn comes, who will speak?

*

In the accidents discussed, the system worked well until identifiable individuals decided to evade their duty. They are protected by defensive mechanisms that stop their actions ever reaching a courtroom - and that is the only place where culpable negligence will be exposed.

Some will say they were following orders - but they were mostly illegal, and they would have been expected to recognise this. Yes, there is a dilemma. Both obeying and refusing to obey might be punished. Effectively, to justify (or get away with) refusal to obey an illegal order one must rely on the law of reciprocity, the principle of treating others as one would wish to be treated. In turn, this relies on MoD having a just culture. It doesn't, so staff face a difficult choice. But obeying a superior does not relieve one of responsibility if a moral choice is possible. Too many choose the immoral route. They are seen as malleable and are favoured over those who make the correct choice. Promoted, their ethos is self-perpetuating. The right kind of people are too busy trying to do their job properly to guard against those to whom self-advancement comes first.

These breaches were identified, but notifications dismissed with malice. Some were in general terms. *Savings are being made at the expense of safety.* Others were specific. *Chinook HC Mk2 isn't airworthy and you are prohibited from flying it.* There was an acute awareness harm <u>would</u> be caused. In each case it was cheaper and quicker to meet obligations. None of this is in doubt, so why does MoD continue to deny and deprecate? The Military Aviation Authority's stated 'mission' is to *'enhance the delivery of operational capability through the continual improvement in military air safety, appropriate culture, regulation and practice'.* Under its auspices, and after allegedly rigorous audit, aircrew and groundcrew have died in aircraft with no valid Safety Cases, and children exposed to unairworthy gliders. That is not a track record. It is a criminal record.

*

Is it too much to ask that staff do their duty? It would seem so. MoD takes exception to such sacrilege and consistently briefs Ministers against those who attempt it.[75] Few in its leadership recognise the shop floor problems. Do we really need people in charge of procurement who have never initiated or delivered a project? And, as Mr Haddon-Cave QC pointed out, one shouldn't employ submariners to procure

---

75 For example, letter 04-06-13-145804-002, 1 July 2013, from DE&S Secretariat.

aircraft.[76] (One assumes he knew a recent Chief of Defence Procurement had been a submariner. Was this a message acknowledging the evidence before him, but too embarrassing to spell out?) Please step back and think of the root causes of the deaths I have discussed. Had any one of those charged with oversight said, *here are the regulations, implement them,* most of the deceased would be alive.

These failures must be tackled head-on. The risk to life is both great and immediate. The lives of our servicemen are not something to be toyed with in some nebulous 10-year plan, diluted at every reorganisation or political reshuffle (as the Covenant itself is). Ten years on from the Nimrod Review, MoD has made little progress. The areas in which it is conspicuously poor are clear. Its refusal to act provides justifiable grounds for believing it will continue to fail. As such, and reluctantly (because I have seen the system work correctly), I believe it is time to transfer responsibilities and authority.

---

76 Nimrod Review, paragraph 24.2 'Undervaluing and dilution of engineers and engineering skill'.

26: Cull the dead wood

According to MoD I have noted only one unlawful act - the refusal to obey an order to make false record. Forgive my dissent. The gravity of proven wrongdoing amounts to an abuse of the public's trust and misconduct in a public office. To whom was this reported? Staff escalated concerns through two separate management chains. Initially, in MoD(PE), by the Directorates of Military Aircraft Projects and Airborne Electronic Systems, to the Director of Procurement Policy. Later, in the RAF, by Deputy Director Avionics (PDS) to Director General Support Management (RAF). The details are set out in full in Appendix 4 of the main submission to the Mull of Kintyre review:

https://sites.google.com/site/militaryairworthiness/their-greatest-disgrace-2016

This evidence disproves Mr Haddon-Cave's claim that the failings only commenced in 1998; and MoD's that they were only identified after Nimrod XV230 crashed in 2006. Both knew the truth.

From 1999 to 2003 the same representations were made to members of the Defence Procurement Agency Executive Board. I set out their responses earlier. Escalation saw a series of Defence Ministers advised - Ivor Caplin MP, Dr Lewis Moonie MP, Adam Ingram MP, Bob Ainsworth MP, Bill Rammell MP and Andrew Robathan MP. Also, Heads of the Civil Service, Sir Robert Kerslake and Sir Jeremy Heywood. The RAF Provost Marshal was also advised (2009-11), specifically on the Nimrod XV230 case.

None took action. Not one. No morals, conscience or credibility.

The original offenders are long gone, but MoD continues to hide behind their rulings. Sometimes progress has seemed likely, only to falter. On 6 December 2000, Ian Fauset, Executive Director 1, conceded there had been wrongdoing. Nevertheless, he upheld disciplinary action for the refusal to make false record, while dealing with the (one would think) more serious offence of issuing an illegal order by offering a pathetic *'we must hope lessons have been learned'*. They were not (and he seemed oblivious to the fact he had to learn more quickly than others). The offenders were not even made aware there *was* a lesson to be learned. They were told they had won - that their right to issue the order, and punish refusal by systematic bullying and harassment, was sacrosanct.

On 9 September 2002, David Baker, Director of Personnel, Resources and Development, chaired a two-hour appeal hearing against this ruling.

He promised a *'forensic investigation'*. Instead, a few days later, having interviewed no witnesses, and refusing to accept a bundle of papers in evidence when offered to him, he advised the Chief of Defence Procurement to (again) uphold the ruling.[77] Seven months later nine aircrew died, victims of the precise violations he disregarded. (The Sea King ASaC mid-air and Tornado/PATRIOT shootdown).

Perhaps even worse, his decision came as no surprise. In 2001 his staff, who presided over interview panels, had taken to asking candidates how they would deal with false record being made in aircraft documentation. If the candidate did not answer 'correctly', he/she was immediately rebuked and told no action should be taken. That, the imperative was to avoid upsetting the offender. Undoubtedly, this question arose from the cases I outline, and was designed to antagonise.

*

Given this depth of official indifference, what can one do? In 2005 MoD issued Personnel Instruction 71/05 setting out two ways of voicing concern. One was the route I have described - escalation, one step at a time, to the Permanent Under-Secretary of State. That just irritated staff, as he never replied (or a lackey buried it in a bottom drawer). The other was to approach newly appointed 'Nominated Officers'. For civilian staff, this was the Personnel Director; who happened to be the immediate successor to the aforementioned David Baker. The Instruction characterised them as:

'Senior members of the department who are independent and impartial, and <u>form no part of</u> the departmental procedures. They can give you one to one advice and direction, and can help ensure that you are treated properly'.

But they <u>were</u> part of departmental procedures - witness the hearing of 9 September 2002. And two of the four Nominated Officers, the new Personnel Director, Richard Hatfield and Director General Commercial, Stan Porter, had formed part of the escalation ladder in 2002. Mr Porter had been advised of the Tornado IFF risk, outlined in Chapter 21; Mr Hatfield had been party to Ministers being advised that refusing to make false record should remain an offence. Neither took any action.

The self-healing Establishment was hard at work.

*

The response of the Scottish legal system was particularly disappointing. (Or perhaps not. Disappointment implies initial expectation). On 16

---

77 Transcript of disciplinary appeal hearing, 9 September 2002.

September 2016 the Lord Advocate, James Wolffe QC, was reminded that the Chinook ZD576 Fatal Accident Inquiry had been grossly misled, by omission and commission. He was asked to consider the evidence accepted by the Mull of Kintyre Review. If, in light of the wrongdoing now revealed, and it being a matter of public interest, whether a legal investigation should be conducted. That was not unreasonable. After all, 29 died. He passed the matter to the head of the Crown Office's Scottish Fatalities Unit, Mr David Green, who took no action.[78]

This attitude continues. The same offices of State have refused to meet their legal obligation to hold a Fatal Accident Inquiry into the loss of five RAF aircrew in Tornado accidents in 2009 and 2012.[79] In the latter case, a mid-air collision over the Moray Firth, MoD failed in its legal duty to notify the North West Wales Coroner that the body of one of the deceased had been repatriated to that country:

'Neither the death of nor the disposal of the body of Flight Lieutenant Poole was ever referred or notified to my office, and I have not been involved in any matters arising from his death'.[80]

Therefore, the Chief Coroner was not given the opportunity to decide who would conduct any Inquest. However, the North West Wales Coroner revealed his own thoughts:

'Inquests into military deaths are rather pointless as they merely regurgitate what has already been made known at the military inquiry'.[81]

This is utter nonsense. As he knows this, he is consciously perverting justice. Lord Philip, in his Mull of Kintyre Review five years earlier:

'A Board of Inquiry was an internal process convened for Armed Services reasons to determine how a serious incident happened and why, and to make recommendations to prevent a recurrence. The Board of Inquiry was not a substitute for a legal inquiry into the cause and circumstances of a death'.[82]

More fundamentally, a military Inquiry is permitted to conceal relevant evidence from interested parties, is judging its own case, and families

---

78 *Inter alia*, letter LP-4 from Mr David Green, Head of Crown Office and Procurator Fiscal Service Scottish Fatalities Investigation Unit, 8 November 2016.

79 Tornado F3 ZE982 in Glen Kinglas on 2 July 2009; and Tornado GR4s ZD743 and ZD813 over the Moray Firth on 3 July 2012.

80 Mr Dewi Pritchard Jones, HM Senior Coroner for North West Wales, e-mail 1 August 2016 12:38.

81 Mr Dewi Pritchard Jones, HM Senior Coroner for North West Wales, e-mail 19 August 2016 11:42.

82 Mull of Kintyre Review, paragraph 3.1.2.

are not permitted to ask questions of witnesses.

Families have every right to expect the law to prosecute offenders, not lend succour. Who spoke for the Mull of Kintyre dead? Not their employers - MoD, MI5 and the Royal Ulster Constabulary. MoD and retired senior RAF officers continue to denigrate the dead pilots. All the families remain in limbo, victims of the greatest Covenant breach of all.

Suggestions

- The Military Aviation Authority has manifestly failed. Its new Duty Holder construct has proven useless, toothless and unenforceable; primarily because postholders do not control the actions of those who manage and carry out pre-requisites, and in any case are not trained in the subject so (again) cannot recognise what has not been done. If MoD will not use its own expertise, then appoint a senior professional team from the Civil Aviation Authority to oversee attaining and maintaining airworthiness (leaving fitness for purpose to the Services). Have the Chief Inspector of Air Accidents sign-off Service Inquiry reports. I would also like to see a Senior Coroner's Officer involved, who are often retired senior police officers, to ensure an unbroken link between what evidence emerges and what is presented in court. (The illegal actions of some Coroners is a separate issue).

- Reinstate the concept of 'trouble-shooters'. As one RN briefing from July 1987 said, these postholders were *literally, worth their weight in gold*. [83] This should be seen as a form of 'special measures'. I acknowledge trouble-shooters are the pariahs of MoD. Nevertheless, they see what is wrong and know exactly how to fix it. At a stroke, they can save time and money, and increase performance, while maintaining or improving operational capability. Okay, that will enrage the Executive Board. But I refer you to the chapter title.

- Make wider use of the System Co-ordinating Design Authority (SCDA) concept, managed by MoD Technical Agencies. In the cases I have set out, who gave prior notifications of systemic failings, risks and hazards? All were Technical Agencies. Of those who made decisions and issued overrules that led to the contributory factors, none were, had been, or could ever be a Technical Agency. Director General Support Management didn't line up and threaten seven

---

83 DGA(N) PAE 123/1, 31 July 1987.

random project managers in December 1992. They were Technical Agencies. That is no coincidence. Only they had identified his fraud. His department then promptly did away with the posts and even the title, immediately and fatally undermining the foundations of the airworthiness and safety management systems.

- Finally, those with airworthiness delegation should be willing to accept responsibility, and have a track record of exercising it responsibly. Lacking these attributes should be a bar to advancement beyond a certain grade. This is not an alien concept in MoD. For example, staff who subscribe to 'Socialist Worker' (a weekly newspaper) are not permitted beyond the most junior management grade - a revealing policy on many levels.

- Notably, the Infantry has adopted SCDA procedures as the basis for its Integrated Soldier System programme - the primary aim being to reduce casualties. The initiative was developed and established in 2001.[84] The entire process is based on the now withdrawn Defence Standard 05-125/2. You <u>always</u> get back to this Standard. It is the Bible. The farcical situation now exists whereby the Military Aviation Authority disagrees with using this unique Standard, whose only purpose is to ensure safety. Yet, the Army openly embraces it. Perhaps the Infantry should have a word?

---

84 DCC2/21/03/0001, 13 December 2001. 'Establishment of a core Soldier System Coordinating Design Authority'.

27: Progress report

The Armed Forces Bill 2011 requires Parliament to produce an annual Armed Forces Covenant Report. A House of Commons Defence Select Committee hearing then takes verbal and written evidence from MoD.

The report must address four aspects of the Covenant - healthcare, education, accommodation and Coroner's Inquests. It usually includes a shorter section discussing what is termed the 'wider Covenant'; issues such as employment, pensions, Reserve Forces, Royal British Legion activities and ceremonial occasions. As I explained at the beginning, the Covenant's original scope and intent has been eviscerated. 'Hard' issues such as providing the tools for the job and reducing the need for the Covenant in the first place are not discussed. This is why I addressed them at length because, lacking discussion, the true picture cannot be seen.

The following analysis cannot, of course, be considered anything other than a snapshot in time. It is intended to offer the reader an insight into the machinations of Parliament, which do not change.

House of Commons Defence Select Committee session, 17 January 2017

The only witnesses were the Parliamentary Under-Secretary of State (Mark Lancaster MP) and MoD's Head of Service Personnel Support (Helen Helliwell). On 16 February MoD submitted a memorandum to the Committee, offering replies to follow-up questions.

Johnny Mercer MP, a former soldier, led vigorously on healthcare. Little progress had been made in managing the transition from being under a Service Medical Officer to a civilian General Practitioner, with numerous examples of military medical records being lost. Nor, on the digitisation of these records, which would make it easier to track the whereabouts of veterans after discharge. (Is progress measured against what records *should* exist, or those that remain?)

MoD admitted much remained to be done on a key commitment, identifying specialist GPs. Mr Mercer pointed out the previous report claimed this task was complete. That this was *precisely the problem with MoD marking its own homework*. In other words, the Committee and Parliament had been deceived. Compounding this, identifying veterans in need was now even more difficult because data on those seriously injured during Operation Herrick (Afghanistan, 2002-14) was no longer published. Mr Lancaster postulated a Freedom of Information request (presumably by the public, as he didn't seem inclined to ask his own staff) might elicit the information.

MoD voiced concern over the dilemma whereby the Covenant promised priority treatment for injured veterans, but civilians with a greater clinical need might do without. That, veterans should not be perceived to have an active advantage over civilians, as it would affect public goodwill. Taken in isolation the point might seem valid, but the policy decision has been made and Mr Lancaster did not produce evidence of any such public opinion. It is for the government to provide resources and the Health Service to implement. For doctors to determine clinical need, not for MoD to interfere and dictate. Immediately, a major problem is evident - the need for someone with authority to grasp the nettle. And for that person to be facing the Committee, not Mr Lancaster.

*

There would seem to be disagreement between the London government and Stormont Assembly over the status of the Covenant in Northern Ireland. Gavin Robinson MP quoted Michelle O'Neill, when Northern Ireland Minister of Health:

'The Covenant has not been adopted here as health care arrangements are delivered on an equitable basis to all members of the community'.

In reply, Mr Lancaster explained the reason - there was no funding. However, during the later Commons debate on 2 February 2017, he replied to the same point with:

'Yes, absolutely, the covenant does apply in Northern Ireland'.

Make your mind up. The two main nationalist parties (Sinn Féin and SDLP) are not prepared to accept the Covenant in its present form, the main difficulty being the contradiction between it and equality laws introduced under the Good Friday Agreement. MoD's official position, as stated by Mr Lancaster, is it agrees with Sinn Féin. Perhaps a more vigilant aide spotted this minefield, leading to his change of story?

*

Ruth Smeeth MP led robustly on education, seeking the same *'deal'* healthcare enjoyed. Given the previous evidence, this could be interpreted as not wanting adequate funding. One must be careful. The Treasury pounces on such slips. Schools across the UK were now rejecting the Covenant. Her main concern was admissions policy for the children of serving personnel redeployed within the UK, and those returning from abroad. What resources were being allocated? MoD replied it was trying to bring postings into line with school terms. This sounds flaccid - Service planners tend to heed operational commitments over school term times. By now in full politician mode (same reply regardless of question), Mr Lancaster reiterated his objection to Service families having a perceived advantage.

Mrs Smeeth also led on accommodation. The same issues arose - lack of new homes, schooling and healthcare for Service families returning from abroad. For many years, Service accommodation has been generally appalling, much of it intended as temporary post-War (1939-45) housing for returning troops. In recent times this has been compounded by tens of thousands of MoD-owned homes being sold off at a huge loss, only to be rented back at vast profit to the new owners. Moreover, the contract to maintain them has failed dismally, with the Public Accounts Committee reporting in May 2016 the situation was *'totally unacceptable'*, calling for the contract to be terminated. An important point was left unexplored. The leaseback contract provides for an imminent large hike in rent. What of the ability of servicemen to pay? The remuneration of junior ranks is historically low. Obtaining a mortgage is nigh on impossible. In fact, many already pay more than the fair market rent, as the accommodation is in such a poor state it does not meet the standards imposed on private landlords or councils. MoD's position seems to rely on spouses acquiring well-paid jobs, begging the question whether military locales can offer them.

*

Finally, the Chairman, Dr Julian Lewis MP, raised the policy of pursuing veterans and serving personnel through courts for alleged offences while in theatre. He apologised, needlessly, for *'stretching the concept of the Covenant a bit, but not beyond propriety'*. (Which is what I've done in this book). He asked MoD what it was doing to protect against spurious claims, especially arising from Iraq and Northern Ireland.

'Why on earth should I want a career, possibly a dangerous front line career, in the Armed Forces if decades after the event I am going to get a knock on the door and find myself hauled up before a court for something that I didn't do wrong in any case?'

Mr Lancaster passed the buck, saying it was not a matter for MoD. Odd, given he had spent the entire proceedings demanding it retain complete control. He ignored the Iraq question, compartmentalising the problem to Northern Ireland, saying it was the responsibility of the Northern Ireland Secretary. The Committee offered nothing, blinded by the wool it was now peering through.

*

The session had lasted under an hour. The feeble report it discussed gives the impression of a Covenant operating efficiently. If it were the first, say six months after the announcement of the Covenant, one might be kinder. But it is 17 years since it was enshrined in Army doctrine. The focus has shifted to what MoD terms the 'Corporate Covenant', whereby companies sign a commitment. The report offers many glossy images of company executives brandishing a pen alongside a Minister, enjoying their 15 seconds of fame. Closer study, however, reveals most are still unsure how they are affected. Frankly, by the second such 'success story' you feel utterly depressed and discouraged.

Mightier than a Lord

At this point, I am reminded of something I witnessed in August 2003. I had occasion to visit a training camp in Wales, as soldiers prepared for deployment to Afghanistan. I was speaking with the Commanding Officer about the comms job outlined in Chapter 22, when he excused himself. A young man in civilian clothes had arrived. He had been seriously injured during their previous deployment, almost losing a lower leg. He could barely walk, but had travelled under his own steam in a desperate effort to go through 'selection' again, and re-join his mates. The CO took him to one side, arm round his shoulder. The medical prognosis was not good. I never found out what happened to him. I wish the Committee, in fact all MPs, could meet him; but I suspect most would suddenly find pressing engagements in their diaries.

Financial assistance to bereaved families

Following his Review into four unexplained deaths at Deepcut Barracks in Kent between 1995 and 2002, in March 2006 Sir Nicholas Blake, a High Court judge, recommended:

'As part of the military covenant with the soldier, the MoD should ensure that the family of a deceased soldier has access to legal advice and, where appropriate, legal representation prior to, and during, the Inquest or Fatal Accident Inquiry'.

Some months later, MoD issued a disgraceful response:

'An inquest is an inquisitorial, non-adversarial fact-finding process of limited scope which does not make findings of civil or criminal liability. It is the general presumption that legal representation is not necessary, and it is quite appropriate for those deemed interested persons by the Coroner to ask questions of witnesses at an inquest without legal assistance'.

(Noting what happened at the Sea King ASaC Inquest in 2007, when MoD complained about the father of a deceased pilot being allowed to ask questions).

The Department of Constitutional Affairs retorted:

'If the MoD maintains the line that inquests are not adversarial, so that families do not need to be represented, this begs the question why MoD needs to be represented'.

The answer, of course, is MoD has committed serious offences and uses its legal representation to divert and obfuscate.

Ministerial correspondence ensued between Harriet Harman MP and MoD, discussing ways to improve matters. Among them:

'Ending the practice of charging families for access to documents, including Inquest transcripts'.

But in his subsequent ministerial statement of 7 June 2007, Adam Ingram MP omitted all mention of legal costs. On 13 March 2008 Ms Harman, by now Leader of the House of Commons, said:

'If bereaved relatives with no legal representation turn up on the steps of a coroner's court and find that the MoD and the Army have a great battery of solicitors and QCs, they cannot help but feel that the position is unfair. We need to give bereaved relatives at Inquests a real sense of fairness and support'.

The general difficulties faced by families were later set out in the Chilcot Report (2016):

'The Opinion Leader [a research consultancy used by the government] *record of the 4 December 2006 meeting...reported that the Coroner's service had not sufficiently met the needs of most families. It identified six main issues:*

- *The time between incident and Inquest [more than three years in some cases];*
- *Not having access to key information;*
- *Insufficient notification of an Inquest, leaving little opportunity to prepare;*
- *Specific problems with the running of the Inquest (including key witnesses not being present, factual errors, and not having the opportunity to ask questions);*

- *A lack of sensitivity in the treatment of families; and,*
- *Cost and logistical issues (including being asked to pay for documents and the difficulty faced by some families in paying for legal representation)'.*

Sir John did not seem to appreciate the first point was largely dictated by the length of MoD's investigation; the Sea King ASaC accident being a prime example. Only a month later the families suffered all these difficulties, and more. And MoD was also responsible for the second point, routinely withholding information and lying to families and courts.

Nevertheless, the general points were well made, but Sir John was ignored. The current situation is that the Legal Aid, Sentencing and Punishment of Offenders Act 2012 repealed an earlier provision - never brought into force - that would have extended legal aid to cover representation at the Inquests of military personnel who died on active service, or in police or prison custody. So, cross-party support (with some honourable exceptions, such as Ms Harman) ensures families are <u>not</u> represented. What price the Covenant?

An important development

The Iraq Historic Allegations Team (IHAT) was formed to investigate allegations of abuse by UK soldiers in Iraq. On 10 February 2017 the Defence Select Committee issued a report giving its verdict. It concluded IHAT had become a:

'Seemingly unstoppable self-perpetuating machine, deaf to the concerns of the armed forces, blind to their needs, and profligate with its own resources'.

(Like MoD itself). The Committee continued:

'Over 3,500 allegations of abuse were taken up by IHAT, many of which were not supported by credible evidence. The report found a range of failings in the conduct of the investigations into those claims alongside a MoD support package which was fragmented, inaccessible and largely unknown. The report concludes that because of this, those under investigation have suffered unacceptable stress, have had their lives put on hold and their careers damaged. The overall impact of this has been the erosion of the bonds of trust between those who serve, and their civilian masters'.

No credible evidence? Failings in the conduct of investigations? Those under investigation suffering unacceptable stress, their lives put on hold and their careers damaged? Erosion of the bonds of trust? We've been here before. The existence of IHAT - established as one of its final acts by the Labour government in March 2010 - was itself a breach of the Covenant. It was recommended that its caseload be handed over to Service police, supported by civilian police, as soon as possible. But these forces exhibit the same traits as IHAT, eschewing natural justice. A typical political move, throwing the problem on a perpetual roundabout.

Johnny Mercer MP, another honourable exception:

> *'Throughout this process there has been an almost total disregard of the welfare of soldiers and their families. The MoD must take responsibility for allowing this to happen. They could have discriminated between credible and non-credible cases yet they lacked the will to do so. They need to get on and immediately dismiss those remaining cases that are based on obviously weak evidence'.*

As if to provoke, even more investigations were announced.

Thankfully, IHAT has now been shut down. But the damage has been done. The bond between servicemen and their political masters has irretrievably broken down. The Covenant is in tatters.

28: A message for the Secretary of State

'An error doesn't become a mistake until you refuse to correct it'.
Orlando A. Battista

The Nimrod and Hercules cases were won with consummate ease. How? By presenting the facts outlined in this book. This strategy was then applied to the Mull of Kintyre case, with equal success.

Conspicuously, members of the public conducted these campaigns. Your department's inadequacies and lies were laid bare. Yet it limps on, seemingly immune to criticism and able to ignore the law at will. It views these as temporary setbacks, not salutary lessons. Redress remains almost impossible.

Serial offences continue to be committed in your name. This misconduct is so far below acceptable standards as to injure the public interest. The perpetrators are reckless as to legality. They include your ministerial predecessors, Cabinet Secretaries and Heads of the Civil Service, as all have condoned this wrongdoing. This political and legal silence has betrayed the dead.

Only you, sir, have the authority commensurate with your responsibilities. Every journey begins with a single step. Your first should be to purge your Department of those who have killed so many. Do your duty. Only then can you say you spoke for the dead.

Author's note

It has been difficult knowing where to draw the line. Most chapters discussing individual cases were written contemporaneously, often shortly after the Board of Inquiry report became available. But it is important not to investigate or write about a single accident, and set the work aside. One must retain records of contributory factors and causes, so others might learn and help prevent recurrence. Investigators must be able to identify repeat failures, which are always evidence of management failings - who must not be allowed to judge their own case.

I had many other cases to choose from. One was so compelling, I decided it deserved its own book, *'Red 5 - An investigation into the death of Flight Lieutenant Sean Cunningham'*. Some emerged late in the day. For example, Yak-52 G-YAKB crashed on 8 July 2016 killing RAF test pilot Flight Lieutenant Alex Parr. The Service Inquiry recommended: *'The Empire Test Pilot School should have access to aircrew publications in English'*. (They were in Russian). Scandalous, given the Director of Flight Safety's recommendation in August 1992 that the RAF cease using captured Argentinian manuals to maintain Chinooks. But the report doesn't say *For goodness sake, not again.*

On 30 August 2017, RAF Hawk T Mk2 training aircraft were grounded after an RAF Valley aircraft suffered electrical failure over the Irish Sea. The unthinkable had happened. Total failure of a 'glass cockpit'. At high altitude, above cloud, they had to descend and hope to identify landmarks. Luck and calmness under pressure averted disaster. MoD entered denial mode. It was implied the 'pause' in flying was planned, due to runway re-surfacing. The real failure, savings at the expense of safety through by-passing maintenance procedures, was concealed. What if the aircraft had crashed into the sea? What evidence would survive? Would MoD repeat what it did to the Chinook ZD576 pilots? *The aircraft seemed okay when it took off, so the pilots must be to blame.* Heels are being dragged. The finger of blame is wagged around, but always pointing away from the guilty.

*

In his Nimrod Review, Mr Haddon-Cave QC dwelt on one central technical and legal point - there was no valid Safety Case. Generating one, and maintaining it, is not rocket science. Yet, MoD and government stood back and let it happen again. Flight Lieutenant Sean Cunningham died in 2011, victim of an aircraft lacking a Safety Case. At least Nimrod had one, albeit poorly constructed. In 2014, Air Cadet Gliders did not have one either. Same project teams, same Type Airworthiness Authority, same RAF Group. Like Nimrod MRA4, and for the same reason, the Vigilant motor glider fleet has been scrapped. Following the Nimrod Review, those responsible must have known the consequence of their actions.

Glossary of terms and abbreviations

Terminology and post titles change regularly in MoD. Those listed are the ones relevant during most of the period discussed.

AAIB	Air Accidents Investigation Branch (UK Department for Transport).
A&AEE	Aeroplane and Armament Experimental Establishment. MoD's aircraft trials establishment at Boscombe Down, Wiltshire. Now part of QinetiQ.
AD/HP2	Assistant Director Helicopter Projects 2, in MoD's Directorate of Helicopter Projects. The Sea King Project Director. Post disestablished in April 1999, with the reformation of Integrated Project Teams.
AEW	Airborne Early Warning.
ALARP	As Low As Reasonably Practicable.
AML	Air Member Logistics. Replaced by Defence Logistics Organisation in 1999.
AMSO	Air Member Supply and Organisation. Replaced by Air Member Logistics in 1994.
ANR	Active Noise Reduction.
ART	Airworthiness Review Team.
ASaC	Airborne Surveillance and Control.
AVRS	Airborne Video Recording System.
BVATE	Blue Vixen Automatic Test Equipment.
CAR	Controller Aircraft Release (see also MAR). Pre-April 1999, the statement by Controller Aircraft to the Service that an aircraft is airworthy at a given Build Standard, listing any limitations. Forms Part 1 of the Release to Service. Mandated upon the Service.
CCWR	Cloud and Collision Warning Radar.
CDR	Critical Design Review.
CPS	Crown Prosecution Service.
DA	Design Authority. The DA holds the master drawing set, whereas a Design Custodian holds secondary masters.

DGA(N)	Director General Aircraft (Navy). A Rear Admiral, head of naval aviation.
DGAS2	Director General Air Systems 2. MoD(PE) 2-Star responsible for Helicopters and Maritime Patrol Aircraft (Nimrod), providing management oversight. Later, Executive Director 1, Defence Procurement Agency.
DGSM	Director General Support Management. A 2-Star Air Officer post.
DHP	Director(ate) of Helicopter Projects in MoD(PE). Responsible for delivery of all helicopters, except Merlin. Post disestablished in April 1999.
DHSA	Defence Helicopter Support Authority. Responsible for the In-Service Support of helicopters. Essentially, the co-locating of Engineering Authorities, although not carrying out all the functions. Disestablished in April 1999, and staff subsumed into Integrated Projects Teams.
DOR(Sea)	Directorate of Operational Requirements (Sea). The London based department seen by MoD(PE) as its customer; who stated the basic requirement and to whom it was delivered. Now, Directorate of Equipment Capability.
DPA	Defence Procurement Agency. Replaced the development and production arms of MoD(PE), although not carrying out all the functions.
DSAC	Defence Scientific Advisory Council.
EWA	Engineering Weapons Authority, part of the RN's Aircraft Support Executive.
FMT	Full Mission Trainer. Used for training ASaC Observers.
FNIPV	Future Northern Ireland Patrol Vehicle.
GPS	Global Positioning System. Both the concept and equipment.
HAS	Helicopter, Anti-Submarine (Sea King Mks 1, 2, 5 and 6).
HC	Helicopter, Commando (Sea King Mk4).
HF	High Frequency (2-30MHz).
HISL	High Intensity Strobe Light.
HSE	Health and Safety Executive. Part of the Department of Work and Pensions.

IDD	Interface Definition Document. For determining the work necessary to achieve systems integration and functional safety. Not to be confused with Interface Control Document.
IFF	Identification Friend or Foe. Radar system that can identify friendly assets, but not foes.
ILS	Integrated Logistics Support. Prior to April 1992, an ILS Manager managed Development, Production and In-Service Support. The meaning changed upon issue of Defence Standard 00-60 (ILS), to part of In-Service Support only (enabling the appointment of serving officers to the role).
INS	Inertial Navigation System.
IPR	Intellectual Property Rights
IPT	Integrated Project Team. In this context the 1999 model. Not to be confused with the 1989 model, which had greater delegated authority.
JTIDS	Joint Tactical Information Distribution System. JTIDS is the bearer platform, Link 16 the data protocol. It is a multinational secure data link system that allows target and operational intelligence to be exchanged between ships and aircraft participating in a particular JTIDS network.
MAA	Military Aviation Authority. Formed in April 2010 after the Nimrod Review, grouping together some airworthiness functions; but not resurrecting those shut down in the early 1990s.
MAR	Military Aircraft Release. Replaced Controller Aircraft Release upon disestablishment of the Controller Aircraft post.
MATS	Merlin Automatic Test System.
MCP	(Directorate of) Military Communications Projects in MoD(PE).
MoD	Ministry of Defence.
MoD(PE)	MoD (Procurement Executive). Split into the Defence Logistics Organisation and Defence Procurement Agency in 1999, while abandoning some functions.
MSU	Mission System Upgrade.

NAS	Naval Air Squadron.
NSM	Naval Service Modification. A form of Service Designed Modification whereby the Design Authority is the RN's Mobile Aircraft Servicing Unit; and the approving authority is the Support Authority, not MoD(PE).
NVG	Night Vision Goggles. Both the concept and the equipment.
PATRIOT	Phased Array Tracking Radar to Intercept on Target
PDS	Post Design Services
PUS	Permanent Under-Secretary of State. MoD's senior civil servant. Not to be confused with Parliamentary Secretaries, who are Members of Parliament.
RAS	Radar Advisory Service. Provided by Air Traffic Control.
RIM	Radio Installation Memorandum. Sets out the basic rules for designing an aircraft installation for a particular avionic equipment.
RNFSAIC	Royal Navy Flight Safety and Accident Investigation Centre.
RSU	Radar System Upgrade.
RTI	Routine Technical Instruction. A type of Service Issued Instruction, only to be used when Design Authority involvement is unnecessary.
RTS	Release to Service. The Master Airworthiness Reference, stating the limitations within which Service regulated flying may be conducted.
RTSA	Release to Service Authority. The named individual responsible for the upkeep of the Release to Service, and the Safety Case reflecting the In-Use Build Standard(s). At a higher level, it can mean the Staff who issue the document.
SCDA	System Co-ordinating Design Authority. The nominated company, sitting above individual Design Authorities, responsible for the safety and performance of a given system.
SD	Service Deviation(s). SDs form Part 2 of the Release to Service, providing authority to temporarily deviate from Part 1 while ensuring the aircraft remains safe.
SKIPT	Sea King Integrated Project Team. Formed April 1999, combining the DHP project and DHSA support offices, but

not all functions.

UHF	Ultra High Frequency (225-399.975 MHz in this context).
UTI	Urgent Technical Instruction. See also RTI.
VHF	Very High Frequency (30-173.975 MHz, with some bands receive-only).

Printed in Great Britain
by Amazon

84566593R00142